FRONTIERS IN
CATHOLIC FEMINIST THEOLOGY

FRONTIERS IN CATHOLIC FEMINIST THEOLOGY

SHOULDER TO SHOULDER

SUSAN ABRAHAM AND ELENA PROCARIO-FOLEY

EDITORS

Fortress Press
Minneapolis

FRONTIERS IN CATHOLIC FEMINIST THEOLOGY
Shoulder to Shoulder

Scripture quotations from the New Revised Standard Version of the Bible are copyright © 1989 by the Division of Christian Education of the National Council of Churches of Christ in the United States of America and are used by permission.

Cover image: "The Three Graces" by Anthony Armstrong, copyright © Anthony Armstrong (www.armstrongnart.net).
Cover design: Laurie Ingram

Library of Congress Cataloging-in-Publication Data

Frontiers in Catholic feminist theology : shoulder to shoulder / Susan Abraham, Elena Procario-Foley, editors.
      p. cm.
  Includes bibliographical references and index.
  ISBN 978-0-8006-6439-8 (alk. paper)
  1. Feminist theology. 2. Catholic Church--Doctrines. I. Abraham, Susan. II. Procario-Foley, Elena.
  BT83.55.F76 2009
  230'.2082--dc22
                                    2009017612

The paper used in this publication meets the minimum requirements for American National Standard for Information Sciences—Permanence of Paper for Printed Library Materials, ANSI Z329.48–1984.

Manufactured in the U.S.A.
13   12   11   10   09   1   2   3   4   5   6   7   8   9   10

CONTENTS

CONTRIBUTORS

Susan Abraham is Assistant Professor of Ministry Studies at Harvard University. She is the author of *Identity, Ethics, and Nonviolence in Postcolonial Theory: A Rahnerian Theological Assessment* (New York: Palgrave Macmillan, 2007). Her current research interests are in the areas of feminist theory and theology, practical theology and culture, and global Christianity between colonialism and postcolonialism.

Rosemary P. Carbine is visiting Assistant Professor in Religious Studies at Whittier College. She specializes, researches, and writes in the fields of comparative feminist, womanist, and Latina/mujerista theologies, theological anthropology, Christology, U.S. public/political theology, and teaching and learning in theology and religious studies. Her manuscript-in-progress, titled *Ekklesial Work: Toward a Feminist Public Theology,* offers an innovative theological take on the intersections of gender, religion, and politics in recent U.S. history.

Teresa Delgado is Director of the Peace and Justice Studies Program and assistant professor of Religious Studies at Iona College. Her interests and scholarship are interdisciplinary in method and scope, utilizing the experience of women, particularly Latinas, to articulate a constructive theological vision both grounded in and critical of Latino culture and the Roman Catholic theological tradition. Her publications include "The Best of Witnesses: Towards a Puerto Rican Theology of Identity, Suffering and Hope," in *Creating Ourselves: African Americans and Latinos/as,*

Popular Culture, and Religious Expression (Benjamin Valentín and Anthony Pinn, eds., Durham, N.C.: Duke University Press, 2009), and"Prophesy Freedom: Puerto Rican Women's Literature as a Source for Latina Feminist Theology," in *A Reader in Latina Feminist Theology: Religion and Justice* (María Pilar Aquino, Daisy Machado, and Jeanette Rodríguez, eds., Austin: University of Texas Press, 2002).

Jeannine Hill Fletcher is Associate Professor of Theology at Fordham University, Bronx, New York. She is the author of *Monopoly on Salvation? A Feminist Response to Religious Pluralism* (New York: Continuum, 2005). Essays include "As Long as We Wonder: Possibilities in the Impossibility of Interreligious Dialogue" in *Theological Studies* 68, no. 3 (September 2007); and "Women's Voices in Dialogue: A Look at the Parliament of the World's Religions" in *Studies in Interreligious Dialogue* 16, no. 1 (2006). Jeannine also serves as the faculty director of Service-Learning at Fordham.

Elizabeth T. Groppe is Associate Professor of Theology at Xavier University in Cincinnati, Ohio. Her work as a systematic theologian uses the tradition to respond constructively to the challenges of our era. She is the author of *Yves Congar's Theology of the Holy Spirit* (Oxford: Oxford University Press, 2004) and articles on a variety of topics, including trinitarian theology and pneumatology. Current projects include the book *Eating and Drinking* for the Practice of Everyday Life series.

LaReine-Marie Mosely, S.N.D., is Assistant Professor of Theology at Loyola University, Chicago. Her research interests include Christology, soteriology, theological anthropology, black theology, black Catholic theology, womanist theology, and the theology of Edward Schillebeeckx. In her present work, Mosely explores the Christian soteriological tradition and African American women's experiences to articulate a Christian theology of salvation in womanist perspective.

Elena G. Procario-Foley is Driscoll Professor of Jewish-Catholic Studies at Iona College. She teaches and researches in Catholic systematic theology with a particular interest in Christology and the soteriological issues confronting Christology in the face of religious pluralism. She focuses on the renewal of Catholic theology as it reshapes its relationship to Judaism. Her manuscript

Children of the Living God: Explorations in Jewish-Catholic Relations is an edited introduction to major themes in the dialogue.

Michele Saracino is Associate Professor of Religious Studies at Manhattan College in Riverdale, New York. She researches the intersections among theological anthropology, contemporary continental theory, and psychologies of the self, and her current work focuses on the theological implications of borders of self, religions, and place. Michele is the author of various essays, and her book *On Being Human: A Conversation with Lonergan and Levinas* was published by Marquette University Press in 2003.

Laura M. Taylor is a doctoral candidate in Theology at Vanderbilt University. Her research and teaching interests include constructive theologies, feminist and postcolonial thought, and theologies of religious pluralism. She is the recipient of the 2006 Catherine Mowry LaCugna Award for New Scholars granted by the Catholic Theological Association of America.

PREFACE

Elena Procario-Foley and Susan Abraham

We understand "frontiers" to mean the inviting horizon of ideas emerging organically from previous ones. Catholic feminist theologians have long been at the leading edges of creative and life-giving thought in Catholic theology, courageously blazing new understandings of being Catholic and of being in community with Church and world. We can only encounter horizons by venturing out. Our ventures were led by able and far-seeing guides and mothers who have led us this far. Therefore, the title of this volume recognizes both the ongoing efforts of Catholic feminist theologians to wrestle with the ever-changing landscape of twenty-first-century Catholicism and the debt the current authors owe to our foremothers in theology. We stand shoulder to shoulder with the feminist, womanist, and mujerista theologians who have gone before us and who stand beside us, forging new paths today.

We offer this book as an introduction to contemporary Catholic feminist theology. Catholic feminism has changed dramatically since Mary Daly's groundbreaking *Beyond God the Father* in 1973. In teaching undergraduates, we find that students (women and men) resist and reject the word *feminism* itself—often with little understanding of what it means. The time is right for a new introduction

1

to Catholic feminist theology. Yet we make no pretensions, as is the general principle of feminist theology, to be the first or last word on the current state of Catholic feminism. We have attempted to delineate a horizon of ideas for a younger generation by being both bold and faithful to our Catholic and feminist heritage.

At the outset of this collaborative work, we consciously avoided two traps. We rejected the perceived need to represent all voices. Not only would that have been an artificial representation of our group, but the attempt to do so would have fallen short; inevitably, some voices would have been neglected. Also, we avoided the trap of trying to address every area of traditional systematic theology and the boundless possibilities of contemporary constructive theology. We realized that a concentrated exploration of key theological foci in the Catholic tradition would serve the reader better than a series of discrete essays.

Consequently, we have chosen to explore theological anthropology, Christology, and ecclesiology as the heart, head, and feet of theology. If God's glory is in living human persons (see Irenaeus, *Adversus haereses* IV.20.7), then theological anthropology is at the heart of a theological enterprise in a new millennium characterized by radical diversity in a global community, which is dependent for its survival on boundary-crossing cooperation. Deep reflection on being human in relationship to each other and to God is a necessary part of a global conversation that wishes to avoid ecological, economic, and military catastrophe. Bending St. Paul's metaphor of the body of Christ, Christology is at the head of feminist theology for better or for worse. Catholic feminists still need to come to terms with the figure of Christ and how Jesus is used or misused by the tradition to support the full humanity of all persons, or to deny full humanity to some. Ecclesiology supplies feet to the theological enterprise. The practice of Catholicism and the efforts of theologians, feminist or otherwise, lack value if individuals do not coalesce into community as the body of Christ and walk in the world as a healing presence. Catholic feminists, however, critique Church structures that do not promote the full flourishing of all human beings, just as much as they demand that social and political structures in our societies work for healing in the world.

The reader deserves a definition of "Catholic feminist theology" at the outset. Briefly defining Christian feminist theology, though, presents a formidable task that is fraught with dangers, given the volume and diversity of Christian feminist theologies that now exist. Nor, as this volume will demonstrate, is there one mode of Catholic feminist theology. Transparency requires that we identify the use of the term in this book as referring, in general, to a stream of feminist thought, which is often referred to as "second wave feminism," and within that wave a type of feminist theology called "reconstructionist."[1] An understanding of the traditional emphases of this type of Christian feminist theology, especially as articulated through Catholic feminist theologians, provides an initial background against which the reader can approach the chapters. Individual authors indicate where they diverge from or add to this approach.

Roughly, over the past forty years, through a variety of voices, feminist theology has summarized the basic themes of feminism in terms of mutual relation/relationality, radical equality, and community in diversity.[2] Identity emerges not in isolation, but from a network of relationships. Relationality "is a way of being in the world."[3] Radical equality affirms the dignity of each human being regardless of one's particularity in terms of ethnicity, race, sex, or religion. Radical equality does not assume an essentialist anthropology, and it rejects theories of complementarity between the sexes. Equality among persons assumes that each person comes to the relationship as a complete human being. Community in diversity is a value that recognizes and celebrates the creativity that arises when equal persons exist in mutual relation.

Christian feminist theology has long recognized a methodology that involves three steps: criticism, recovery, and reconstruction.[4]

The theologian first needs to assess the prevailing situation in which she finds herself. The feminist theological critique yields the position that structures within Christianity have historically been patriarchal, hierarchical, and damaging for women's full flourishing. To address the situation, feminist theologians scour the tradition to recover elements of the tradition that have been suppressed that are beneficial to women. With a more complete view of the Christian tradition in hand (for good or ill), the feminist theologian reconstructs a Christian narrative that demonstrates the inclusivity of mutuality, equality, and diversity.

Thousands of pages have been written to explore the ideas in these two paragraphs. The reader is invited to recognize these themes and methods in the pages that follow. We offer the reader one more interpretive rule for Catholic feminism. Elegant in its simplicity, wisdom, and brevity, Catholic feminist theologian Rosemary Radford Ruether provides a powerful criterion for pursuing feminist analysis in theology: if something promotes one's full humanity, then it is of God; conversely, if something is destructive of one's full humanity, then it is not of God.[5]

With these principles in hand, the reader can navigate the pages of this book, while also recognizing that theological anthropology, Christology, and ecclesiology are not distinct enterprises functioning separately from one another. To use traditional language, reflections on grace, salvation, and praxis cannot be analyzed as separate categories. There is a surfeit of wisdom that overflows and overlaps each theological category—each illuminating and enriching the other. In this regard, Catholic feminists firmly stand in continuity with the theological tradition. Theological roundtables at the end of each section demonstrate the fluid and necessary interchange among the three theological foci. The roundtables are written by the authors of the preceding section to exemplify further the fruitful interchange among theological categories and the collaborative nature of feminist theology. Questions at the end of each section and suggestions for further reading offer additional guides to the essays.

This book has its origins in the Workgroup for Constructive Theology. We thank all the members for their advice and support. We thank especially Serene Jones, now the president of Union Theological Seminary in New York City, for her prescience when she looked at the group of us over dinner and said, "There's a book in you. Figure it out!" We thank Michael West, editor-in-chief at Fortress Press, for encouraging us, persevering with us, and providing us with expert guidance. We thank, by way of dedication, two sorely missed pioneers of Catholic feminist theology: Catherine Mowry LaCugna, whose volume *Freeing Theology* inspired us early in our theological careers, and Anne E. Carr, who died as we were finalizing our plans for this work. Their impact on Catholic feminist theology is incalculable, and their early deaths impoverish us. Finally, we thank all of our family members and friends, too numerous to list, who have shared the growing pains of this volume. Each of us has endured significant life changes within our families throughout the writing of this book—births, deaths, major illnesses, employment changes—and we have stood together throughout, shoulder to shoulder.

Part One

THEOLOGICAL ANTHROPOLOGY

Chapter 1

MOVING BEYOND THE "ONE TRUE STORY"

Michele Saracino

From Augustine to Rahner, from Aquinas to Lonergan, Roman Catholic thinkers have long struggled with fundamental questions about human existence, including the goodness of creation, the need to enact freedom responsibly in a world plagued by suffering and brokenness, and the importance of engendering right relationships with God and others. Traditionally, these basic axioms have been framed in terms of *nature* and *grace.* It is not too strong to suggest, however, that these categories yield truncated notions of the human person as they breed binaries in which some individuals and groups are cast as closer to nature and, consequently, as less able to participate in God's offer of grace, while other individuals are typed by their nature as more capable of living a grace-filled life. In the latter half of the twentieth century, black, feminist, womanist, Latina, liberationist, and queer theologians have demonstrated that women and other "others" are often the ones relegated to the status of less-graced beings, legitimizing their oppression and exploitation by more privileged groups in both ecclesial and secular contexts. Without a doubt, binary thinking cannot and should not hold. Less reductionist and totalizing categories are necessary for understanding what is at stake in being human with others in the twenty-first century—ones that account for the diversity of experiences and the complexity of our identity in relation to God and others, ones that avoid the social sins of oppression and exploitation.

The notion of "story" is one such category. Stories profoundly shape who we are, what we want out of life, and how we are connected to others. Michel de Certeau puts it most eloquently when he writes that stories arrange our sense of reality in that "they traverse and organize places; they select and link them together; they make sentences and itineraries out of them. They are spatial trajectories."[1] Speaking about theological anthropology through the discourse of story also reveals how, in the contemporary globalized world, individual and group identities cannot be contained by binary logic because they more often than not are plural. We find ourselves playing a variety of roles and reciting a diversity of scripts all at the same time—a plurality that complicates the most basic theological assumptions about being human. Some of us are students, sons, and African Americans. Others of us are teachers, mothers, and Christians. Not defined exclusively by any one category or narrative, we are all in some way or another hybrids—collections of various stories related to our life experiences, family origins, gender, class, religion, and so on.[2] This has always been the case. Still, increased communication technology and multinational industry have shed new light on our hybrid reality, clarifying how we live with and among those with multiple stories, some of which either resonate with or contest our own. In order for life-giving relationships with others to endure, humanity is obligated to move beyond the potentially totalizing categories of nature and grace and engage the plural and enmeshed qualities of human existence—in other words, to claim its hybridity.

DEFINING HYBRIDITY

Hybridity is not a new term. Gregor Mendel's foundational research on genetic crossings in plant life provided one of the first definitions of hybridity.[3] More recently, in the humanities postcolonialist theorists have invoked the notion of hybridity to signify identities that cannot be reduced to any one static homogenous concept or story.[4] Even political leaders strive to consider a hybrid sense of humanity. When the former senator from Illinois, and now the forty-fourth president of the United States of America, Barack Obama, was under fire for being part of Reverend Jeremiah Wright's church, a pastor associated with what some have considered to be hate speech against white Americans, Obama, the son of a "black man" and a "white woman," responded by retelling his own hybrid story:

> I can no more disown him [Rev. Wright] than I can disown the black community. I can no more disown him than I can disown my white grandmother, a woman who helped raise me, a woman who sacrificed again and again for me, a woman who loves me as much as she loves anything in this world, but a woman who once confessed her fear of black men who passed her by on the street, and who on more than one occasion has uttered racial or ethnic stereotypes that made me cringe. These people are a part of me. And they are part of America, this country that I love.[5]

Together with these scientific, philosophical, and political trajectories, Christianity has much to contribute to the conversation about human identity being composed of many stories, particularly in relation to the doctrines of creation and Christology.

HYBRIDITY

Hybridity is the mixing that brings forth new forms from previously identified categories. The term has roots in the modern usage of taxonomies for organizing information about the material world, and is characteristically used in the natural sciences (for example, in botany). The term has been claimed by postcolonial and feminist thought to refer to identities that cannot be captured by static categories. It describes the experience of having no fixed or pure identity, and instead occupying various social locations or stories simultaneously.

CREATION AS PLURAL

One cannot utter the notion of hybridity without turning to scripture and interrogating the two paradigmatic, canonical creation stories found in Genesis 1 and 2. Both these narratives enrich and challenge one another and, as a result, counter any commonsense notion that there is any "one true story" about what it means to be human. Turning first to the account in Genesis 1, men and women are described as created equally in God's likeness, "in the image of God he created them; male and female he created them."[6] For feminists, this often is regarded as the great equalizing text in that God is portrayed as making both genders good and sacred. However, here I want to move beyond issues exclusively pertinent to gender and assert that being created in God's image and likeness underscores the theological idea that human beings carry the story of the divine within them. Human beings, therefore, are by nature hybrid, and what's more, their hybridized identity is regarded as good in and of itself. Accordingly, any resistance to the goodness of our multistoried selves becomes a potential site of brokenness, rendering sin an important category in thinking through theological anthropology.

In Genesis 2, Christians are faced with another paradigmatic account of human creation, one in which a female is created from a male: "So the Lord God caused a deep sleep to fall upon the man, and he slept; then he took one of his ribs and closed up its place with flesh. And the rib that the Lord God had taken from the man he made into a woman and brought her to the man."[7] Even when interpreted metaphorically, this story can be read to be problematic, since it has been used to classify women as derivatives of men, concretizing a gender dualism that is already rife within Roman Catholicism, as well as in secular consumerist culture. What if, however, we play with the idea that in forming a female from the male body, women carry within them the story of a lonely soul, of another's suffering? In making another human from the first, God creates a hybrid being, who recognizes the story of the other as connected to her own and, as a result, is enabled to have compassion for him. One might even add that in a way the female creature best symbolizes our plural existence, because in addition to being hybridized by the image of God, she is crossed and complicated by another other's story, namely, that of her partner.

There are other talking points about hybridity within the doctrine of creation. God makes difference sacred by creating a diversity of creatures, all of which are labeled as good. Connected to that plurality of diverse creatures is the sacralizing of the interdependence among them, since all creatures are dependent on their creator for every moment of their existence, rendering being dependent and feeling vulnerable normative. Interdependence carries over to the relations among creatures. Human beings are dependent on all the plants and animals of the earth, and the earth is vulnerable to the actions of all of creation. Being dependent and vulnerable is an essential aspect of claiming hybridity, in that in telling our stories we have to admit our connections to and differences from one another. And, finally, the theological idea of "sacramentality" itself, specifically the notion of God's presence in the created and finite world, illuminates human existence as hybrid in that there is a constant exchange between the sacred and the everyday.

JESUS AS HYBRID

Teachings about the person and work of Jesus Christ provide additional talking points for making the case that hybridity is a normative dimension of human existence. Christians are hard-pressed to ignore the many stories of the historical Jesus: he was a Jew, a man, a friend, and a son, incarnating a hybridity that landed him in trouble on more than a few occasions and, at other times, became the cause for celebration. In most instances, however, the effects of

Jesus' hybridity remain ambiguous at best. Few can forget John's portrayal of the wedding at Cana, when Mary demands that her son alleviate a wine shortage: "When the wine gave out, the mother of Jesus said to him, 'They have no wine.' And Jesus said to her, 'Woman, what concern is that to you and to me? My hour has not yet come.'"[8] While this text can be interpreted in any number of ways, even as a rebuke of Jesus' mother's assumptions, it is most interesting for our discussion to read it as Mary calling Jesus to attend to another one of his many stories. Although it is ultimately not up to her to decide when and where he needs to intervene, her request acknowledges that he is not merely the party guest in this context, but in many ways he serves in the role of the host—the one who can save it from ruin.[9] Arguably here, Mary points to Jesus' hybrid identity. While most of us do not have the power to change water to wine or save the world, analogously we play different roles in our lives, all of which come with particular responsibilities and challenges when trying to create and maintain right relationships with others.

Beyond his many-storied historical self, Jesus was actively engaged with others and their stories. In each of the Gospels, Jesus is illustrated as an *other-oriented* person, someone who is consistently engaged with and transformed by the stories of others. He does not hide behind one fixed identity; in fact, he constantly challenges the privilege of the "one true story." One example of Jesus' other-oriented style can be found in the Gospel of Luke where Jesus asks his host, and really all of us, to invite others to our tables, not just the ones with the same old stories: "When you give a luncheon or a dinner, do not invite your friends or your brothers or your relatives or rich neighbors, in case they may invite you in return, and you would be repaid. But when you give a banquet, invite the poor, the crippled, the lame, and the blind. And you will be blessed, because they cannot repay you, for you will be repaid at the resurrection of the righteous."[10] Christians have interpreted this text among others in terms of the call for "table fellowship," creating the possibility for each one of us to open to others through their many stories, some of which are enmeshed with our own.[11]

References to human existence as plural and enmeshed are not limited to the historical person of Jesus. One only needs to examine the doctrine of the incarnation, which asserts that "Jesus Christ is fully human and fully divine . . . one [person] . . . existing in the two natures . . . without confusion, without change, without division, without separation," to find another significant talking point for realizing what is at stake in claiming hybridity.[12] In the incarnation, as Jesus takes on simultaneously the "spatial trajectories" of humanity and divinity, the mysterious and the mundane live in proximity, and relationships with otherness are graced and made sacramental. Most importantly, this hybrid relationship between the divine and the human is salvific. In reflecting on our own hybridized existence, Christians might contemplate the mystery of Jesus' hybridity, not with any fixation on locating any one pure or true story about his divinity or about his humanity, but about being opened to hope and redemption by the rich interplay between these stories.[13]

Finally, in Jesus' death and resurrection, hybridity manifests even more profoundly as Christians proclaim that through the cross Jesus takes on the stories of many, including those of the most stigmatized of his time: women, children, the sick, and the outcast. He takes them on by making them important, by de-centering his own need for survival in order to secure theirs. He dies for all of humanity—not just for mine or yours, but for everyone's stories. Like Jesus, who takes on the stories of many, Christians are called to bear the other's story as their own, largely because it is theirs too. As Jesus becomes the one who shoulders the burden of all our histories and refuses to take shelter in any one story, in any one home, Christians are elected to model Jesus' humble posture, not by merely trying to transcend self, but through carrying the weight of many in their own hybrid selves. One might want to push even further and argue that resurrection is the hope for all of our stories to be acknowledged, even if they have to be rewritten or relinquished in an act of reconciliation toward another.

In suggesting that the Christian tradition demonstrates hybridity as a normative dimension of human existence, in which one is called to forfeit a single, fixed, and pure story about oneself to make room for another, I realize that I am treading on dangerous terrain. After all, don't some individuals and groups have more to relinquish than others? Moreover, is it fair to say that everyone experiences hybridity the same? Certainly not, since for some, embracing their identity as hybrid is not a choice but something they are forced to do and are stigmatized because of it, including those peoples and cultures fragmented and broken by conquest and exile.[14] These hybrids have been dehumanized and demonized by more powerful groups because they do not have one pure story or one idealized identity in their background. Other groups are robbed of the right to call themselves hybrid altogether, even if they wanted to claim the name. African Americans, in many ways, have been essentialized to such an extreme by white supremacist ideology that there is little room for them to be conceptualized as anything else than other. This reductionist thinking allows privileged groups to resist acknowledging that African Americans are comprised of multiple stories, some of which overlap and intertwine with their own.[15] While being vigilant about these particular experiences, I argue here against interpreting hybridity in any commonsense manner, and instead propose that none of us are free from the responsibility of acknowledging our hybridity or that of others. As we begin to claim our hybridity, we will see that we all have idealized stories we need to surrender in order to make room for those of another. The mere realization of the fact that "we are all hybrids" can lead to an existence in which we shed the arrogance of having the "one true story," overcome our blindness to other stories, and ultimately acknowledge that our many-storied selves are connected to those of others. These concessions create the possibility for living in the image of God, honoring the incarnation, and emulating Jesus' other-oriented activity—in other words, for being human in a world with others.

THE COST OF HYBRIDITY

With all our heightened attention to the plural and enmeshed reality of human existence, it still is tempting to live as if our identities are singular and pure, not trespassed and challenged by the stories of others—that our story is the one, the only, and the true story. In fact, there is an undeniable cost to claiming hybridity, namely, that of giving up the "one true story" that provides us with a security blanket, shielding us from appearing or feeling vulnerable, and permitting us to avoid the responsibility of dealing with another's stories. It is hard to deny that life would be somewhat easier, at least in the short term, if I could really buy into the idea that my story of being a Christian is the most important one in my life, or that I am a mother first and foremost. If either of those scenarios were the case, I could make ethical decisions quite easily and organize my social relationships accordingly. I would feel like I have a modicum of certainty and control in my life. Nevertheless, being human from a Christian perspective demands that one cease longing for total control and embrace the reality that our freedom and responsibility are always directed in service of another and their complicated stories. Any denial of that obligation defies our God-given plural and social—or what I haven been calling hybrid—nature, leading to brokenness in individuals and communities.

Some feminist theologians, including myself, are inclined to resist the discourse of "sin" because it has been used to devalue women, starting with Eve as the locus of human transgression. However, one cannot adequately attend to the plurality of identity without sustaining, in the words of Serene Jones, "serious reflection on the depth to which persons can 'fall' in their brokenness and their participation in the breaking of others."[16] Sin is an important piece in the discussion of anthropology, because when people refuse to engage their freedom in a way that respects their social relationships with all of creation, they risk refusing the call to live in the image of God and honor the incarnation. In the midst of hybrid existence, sin occurs when we fail to attend to the needs, feelings, memories, and stories of another. We sin not necessarily because we are mean-spirited or even because we are consumed by hubris, but perhaps, as Bernard Lonergan explains, because such sin is a result of scotoma, of being blinded to our hybrid existence. We experience this blindness as bias, which prevents us from having insights about ourselves that would reveal our negative feelings toward others. Fear, prejudice, and anger permeate our biased outlooks, prohibiting us from acknowledging how our individual and group stories are multiple and enmeshed with those of others.[17] Overcoming the brokenness among individuals and groups that results from scotoma is an important dimension in claiming one's hybridity and building right relationships with others.

Without a doubt, theological anthropology can be read in terms of living among others with many stories. The question before us now is: how do ordinary persons, begin to consider the effects of their stories on others, to claim their hybridity? In a way, it begins with autobiographical storytelling that seeks to be as honest and responsible as possible—to tell one's stories in a way that invites others into one's life.

STORYTELLING AS PRAXIS

I consider myself a laywoman, a feminist, and a Roman Catholic (not necessarily in that order), and not surprisingly, some of these stories compete with others for my time and energy. More often than not, any one of my stories seeps into that of another, resulting in a situation permeated with ambiguity and internal emotional conflict. As a lay Catholic feminist theologian, I am also a mother, and every so often when I mother my two children, I feel as if I am neglecting my students and colleagues; or when I tout my professional story, I feel as if I am ignoring the needs of my family. From another angle, from time to time when I embrace Roman Catholicism, I feel as if I am falling short of my feminist ideals.

This is not the end of the responsibility to others that my stories bring. In being a laywoman, a feminist, and a Catholic in an ecclesial context, I hold certain privileges that the women before me did not. It is not too strong to suggest that a laywoman in today's world can wield as much or more power as any woman religious, whereas in the past this power dynamic may not have been present. This volume on Catholic feminist thought is written largely by laywomen, virtually destabilizing and marginalizing the previously privileged stories of women religious who came before. These shifts in power in relation to our stories must not be swept under the table to which we are called. Undoubtedly, talking about these issues is not always comfortable or desirable. I would like to think I secured my place in this book through my own merit. Claiming hybridity forces me to realize that I am always connected and indebted to others, some of whose stories are now occluded by my own. In order for right relationships of human flourishing and trust to emerge—to stand shoulder to shoulder with one another—human beings in general, and Christians in particular, have a responsibility to enact their freedom by being honest about these tensions and by being vigilant about how our stories overlap and intertwine with one another. As long as we hold on to singular, un-trespassed stories about ourselves, our religion, culture, and nation and, consequently, ignore the reality that many of our stories merge and conflict with that of another, we fall victim to sin.

Beyond these intensely personal stories, some of my stories are more politically charged, like that of being a Christian in the United States. After 9/11, many U.S. citizens, and many of them Christian, have adhered to a certain role when identifying themselves: the helpless victim of an unfathomable attack.

Feeling victimized by terrorists who can be anyone, strike any-where, and at any time has led to unending discourse and anxi-ety about the need to survive in this uncertain world. These fears over survival have had disastrous effects, legitimizing inhuman and unjust acts across the globe. Claiming hybridity in the midst of the affective overflow of 9/11, including U.S. military engage-ments around the world, requires great courage and stamina in order to analyze how the roles of victim and perpetrator are cast, and to consider whether, and if so how, the stories about the vic-tims and the perpetrators overlap and intertwine. There is very little wiggle room in the public sphere to imagine these roles and stories as overlapping, that the one who has been hurt may be connected (if only de facto) to those who are responsible for caus-ing the injury; in other words, there is limited tolerance for being responsible for hybrid existence within the backdrop of global fears about terrorism. Like that of any story that wields a total-izing and hegemonic appeal, Christians must resist patriotism based in the ideology of victimhood and grapple with the stories of others, even the stories belonging to those typed as perpetra-tors. They must do this not to be in style with the latest theories about identity as multiple, but rather to avoid the sin of scotoma. Holding on to the primacy of one story at the expense of being blind to all others refuses to honor the good of all of creation, the mystery of the incarnation, and the right relationships between God and humanity and among all of creation modeled in Jesus' other-oriented activity.

MATERNITY AS A METAPHOR
FOR HYBRIDITY[18]

Unlike at any other moment of my life, when I was pregnant with my two children, I felt hostage to the other and challenged by the multiplicity of stories that informed my identity. For those few months, I was concretely hybrid. Maternity is *one* way to speak about what is at stake in claiming hybridity as a theological meta-phor, one that is responsible to having overlapping and contesting stories that complicate our relationships with others.

MOTHER ISSUES

As one might already imagine, speaking about hybridity in terms of maternity and motherhood is not without problems. My work could be read as myopic, as there are countless people who cannot be mothers, including women who strongly desire to do so but are unable for a whole host of biological, economic, political, and tech-nological reasons. My work also raises the question of whether my telling of this particular story excludes others. Or put more starkly, does even uttering the word *mother* in either a theological or aca-demic setting further oppress women who feel either exploited by that story or alienated from it? My intention is not to occlude or erase any of these stories or hurt anyone, but to put forward one metaphor among many that further illuminates the very compli-cated process of being Christian in today's world of plurality.

Others may label my invocation of the specter of motherhood as essentialist in that by suggesting that women have the potential to experience a certain role, I am reducing them to that specific role, namely, that of mothering. With the tendency toward essential-ism as insidious as it is in an ecclesial context, and even more nar-rowly as defined by Roman Catholicism, I do not take this charge lightly. As Mary, the virgin mother, is cast as the perfect impossi-ble role model, and as reductionist connotations about Mary and motherhood are embellished by spousal, heterosexist imagery that concretizes unequal and potentially harmful power relationships within the church, I too have wondered if Christians have any more room for another mother.[19] I hope by the end of my essay it becomes clear that the anthropology I espouse purports precisely the opposite, specifically, that there is always room for another's story at the table, and that welcoming another has the potential to dislodge the dominant glamorized reading of motherhood in the Christian traditions as well as within everyday culture. In other words, I seek to complicate those insidious narratives that fabricate the "mommy myth" about an idealized woman with an unending reservoir of love, who sacrifices without complaint and never loses her temper.[20] Therefore, if I am engaging in essentialism, I hope it fits the label of what some feminists categorize as "strategic," and that by rethinking maternity as a metaphor for hybrid existence, I can begin to chip away at the primacy of that one oppressive story about motherhood that blinds us to the many other stories of maternity, including those which uphold the reality that for some, it is not important to become a mother at all.[21]

MATERNAL HYBRIDS

From conception forward, a woman is hostage to an other who continually encroaches upon and de-centers her one private story, her soliloquy. Physical symptoms such as nausea, vomiting, fatigue, and fetal movement, commonly referred to as quickening, concretize this changing dynamic. Even if the pregnancy is interrupted, her story is trespassed and multiplied. Julia Kristeva writes of this process of emerging hybridity:

> Cells fuse, split, and proliferate; volumes grow, tissues stretch, and body fluids change rhythm, speeding up or slowing down. Within the body, growing as a graft, indomitable there is an other. And no one is present, within that simultaneously dual and alien space, to signify what is going on. "It happens, but I'm not there." "I cannot realize it, but it goes on." Motherhood's impossible syllogism.[22]

With these bodily changes come emotional uncertainty and fear of what the other will bring. When I was expecting my first child, feeling him "kick" for the first time was so exhilarating, as each movement symbolized another dream that I had for his future. With my second child there was a strange apprehension that accompanied each poke and hiccup. I realized that my story was no longer my own and that I was enmeshed with that of another's story, over which I had very little control, yet toward which I had a momentous obligation.

One might think birth, which is an undeniable act of separation, clears up the physical or emotional ambiguity in the encounter between mother/self and fetus/other. Yet, separation on either level is never really possible when everyday life is shaped by the needs, feelings, memories, and stories related to that of another. A mother's story seems indelibly marked by the otherness that was part of her either for a short while or for nine months five times over. Whether there is a "strong effect" or a "vague awareness" between the mother and the fetus, the "leaky boundary" between them makes their relationship difficult to navigate, as one spills over onto one another, creating as close as humans can get to living-hybrid existence concretely.[23] One needs to be honest about that challenge as they claim their hybrid existence and, as a result, realize the gravity of being interconnected with others and making responsible decisions accordingly—choices that are not necessarily based in accepting the other automatically without attending to the stories of all the parties involved.

"Ambivalence" about the stories of motherhood is not always tolerated, and in many ways it "remains a taboo subject."[24] It is not as if women, including theorists, theologians, and ethicists, do not express mixed emotions about conception, pregnancy, and parenting; rather, it is tough for them and others to hear.[25] One might say that there is a blindness to the other stories about motherhood. Many people cringed when Adrienne Rich used the term "monstrous" to describe her experience of motherhood in the feminist classic *Of Woman Born: Motherhood as Experience and Institution*.[26] It is not as if everything about mothering is horrible; on the contrary, everything about mothering is ambiguous. Rich writes: "The bad and the good moments are inseparable for me. I recall the times when, suckling each of my children, I saw his eyes open full to mine, and realized each one of us was fastened to the other, not only by mouth and breast, but through mutual gaze."[27]

This snapshot of the intricate interdependence of maternity has the potential to highlight the multitude of complexities that hybrid existence brings. In a fascinating way, the interplay between the painful and the pleasurable moments and the multiplicity of overlapping and intertwining stories, which are both endemic to motherhood, bring to bear the most fundamental challenges of being human in a world with others. Claiming our hybridity is not easy, nor is it immediately rewarding; rather, in many ways, like being a mother, it is "complex and profound and terrifying."[28] Yet it seems our only option. By resisting any "one true story" about idealized motherhood, or more pertinent to our discussion, about what it means to be human, we become liberated and, dare I say, "graced" to celebrate and embrace even more fully the goodness of creation, the centrality of human freedom, and right relationships with God and others in our everyday lives.

Chapter 2

THIS IS MY BODY . . . GIVEN FOR YOU: THEOLOGICAL ANTHROPOLOGY LATINA/MENTE[1]

Teresa Delgado

As a Roman Catholic Latina, I've spent my entire life gazing upon the crucifix of Jesus' bloody and broken body strung up on the cross, the mode of execution for a criminal of his day. I see beyond the sculptor's rendering of a religious icon and imagine what it would have been like to nail a body onto a tree, with flesh ripping from the weight and gravity. I have that gruesome vision as I hear the words of institution, stated and restated at every Sunday Mass, which affirm the meaning and purpose of that tragic death as freely given, offered for our salvation, a sign of the relationality and grace of God: "This is my body, which is given for you" (Luke 22:19).

These words took on new meaning when I heard testimony of women and young girls from Latin America and the Caribbean, sometimes as young as ten years of age, recount their stories of being trafficked across the borders within Latin America or into the United States. They spoke of the terror of being taken from their homes, some without knowledge of where they were going, deprived of sleep and food, raped, and beaten, often to settle some debt held by their very own family. They spoke of being sold into sexual slavery so that their bodies and their sex could be used as

25

a commodity to save their respective families from financial ruin. This is my body, which is given for you.[2]

The words took on new meaning yet again when I heard the testimony of young Latinas in the United States who had contracted HIV from their boyfriends or husbands with multiple sex partners who refuse to use condoms, unable to confront these men for fear of being beaten, abandoned, or both. Their culture had taught them that good women don't assert their sexual needs and certainly don't contradict those of men. Good women are supposed to serve their men, in the kitchen and the bedroom, even at the expense of their own health. This is my body, which is given for you.[3]

This essay will explore the ways both Catholicism and Latin American/Latino culture have shaped what it means to be human in general and woman in particular. It will investigate how that particular meaning ascribed to "woman" has led to, and perpetuated, abusive and self-sacrificial characteristics as constitutive elements of women's humanity. This essay will identify how these can be both resources for renewal, as well as occasions for distortion when filtered through the lens of particular cultural identities bound by sexuality and gender, using the classic Christian anthropological categories of relationship and grace.

For Latin American and Latina women, the religious and cultural foundations of sexuality have dominated their self-understanding, exacerbated by the double scourge of an increasing rate of HIV/AIDS infection and human trafficking. Using the womanist critique of Christian atonement and sacrifice, as well as the Latin American feminist critique of culture, I will explore what it means to be human in the physical bodies that women inhabit, especially when the particularity of "woman bodiliness" entails the religious and cultural mandate to "give up" our bodies for the sake of others: as mothers, objects of sexual exploitation, and commodities for sale. This will include a critique of fundamental Roman Catholic moral theology, where the notion of sex/sexuality as a means to a greater good can serve to perpetuate the abuse of women's sexual bodies. I will conclude with a new vision of theological anthropology *latina/ mente* that critiques both Latin American culture and Roman Catholic theology while reclaiming from both that which values the physical/ sexual bodies of Latin American and Latina women as women.

THE CROSSES WE BEAR LATINA/MENTE: TRAFFICKING AND HIV/AIDS

The Christian tradition in general and the Roman Catholic Church in particular have a responsibility to address the dual crosses of human trafficking and HIV/AIDS that Latin American women and Latinas in the United States have been burdened to bear in the twenty-first century, given that our tradition is founded on a belief that God took on a bodily form through Jesus to affirm the goodness of humanity and to live with us and die for us: this is my body, which is given for you. The statistics for both human trafficking and HIV/AIDS, as distinct yet intimately related scourges, are staggering. The Central Intelligence Agency of the United States estimates that 50,000 persons are trafficked into the United States annually, 15,000 of whom are enslaved Latin Americans. By these estimates (2003 CIA report), the majority of these are women and children used for organized sex trafficking, representing a $10 billion industry. The United Nations Office on Drugs and Crime (UNODC) has made explicit the connection between human trafficking and HIV/ AIDS transmission by stating:

> Many girls and women are being trafficked for the purpose of sexual exploitation and it seems highly likely that they are forced into unprotected sexual acts with multiple partners, and this is a significant factor in the spread of HIV. HIV/AIDS has received little attention in efforts to address trafficking in persons, and therefore at the moment specific HIV/ AIDS prevention and care services hardly exist for these people. While many national HIV/

HIV/AIDS AND LATINAS IN THE US

According to the Centers for Disease Control, HIV/AIDS is the fourth leading cause of death among Latinas in the United States ages 35-44. High risk heterosexual contact accounts for 80% of transmission for all women and adolescent girls (2005).[1] Latinas constitute 16% of HIV/AIDS cases among women in 33 states. In 1999, the *Los Angeles Times* reported that, according to Dr. Chuck Henry, Director of the Los Angeles County Office of AIDS Programs and Policy, the rate of infection among Latinos in L.A. County had risen from 26% (1991) to 43% (1998).[2] Again, these statistics underestimate the number of Latinas actually infected, since many go unreported due to illegal immigrant status, lack of access to medical care, and the clandestine nature of sex slavery and human trafficking.[3]

---

[1] However, among the diverse Latin groups, Puerto Ricans were more likely to contract the infection via intravenous drug use than high-risk heterosexual contact; see "*HIV*/AIDS among Hispanics/ Latinos," Centers for Disease Control, August 2007.

[2] Jeffrey L. Rabin, Jocelyn Y. Stewart, "AIDS Emergency Declared among County's Minorities," *The Los Angeles Times* (9/29/99); this report also described the proportion of African Americans diagnosed with AIDS grew from 18% to 25% during the same period. Cases in the Asian/Pacific Islander group and among Native Americans grew from 1% to 2%.

[3] Centers for Disease Control HIV/AIDS Fact Sheet, August 2007; The Council on Hemispheric Affairs (March 2006) has stated: "By the end of 2005, the United Nations (UN) estimated 1.8 million Latin Americans were newly infected with the disease that claimed the lives of some 200,000 that year. In the Caribbean, where the epidemic ranks second only to Sub-Saharan Africa's in its tenacity, AIDS killed an estimated 24,000 in 2005, becoming the leading cause of death among adults aged 15 to 44. AIDS further compounds the region's already overwhelming problems of poverty and underdevelopment, as it often strikes victims in the most productive years of their lives, leaving them unable to contribute to their personal and national economies. Furthermore, AIDS disproportionately strikes poor communities as they not only contain high-risk groups like prostitutes and drug users, but also have less biological resistance, as malnutrition and poor health care have been linked to an increased likelihood of contracting AIDS. 'The relationship between poverty and AIDS and AIDS and poverty is bi-directional,' warned a 2002 UNICEF report."

AIDS plans include policies and programs addressing sex work, issues such as trafficking in persons, coercion into sex work, rape and sexual violence are usually not addressed. General responses addressing HIV/AIDS have little impact on trafficked persons due to the clandestine nature of human trafficking, and because people who have been trafficked are not usually reached by services.[4]

We can conclude that simply *being* a Latina or Latin American woman in the twenty-first century puts her at an incredible risk of having her bodily integrity compromised by the double scourge of human trafficking and HIV/AIDS. One cannot speak about what it means to be a human being in relation to God and others, the goal of theological anthropology, without taking seriously the lived historical context in which our human bodies are situated. And Latin American women's bodies, as well as those of their sister Latinas in the United States, are bodies under siege. If we are bold enough to recall those words—"This is my body, which is given for you"— then we are affirming a belief that Jesus' life, death, and resurrection in his particular time and place has something to do with our own. In other words, what happens to and with our bodies in this time and place is supposed to matter.

WHAT DOES IT MEAN TO BE HUMAN? FROM CATHOLIC CHRISTIAN THEOLOGY: RELATIONALITY AND GRACE

Two classic themes that emerge from a Catholic Christian theological anthropology—relationality and grace—have both limited and provided significant resources for claiming the full humanity of Latinas and Latin American women within Catholic feminist theology.

RELATIONALITY

"The human body in its original masculinity and femininity according to the mystery of creation . . . is not only a source of fruitfulness, that is, of procreation, but has 'from the beginning' a spousal character, that is, it has the power to express the love by which the human person becomes a gift, thus fulfilling the deep meaning of his or her being and existence. In this . . . the body is the expression of the spirit and is called . . . to exist in the communion of persons 'in the image of God.'"[5] This statement summarizes the core doctrine of Catholic theological anthropology in that the human person is fully realized in relation to others, in communion with the other in a complementary fashion. Anthropological complementarity of male and female is fundamental to the classic Roman Catholic doctrine of humanity. While this is not exclusive to the sexual realm, sexuality is implied here as a unique condition in which the human body is reciprocated with another human body in the form of "spousal" unity.[6]

The image of God, or *imago Dei*, is the primary source of our relationality, and that image does not necessarily convey a complementary nature, according to a number of contemporary Latino/a theologians. For example, Michelle A. Gonzalez, in her exceptional introduction to feminist theological anthropology, *Created in God's Image*, contributes to systematic theological anthropology by insisting that *imago Dei* anthropology is grounded in the Trinity and is therefore relational. She states, "Through our relationship with God, our fellow human beings, and the rest of creation, we reflect the image of God within us. The human being is not self-contained but rather is constituted by relationships."[7]

If we believe in a triune God as creator, redeemer, and sustainer who has created humanity after God's likeness, then we are called to "be in relation" as intrinsic to our very being. We cannot exist solely unto ourselves, despite our gift of free will, which includes the possibility to reject the other and even God. We fall away from the image of God when we fail "to live according to the ends for which we were created."[8] That end includes our interdependency and relationality with others.

Roberto Goizueta, particularly in his book *Caminemos con Jesús*,[9] speaks of the intrinsic communal nature of our humanity when viewed through the lens of Latino culture and experience. Goizueta asserts the human person is fully actualized in communion with others; in fact, "the community is the birthplace of the self."[10] This notion of community is concrete and tangible; it is the cultural environment and locus of relationships that extend beyond nuclear familiarity. In fact, one cannot be fully human, from a Hispanic/Latino perspective, without "being in relationship with others, and to be in relationship with others is to be *'acompañado.'*"[11] To be a Catholic Hispanic human person is to see oneself reflected in Jesus (who we are) and to accompany Jesus through our life praxis (how we are called to live). Our relational being cannot be separated from our relational doing. Again, that relationality is not centered upon or limited to a complementary understanding of relationship. On the contrary, like Gonzalez, Goizueta maintains that the human person can only be actualized within a community that extends far beyond the limit of the other. This assertion is a distinct departure from the classic model of complementarity in Catholic anthropology.

GRACE

The theological anthropology of Catholic theologian Karl Rahner has been a central focus for numerous contemporary theologians, including Gonzalez and Miguel Díaz, who have reflected in particular on the way Rahner formulated his understanding of human nature as grounded in the universal possibility of God's grace infused into the particular experience of the everyday. As Gonzalez writes, "Rahner argues that we are oriented toward the horizon that we know as God and that the ground for the reception of grace is in the structure of the human. Within us is the experience of grace."[12] In other words, it is God alone who offers God's infinite grace to us, accessible if we so choose to access it by our freedom and autonomy.

Miguel Díaz offers a similar analysis of Rahner's theological anthropology as a source for constructing a dialogue between his and U.S. Hispanic perspectives, given their valuation of the particular as a locus for God's saving grace, and the universal accessibility of that grace. Although we can look to the person of Jesus as the exemplar of God's intercommunication with humanity, we can also examine our own lives and experiences as the potential place for the universality of God's grace to pervade. "Rahner makes very clear that as a result of God's universal offer of grace, God's solidarity with all humanity in Christ, and the essential constitution of the human as hearer of the Word, all human activity, even if unthematic and implicit, is religious activity."[13]

These two pillars of classic Christian theological anthropology—relationality and grace—are foundational and unwavering elements of what constitutes our human nature as beings created by God, redeemed by Jesus, and sustained by the Holy Spirit. Latino/a theologians cannot divorce themselves from these same categories if they are to take seriously the cultural and social context from which a theological anthropology latina/mente is shaped.

DOUBLE CROSSED: DISTORTIONS OF THEOLOGY AND CULTURE

Latin American women and Latinas in the United States, through their experience of suffering by human trafficking and HIV/AIDS, live out their humanity in a way that seems to be a far cry from the idealization of anthropology as posited by the Catholic theological tradition and even by that of contemporary Latino/a theologians. Given that the majority of Latin American women and Latinas emerge from a predominantly Christian backdrop, the question becomes whether the religious and cultural traditions have created the conditions that allow this "double cross"[14] to permeate and stake a stronger claim upon the lives of women. Why is it that families sell their own daughters to traffickers, when these same families pray to a God in whose image we have been created? Are not these daughters made in that image and, as a result, worthy of a life of justice, love, and freedom? Why is it that women resign themselves to be bound to their husbands, boyfriends, or other male companions who put their physical/sexual bodies at risk, when these same women pray to a God whose grace is universal and accessible to all? Are not their bodies deserving of the infusion of God's grace that privileges the "least among us"?

The problem with the classical understanding of theological anthropology is that it has not only disallowed a critique of the ways relationality and grace have been distorted, but it has also fueled that distortion in relation to women's lives in two distinct ways. First, the central focus of complementarity as a constitutive element of our human relationality has emboldened a hierarchical ordering of male/female relationship when filtered through the context of Latin American and U.S. Latino culture, with dire consequences for women. Second, the privileged place of the Virgin Mary as the exemplar of the human manifestation of God's grace for women ("Hail Mary, full of grace") has bolstered the belief that women's humanity is actualized when the will of another is made a priority ("Let it be done to me according to thy will"). Both interpretations have created distortions of the true meaning of grace, leading to an understanding of humanity that accepts injustice and violence against women.

In this sense, Latin American women and Latinas not only bear the dual cross of human trafficking/sex slavery and HIV/AIDS, but have been double crossed by our Latino cultures and religious traditions, both of which have emphasized the role of woman as one who sacrifices herself for the good of others. This emphasis on self-sacrifice, even at the expense of one's physical body, is a distortion of the true meaning of relationality and grace when viewed through the lens of love and justice, for self and community. This distortion has served the domination and commodification of women's physical bodies, in spite of the best attempts to interpret that culture and theological tradition in ways that affirm women's full humanity.

FROM LATIN AMERICAN CULTURE

WE ARE, THEREFORE I AM

Latin American women and Latinas learn at a very early age to put the community before individual, the family before the self. This familial and communal experience is so central to Latin American culture that we often put our individual needs and desires aside to satisfy the needs and desires of our families. And this is not necessarily a destructive thing; it can act as a corrective to an overly individualistic society that values and rewards competition and "win/lose" dynamics. Our bodies become the vehicle through which a greater good is attained.

The testimonies of trafficked women demonstrate that some are willing to risk their lives in the exchange for the financial well-being of their families. They convince themselves that this is only a temporary, short-term arrangement to pay off a debt, to care for a younger sibling or an older parent, so that they will not have to endure the same. In other words, her body becomes the vehicle through which a greater good is attained, namely, economic "salvation." The work being performed becomes a violation of bodily integrity, devoid of any human dignity, since neither the woman nor the work is valued intrinsically. Her body becomes a means to an end, a commodity for exchange, an exchange that can be justified when seen as a way of showing love for another: there is no greater love than this, our Christian tradition has taught us. In other words, when the needs of the community are placed before the needs of the self, it is not difficult to see how one can interpret that self-sacrifice as a means to a communal good. Even the communal nature of relationality so emphasized by Latino/a theologians runs the risk of becoming a detriment when taken to such an extreme.

MARIANISMO/MACHISMO

The dual cultural dynamic of *marianismo* (the idealization of the obedient woman as reflected in the Virgin Mary as exemplar) and *machismo* (the idealization of the dominant male hero) have perpetuated the dominant role of the heterosexist male, embodied by fathers, brothers, husbands, and boyfriends, who maintain the final authority for women who must remain docile and accommodating in order to sustain "calm" familial relationships.[15] Ivone Gebara speaks directly to the dynamic of sacrifice, fear, and guilt in the lives of women in Latin America in whom it is instilled, from a very young age, to accept the imbalance of power and powerlessness between men and women. In this context, culture and religion intersect in a way that perpetuates the belief that women, in order to be considered good, must be unquestioningly obedient. Gebara explains:

> Living in sacrifice is living in obedience to the will of the Father. And living in obedience to the will of the Father means living in obedience to his Son, represented by father, husbands, brothers and men who hold social and religious power. The ideology of sacrifice, imposed by patriarchal culture, has developed in women training in renunciation. . . . Women in many ways are made to serve others.[16]

FROM CATHOLIC CHRISTIAN TRADITION

The Christian traditions and popular beliefs regarding Jesus and sacrifice have not served Latin American women and Latinas any better than their culture. The Catechism of the Roman Catholic Church is very clear about the atoning nature of Jesus' death.[17] Jesus substitutes his obedience for our disobedience, the new Adam whose life is given "as a ransom for many" (Matt. 20:28). His suffering frees us from suffering; his death brings us new life. With this substitution theory of atonement, we are taught to fear direct retributive punishment for some wrongdoing and rationalize our own suffering as the result of some wrongdoing, even when we cannot identify it directly. In this sense, the innocent person may receive the brunt of suffering and punishment, thinking that she must have done something wrong to deserve it.[18]

Here we see the consequences of what Eleazar Fernandez has termed "disembodied knowing," a universalizing of principles and norms that does not take into account how the application of those principles and norms affects our very bodies. Our Christian doctrines need to be critiqued through the lens of an embodied epistemology, a way of knowing that "sees reality through the con-figuration of our bodiliness and seriously considers the effects of ideas as they bear on bodies and vice versa, especially the disfig-ured bodies of the marginalized. . . . It pays attention to radical plu-rality, particularity and the differences between human beings."[19] A theological anthropology that does not address the way in which its categories of relationality and grace affect the real bodies of real human beings deserves neither adherence nor reverence. What it deserves is an overhaul, a total-body makeover, guided by the way Latin American women and Latinas, in this case, have absorbed the legacy of that doctrine to their disadvantage.

UNRELATIONALITY: DISTORTIONS OF THE IMAGE OF GOD

Fueled by the distortions within Latin American cultural and Catholic traditions around the notions of sacrifice, Latin American women and Latinas in the United States bear the double cross of sex slavery/trafficking and HIV/AIDS as a consequence of a belief, in part, that they need to atone for the evil of the community of which they are not only a part, but also that has shaped their very sense of self. The various interpretations of the category of relation-ality, as complementary and/or communal, share common ground that the human being is relational when understood as reflective of the image of God. Fernandez confirms the postmodern turn on the Cartesian formula by centering the self in terms of our emotional connection with others and the world, rather than in terms of our ability to reason, the traditional anthropological distinction between humanity and the rest of creation. He states, "Relationship is con-stitutive of who we are and what we can become. Relationality, not rationality, is decisive for our humanity."[20]

Unfortunately, women have been short-changed on both fronts—relationality and rationality—and this is no different for Latin American women and Latinas when examined through the lens of patriarchy. The classic Roman Catholic emphasis on comple-mentarity as a fundamental element of our humanity has still rel-egated women to the lower of the hierarchical ordering of male and female, despite John Paul II's insistence on the valuation of both sexes in distinct, yet equal, ways.[21] This is nowhere more visible than in the division of labor within the institution of the Church itself: the priest takes on the symbolic manifestation of Jesus as priest, prophet, and king. Jesus as the suffering servant, the one who gives his life for many, seems to be the distinct role reserved for women, since only men can take on the priestly function. In other words, complementarity becomes a source of unjust relation-ship that accords men the benefit of one aspect of God's image and relegates women to another, without any regard for the way a par-ticular cultural context, namely, machismo/marianismo, can has-ten that distortion.

Despite the attempts of more contemporary theologians to emphasize community as a critical component of one's human rela-tionality, as opposed to complementarity, this too has its downside. The privileged place of community for many marginalized iden-tities has served as a corrective to the individualistic and univer-salizing legacy of modern eurocentric Christian theologies. In that sense, the emphasis on community has served an important bal-ancing role. However, even communities from which we emerge and to whom we feel accountable are not immune to the systemic evils, as Fernandez suggests, of interconnected oppressions.[22] We must remember that it is members of one's community who are trafficking their very own; we must not forget that those men who have multiple partners and completely disregard safer sexual practices are doing so, in large measure, with women from their own communities. It is one thing to look upon another group, different from one's own, and question its humanity; both colonization and slavery succeeded for many years because of the ability of the colonizers and slaveholders to obscure the humanity of the other. Yet it is no different within respective communities when those who benefit from such obfuscation (Latin American men and Latinos, Roman Catholic priestly hierarchy, etc.) are able to maintain their power status by doing so. Gonzalez's work is instructive when she claims that our understanding of relationship is not uncritical or romanticized. "Not all relations reflect the image of God. Instead, relationships are judged against the norm of Jesus' concrete life, ministry, death and resurrection. Through our mirroring of Jesus' justice-infused ministry we grow in the image of Christ and, consequently, in the image of God."[23]

DIS-GRACE: DISTORTIONS OF OUR DEPENDENCE ON GOD

The Christian tradition has affirmed some essential meanings of God's grace. First, God's grace is universal, that is, it is available to all of God's creation at all times in infinite measure. There is nothing that we can do to earn God's grace; it is not in our human power to control the grace of God which is beyond our manipulation. At the same time, the Christian tradition maintains that we can make ourselves more accessible, more open, to the grace of God by our submission to God's will, our obedience to God's laws, and our dependence on God's forgiveness and mercy. In doing so, we open the window of our hearts to allow the refreshing breeze of God's grace to sweep over us. Grace is God-being-for-us in a way that we cannot be for ourselves; we are not the source of our own, or others', salvation. In this way, grace connects the lifespan of Jesus, including his cross, to our own lifespan and our own crosses.[24]

This intimate connection of Jesus' life to our own lives through the vehicle of God's grace will necessarily come to us by way of our lived, historical, and contextual reality. We cannot separate our experience of God's grace from our cultural experience, even though the former is not bound by the latter. "There is no acultural Christianity," in the words of Orlando Espín; in its form and expression, Christianity is bound to culture. Grace may not be bound by culture because it comes from God and is therefore infinite.[25]

Within the particular cultural experience of Latin America, the image of the Virgin Mary is upheld as the shining example of what it means to be a "grace-filled" human being, that is, one who has maintained the characteristics of submission, obedience, and dependence upon God's will to receive the universal gift of God's grace. John Paul II's anthropological vision is inseparable from his Mariological vision. "Mary's divine motherhood is . . . a superabundant revelation of that fruitfulness in the Holy Spirit to which man submits his spirit when he freely chooses continence 'in the body . . . for the kingdom of heaven.'"[26] Traditional Roman Catholic theology has asserted that "if every woman were an image of the Mother of God, a spouse of Christ and an apostle of the divine Heart, she would fulfill her feminine vocation no matter in what circumstances she lived and what her external activities might be."[27]

This understanding of female humanity has been the dominant and authoritative understanding for Latin American women and Latinas who have been shaped within a Christian context of Latin American culture. Therefore, to be a Latin American woman or Latina is to be judged against this vision of the "grace-filled" woman, namely, the Virgin Mary, who submitted to the will of the Father, gave her body for the Son, and allowed herself to be impregnated by the Spirit. Obedience to a male image is the fundamental starting point for female humanity. To be "full of grace," then, is to mirror Mary in one's own life: giving up one's autonomy to answer a larger, more meaningful call.

This emphasis on submission, obedience, and dependence, as the fertile ground within which God's grace is sown, has violent implications for Latin American women and Latinas. Ivone Gebara asserts that "[t]he symbols of love and power are unfailingly male and tied to obedience. A culture of obedience has developed differently for women than for men. We must recognize that the hierarchy in society is a sexual one crisscrossed by others."[28]

What does it look like, then, when Latin American women and Latinas, shaped by such notions of God's relationality and grace, confront the scourges of human trafficking and HIV/AIDS? If she has been raised to believe that women are to emulate the virtues of Mary and model themselves after the suffering servant as a reflection of her openness to God, then she will accept her suffering at the hands of the traffickers and those raping her body because these are her crosses to bear. It is a distortion of a doctrine that says only God can save us; we cannot save ourselves. But it is a useful distortion when perpetuated by those who benefit from obedience and submission in both our culture and our church. If she has been raised to believe that women are dependent upon and "obey God the Father, to follow Jesus the Son, and to be open to the Spirit that impregnates"[29] her, she will accept the notion that she needs a male figure in her life to take care of her, economically and otherwise, regardless of the way he may abuse her body. She must fulfill her conjugal duty to be open to her man's sexual needs, regardless of whether such openness will lead to her own illness and possible death.

The models of how women are called to live into their full humanity have been unrelational and disgraceful when we examine how these have manifested themselves in the lives of Latin American women and Latinas through the lens of their double crosses of human trafficking and HIV/AIDS. While it is true that men have had to contend with a distortion of relationality and grace, which has led to an emphasis on submission and suffering through heroism,[30] I hope to have made clear that the norms of a culture and church tradition that lead to such bodily violence against women are distinct, insidious, and must be dismantled at the very core. The questions then become: What are we left to retrieve? What are we left to uphold?

CLAIMING THE TRADITION ANEW

I believe that we can reclaim the Christian tradition of theological anthropology, inclusive of the categories of relationality and grace, in a way that dismantles the oppressive structures upon which human trafficking and HIV/AIDS have been allowed to flourish unchecked. We need only look to our African American sisters who have for twenty-five years waged a fierce theological critique against that which has compromised their bodily integrity through the legacy and current manifestations of slavery, sexual exploitation, and forced surrogacy.

USE OF WOMANIST CRITIQUE OF ATONEMENT

Latin American women and Latinas in the United States are called to form bonds of solidarity with African American women through our common experience of slavery and sexual subjugation. Through this shared bond, both communities of women can stand together as witnesses against not only the legacy of African American slavery, but its present manifestation through human trafficking and the HIV/AIDS crisis.[31]

Latin American women and Latinas in the United States can look to African American womanist theology as a resource to critique Christian atonement theology. In particular, Delores Williams and JoAnne Terrell have contributed tremendously to atonement theories by critiquing traditional notions of surrogacy and sacrifice, making clear that the formulations of atonement theory have few, if any, resources to be claimed by African American women.[32] Cast through the lens of African American women's experience of their bodies, defiled by slave surrogacy and sexual exploitation (was not Hagar a sexual slave?), Williams affirms that

> God did not intend the surrogacy roles they have per-
> formed. God did not intend the defilement of their bodies
> as white men put them in the place of white women to
> provide sexual pleasure for white men during the slavoc-
> racy. This was rape and rape is defilement. . . . Humankind
> is redeemed through Jesus' ministerial vision of life, and
> not through his death.[33]

Similarly, JoAnne Terrell asserts that the cross, for African Americans, is a confrontation with theodicy, an experience that is all too real in the life and premature death of so many in the black community.

> [T]he cross, in its original sense, embodied a scandal that
> something, anything, good could come out of such an
> event. Seen in this light, Jesus' sacrificial act was not the
> objective. Rather, it was the tragic, if foreseeable, result of
> his confrontation with evil. . . . Anyone's death has saving
> significance inasmuch as we learn continuously from the
> life that preceded it.[34]

Using the experience and critique of African American women as a guide, Latin American women and Latinas must maintain a suspicious stance against anything within both the culture and Christianity that even leans in the direction of sacrifice for the other, even for the community, when one's own autonomy, freedom, and bodily integrity are compromised.

USE OF LATIN AMERICAN FEMINIST CRITIQUE OF PATRIARCHY

Latin American women and Latinas must also resist sexual con-
structs, dismantling the dichotomy of marianismo/machismo and uprooting them both from their cultural and religious foundations.

The sexual/political/economic critique from Argentinian theologian Marcella Althaus Reid is most instructive, as she seeks to undermine the constructs of Roman Catholic moral theology that set up sexuality, particularly complementarity, as a means to an end—namely, the Church's insistence on the distinct sexual roles between men and women. Reid challenges the dualistic nature of Christian theological discourse to suggest that it is not the universal norm for sexual self-understanding. Part of this challenge centers on the role of the Virgin Mary, but the "work concerning a serious criticism of Mariology has not yet started [in Latin America], perhaps because Mariology fulfills such a crucial role in the patriarchal order of our society."[35]

Claiming the tradition anew also requires us to critique global and domestic economic systems and structures that force families to sell off their own daughters for economic gain, that instill the fear of being abandoned by men so as not to lose one's economic status (feminization of poverty), and that encourage high risk/high reward lifestyles that threaten health and life, such as allowing men to pay more for sex without the use of a condom. This economic reality of globalization is linked explicitly to a patriarchal system that idealizes the Virgin Mary and elicits benefits from perpetuating her "virtues" among Latin American women and Latinas. Reid emphasizes that "Mariology sacralizes and dictates how to be a woman in Latin America and works as the cornerstone of the feminization of poverty in the continent."[36]

RECONSTRUCTING A CATHOLIC FEMINIST THEOLOGICAL ANTHROPOLOGY LATINA/MENTE

Is it possible, then, to construct a theological anthropology that is life-giving and liberating for women, in a way that does not perpetuate the distortions of "unrelationality" and "dis-grace"? I am led back to the words at the onset of this essay, the words that provoked my reevaluation of theological anthropology: "This is my body, which is given for you." How can Latin American women and Latinas say these words without allowing their bodies to be exploited, ravaged, commodified, devalued, and discarded as we have seen with human trafficking and HIV/AIDS? She must begin by refusing to internalize the way in which both culture and theology has distorted our bodies. She must refuse to accept both the cultural and religious legacies of her community that dictate the sacrificial offering of her body. She must refuse to allow the words of Jesus—"This is my body, which is given for you"—to become a death sentence. I believe this refusal is possible only when we consider the intersections of human nature and sexuality as these are embodied by women. In other words, reconstructing a Catholic feminist theological anthropology is an act of resistance to the sexual crosscurrents of our culture and theology. Our resistance to being double-crossed by our culture and our theology must be sustained on many levels.

First, we must resist a theology of the cross that glorifies or exemplifies the sacrificial suffering of Jesus as means to a salvific end. On the cross of Jesus, we are faced with multiple dimensions of human suffering and evil, kept in place by nails and swords, penetrating the body until blood and water emerge. But when viewed through the lens of Latin American and Latina women who are faced with human trafficking and the sex trade, and the compounded prevalence of HIV/AIDS, they too are wounded by nails and swords, penetrated in places where blood and water emerge. Rather than defining her body in terms of sacrifice and suffering in that moment, her body becomes the ground of resistance to evil and sin; her scars mark the territory of many acts of defiance. When we understand sacrifice and suffering in this way, we see reflected in the pool of blood at the foot of the cross of Jesus the evil structures, relationships, and institutions that put him there in the first place. Therefore, any attempt to sacrifice her body is no longer viewed as a cross she is called to bear, but a cross that indicts those who would impose it upon her. In this case, we must indict the traffickers, the communities that act in complicity with them, the men who pass HIV on to their partners, and the church that refuses to view condom use as protection of life. The list of accomplices runs long.

Second, a new feminist theological anthropology must expose the way the Catholic emphasis on the Marian ideal has created the conditions, in part, for women to accept their own self-deprecation, sacrifice, and passivity. It is not enough for us to redefine the Virgin Mary simply by recasting her in a different light or by showing her to be just as woman as we are. On the contrary, a new feminist theological anthropology that takes seriously the lives of women as they are embodied in their sexuality must also reexamine the Virgin Mary in terms of her sexuality. Rather than defining her body as a vehicle for the salvation and life of others, her body becomes the source and celebration of her own life as it is lived in relation. When viewed through the lens of human trafficking and HIV/AIDS, a new Mariology must then challenge the presumption of obedience as a precondition for God's grace; we can no longer be obedient when faced with the defilement or negation of our own bodies.

Third, a new feminist theological anthropology must also break open the categories of sexuality and suffering. It must explore the connections between sex/pleasure and sex/suffering for women, debunking the theological and philosophical notions of the female as a passive receptacle for male agency. Our inherited Roman Catholic tradition has emphasized that women's bodily integrity can only be maintained by denying sexual pleasure as a virgin or subverting sexual pleasure for a higher good as a mother/wife. If the tradition claims that to be a virgin is to maintain bodily integrity, then that formulation would also claim that having sex is to lose bodily integrity. A new feminist theological anthropology must reject those binaries and transform the relationship of women to sex that is not defined by patriarchal culture centered on male pleasure or by a patriarchal church centered on male holiness. Rather, sex becomes a relationship of giving/receiving pleasure as a gift to other and self. Her body, especially the sexual expression of her body, can be seen as an affirmation of God's goodness in creation, a reflection of the image of God in the flesh. Both relationality and grace, as constitutive elements of a new anthropology, are precisely about the giving and receiving of an incarnate gift.

THIS IS MY BODY . . . GIVEN FOR YOU *IN MEMORY OF ME*

This essay has been my attempt to articulate a theological anthropology that takes seriously the lived reality of women's bodies in the twenty-first century when scourged by human trafficking and HIV/AIDS. To do this, I have critiqued both Latin American culture and Roman Catholic theology for their silence and complicity in relation to these two assaults on women's bodies. It is, admittedly, a preliminary attempt to open up a discussion of the moral norms of sexual expression, in terms of the categories of relationality and grace, in a way that helps Latin American women and Latinas discern, with a critical and suspicious eye, that which seeks to create idols of power and authority against the integrity of their physical and sexual bodies.

It has been virtually impossible for me to envision this new theological anthropology latina/mente without drawing into the conversation other related theological themes, such as sexual ethics, soteriology (doctrine of salvation), theodicy (relationship of evil and creation), eschatology (doctrine of the future end-time), and most notably Christology (the doctrine of Jesus). It is not an accident that I began this journey with a reflection of Jesus' body on the cross, using it as a metaphor to lift up the suffering of Latin American women and Latinas. Who we are, how we suffer, and what we hope for, as human beings, is tied up with Jesus' life, death, and resurrection, if we affirm the words that Jesus proclaimed the night before he took up the cross: "This is my body, which is given for you." But we mustn't forget the words that follow his prophetic proclamation: "Do this *in memory of me*" (emphasis added). That memory of Jesus requires that we look at his lifespan through the lens of love and justice, and evaluate our own lives in relation to that lens. An emphasis on sex and sexuality must also be added to the dialogue within Christian theology from a Latin American women's and Latina perspective. Althaus-Reid and Gebara have begun to break into that dialogue in relation to the Roman Catholic legacy of Mariology, but much more work needs to be done in this regard.

Latin American women and Latinas must strive to remember the disembodied relationality and grace that have been the legacies of the tradition of theological anthropology in a way that values their bodies and their sex. The only way that Latin American and Latina women can adequately attend to a theological anthropology that takes their lives into account is to hold together the interconnectedness of relationality, grace, and sexuality. To this end, we are no longer called to carry a double cross that continues to weigh our bodies down for the good of others. On the contrary, we are called to unbind those three elements of our humanity and to break an unholy silence that restricts the cries of injustice. We can dream of a new way of being relational, graceful, and sexual by lifting our voice in protest, of gaining the strength we need to be who we are created and called to be: the relational, graceful, and sexual image of God.

Chapter 3

WOMANIST WAYS OF BEING IN THE WORLD[1]

LaReine-Marie Mosely

Womanist ethicist Emilie M. Townes has written about how black folk have been dehumanized and commodified in the United States. Some have treated them as statistical social problems; others have rendered their identity and cultural gifts property by exploiting black bodies, images, and ideas for financial gain.[2] This complicates the identity formation of African Americans in general and African American women in particular. By taking on these and other distortions, black women have named and affirmed themselves as the children of God that they are, thus celebrating an inner resonance or integrity that can be properly called womanist.[3] Christian womanists know that Jesus walks with them and that God desires their human flourishing. They are not property. Their identity is derived from the consolation of such divine accompaniment. Traditional issues surrounding the convergence of human nature and grace have never been their concern. Rather, womanists engage their critical cognitive consciousness to navigate in a world where some would call their full humanity into question. The story that follows reveals a womanist way of being in the world, of being human, of being in process, of growing further into one's identity amid the never-ending influence of family, community, society, culture, and history.

My worst nightmare came true sooner than I ever could have imagined. My dear, smart, seventy-one-year-old mother, who has been suffering from Alzheimer disease for some time, didn't recognize me the other day. Not only did she not recognize me, but there were times when she thought that my sisters and I were trying to trick her. Isaiah 49:15 says, "Can a mother forget her infant, be without tenderness for the child in her womb? Even should she forget I will never forget you." Here, the woman who gave me life does not consistently recognize me. My identity is so linked with my mother—clearly the most influential woman of my life—a woman who once shared with me that her Catholic faith has been the one constant in her life. Sometimes I do not know how I will endure this long good-bye. Right now I am numb. Later I will be in tears. In some ways I do not know who I am. My core identity has been called into question. Similarly, my multiple marginal roles as an African American woman religious who is a theologian in the Catholic Church in the United States prompts me to face daily my ambiguous identity and my frequent queries regarding my sense of self.

Right now, in the progression of my mother's disease, there are times when she recognizes me and times when she does not. When my name rolls off her tongue, it makes my day. She's my mother and I am her daughter, and all's right with the world. Gone are my mother's agitation, anxiety, and incessant pleas to go home. The joy is so great when I hear her call me by my nickname and when I call her Mom or Mommy and she doesn't call it into question. When my mother does not recognize me, my world comes to a halt. I am numb and begin looking for pictures or anything that will help her make the link to my identity. Last month while visiting my mother, my eyes filled with tears when I realized that she did not think I was her daughter. True to her gentle spirit, she hugged me, patted me on the back, and asked me how my mother was.

And so, there is an ebb-and-flow that now characterizes my life with my mother. Something similar has been happening in my relationships with my Church, my religious community, and my nation. This Church does not consistently recognize me and other black Catholics and celebrate our identity as *imago Dei*.[4] That hurts deeply. But just as there is great joy when my mother recognizes me, there is also great joy when my Church recognizes and celebrates my community and our rich black Catholic heritage.[5] The ebb-and-flow that is my life as an African American woman religious is marked by the joy of our common seeking of Jesus Christ, along with the realization and subsequent disappointment that for so many of my religious sisters racism and white privilege are simply not on their radar. As one African American woman among many in the United States, I, too, try to transcend this nation's assumptions that we are mammies, Jezebels, and welfare mothers.[6] We wrestle with these stereotypes that we sometimes imbibe, thus compromising our true sense of self. Such was the case when New York "shock jock" Don Imus called the members of the Rutgers women's basketball team a bunch of "nappy-headed hos." Sociologist Michael Eric Dyson translated what many of us already knew: "nappy was a stand-in for black female ugliness."[7] Just a few years later, First Lady Michelle Obama appeared on the national scene and began to undo two centuries' worth of dangerous falsehoods about black women. Her presence as a devoted wife, mother, lawyer, administrator, and Ivy League alumna begs for new and fitting ways to image African American women. The iconography of black women in America is changing in new and exciting ways with the potential of empowering black women to identify and celebrate the goodness and possibilities of their humanity in relationship with God.

In my journey toward renewed identity at this important juncture in my life, I join African American writer and activist Alice

Walker and set out in search of our mothers' gardens. In her essay of the same title, Walker marvels at the fruitfulness of our mothers' gardens despite the effects of racism. These mothers and "other mothers" recognize me and will shed light on my path. These womanists will show me the way, and their ethos will be mine. In fact, it is already mine. A womanist theological ethos "signals a perspective or approach that places the differentiated (for example, religious, personal, cultural, social, psychological, biological) experience of African American women at the hermeneutical center of theological inquiry and research, reflection, and judgment."[8] A womanist imagination taken to heart will reveal new ways to engage theological anthropology. Theological inquiry on what it means to be human against the backdrop of black women's lives will certainly attend to their bodiliness and their embodiment as God's image in black.[9] First, I will provide a thumbnail sketch of two modern thinkers. Second, I will critique dimensions of this theological anthropology. Third, I will begin to formulate a womanist theological anthropology that will transcend suffocating historical and cultural circumstances, to enact graced and life-giving insights that honor African American women's humanity as God's unique meeting place. Before embarking on the three main parts of this chapter, I will say more about womanism.

WOMANISTS IN SEARCH OF OUR MOTHERS' GARDENS

The year was 1983 when Pulitzer Prize winner Alice Walker published her first nonfiction collection of essays, *In Search of Our Mothers' Gardens: Womanist Prose*. As the story goes, at the behest of Walker's editors, she provided a dictionary-style definition of the word womanist in four parts. Derived from a black folk term, womanish, as in, "You acting womanish," Walker explains that such a statement would be spoken by black mothers to their female children who are "trying to be grown," that is, displaying typically "outrageous, audacious, courageous, or *willful* behavior." In a word, a womanist is "a black feminist or feminist of color."[10] Nevertheless, not all black feminists self-identify as such. Second, Walker then affirms womanists as female-loving and/or male-loving women who value diversity and the well-being of her sisters, whose ability to dream a new world on new terms is inestimable.[11] Third, Walker embarks on a litany of things womanists love. These include music, dance, the moon, the Spirit, love, food, roundness, struggle, the Folk, and herself—*regardless*. Fourth, Walker concludes her entry just the way she started it, by describing a womanist relationship to a feminist. She says, "Womanist is to feminist as purple is to lavender."[12] This differentiation suggests the depth and complexity of black women's experiences in the United States and beyond, due to the interlocking oppressions of racism, sexism, and classism and their creativity in navigating this treacherous terrain.

When African American female seminary and theology students, theologians, ethicists, and other scholars of religion encountered womanism, many of them adopted it as a way to describe the work of those who put black women's experience at the center of their theologizing. Jacquelyn Grant, Katie Geneva Cannon, Delores S. Williams, Cheryl Townsend Gilkes, Emilie M. Townes, Linda E. Thomas, M. Shawn Copeland, Diana L. Hayes, and Jamie T. Phelps are among those women who have donned the mantle of womanism. Womanist theology can also be understood as a critique of black women's exclusion by the practitioners of black and (white) feminist theologies.

Womanist theologians' signature move to place African American women at the center of their theologizing converged with these theologians' need to critique the failure of black theology and feminist theology to include and take seriously black women's experiences of God and the world. The early voices of black theology needed to be shown their unconscious racism, and early feminists and feminist theologians needed to be reminded that Caucasian women's experiences were not normative.

African American female religious scholars who write in womanist perspective expose the tripartite nature of black women's oppression and affirm their right to speak for themselves, about themselves, on their own terms. In an article honoring the twentieth anniversary of black women's participation in a preconference consultation at the American Academy of Religion and Society of Biblical Literature annual joint conferences, Katie Geneva Cannon observes:

> For us to bring to the surface the inconsistencies between our real-life biotexts and the people, places, and things that represent dissenting opinions regarding our existential experiences, we must share reliable information that can be accurately assessed. These types of "aha" moments suggest confrontations between historical facts that members of the dominant race formulate as truth and the juxtaposition of our daily realities that are incongruent with such explanations.[13]

Without bypassing their own autobiographical contributions, womanist scholars excavate and retrieve oral and written narratives that transcend the "restrictive identities"[14] meant to contain black women and their communities and weaken their spirits. Womanist scholars engage in critical race theory to name and analyze the present state of affairs. Knowledgeable of and conversant with this cluster of information, womanist theologians and scholars of religion turn to theology to critique its collusion in the oppression of black women and their communities and to retrieve life-giving dimensions of the tradition that can liberate minds, hearts, and spirits. For those who write in Catholic womanist perspective, they query, "Can Catholic theology specifically enhance womanist critique, that is, can it permit us to engage in a sharper challenge of the Christian tradition, black theology, and feminism?" The critique and challenge of this particular essay is centered on Christian theological considerations of being human in the context of black women's experience. To this we now turn.

THE MODERN DEBATE BETWEEN NATURE AND GRACE

Traditional understandings of Christian theological anthropology begin at the intersection of (human) nature and grace, that is, the natural and the supernatural. The convergence of these two categories was discussed and debated from the Counter-Reformation until the middle of the twentieth century. During this time, theologians spoke hypothetically about "pure nature," that is, the human person apart from or unaided by grace or God's life. This theoretical move proved to be very problematic, because there is no such thing as the human person as "pure nature," because the world is imbued with God's life and presence. Similarly, theologians pondered super-nature or the supernatural, that is, grace or God's life. Consider the following statements:

> The life offered by grace is said to be "supernatural" in three senses: a) God's being is ontologically superior to all created being; b) a direct and perduring relationship with God surpasses human cognitive and affective capacities; and c) life with God under grace is freely given and beyond all claims or requirements that flow from human nature itself. In a word, the life of grace transcends the being, powers, and exigencies of the human person.[15]

As you can see, it was important for theologians engaging the issues of nature and grace to distinguish between God and God's creation in very concrete ways. The creator God's being is superior to that which God creates in complete freedom and love. Additionally, God initiates "a direct and perduring relationship" with humankind despite God's transcendence that far "surpasses human cognitive and affective capacities."[16] This theme of God's loving relationship with God's creation would eventually displace the obsession with nature and grace and break open new understandings of theological anthropology in the second half of the twentieth century and beyond. This was a significant move, because by dichotomizing nature and grace, some began to think of grace as extrinsic to nature and superadded.

With a greater attention to historical consciousness and personalism, and a shift to grace as the new starting point, conversations about theological anthropology changed dramatically during the middle of the twentieth century. The contribution of German theologian Karl Rahner (1904–1984) was distinctive in this regard. By expounding on the human person's innate desire for God, called the supernatural existential, he promoted new understandings of a God who is part and parcel of the human order and gratuitous by God's very presence. It has been noted that "in the twentieth century no Catholic theologian has done more than Karl Rahner to restore the theology of grace to its position close to the center of Christian thought."[17] Through Rahner's influence, people began to equate grace with God's self-communication to humanity. This self-communication occurs in history within time and space as an offer of grace and salvation. "Against the implication that grace is scarce, then, or that there is no salvific grace outside the Christian sphere, Rahner argues theologically to the universality of grace on the basis of the universality of God's saving will."[18] And through Rahner's theological contribution people began to view grace as something that could be experienced in the context of actual self-transcendence. The implications for this move reverberated in Western theological circles.

Long before Rahner's contribution, African-descended women knew God as "an all-pervading reality."[19] African theologian Mercy Amba Oduyoye explains further:

> God is a constant participant in the affairs of human beings, judging by the everyday language of West

Africans of my experience. A Muslim never projects into the future nor talks about the past without the qualifying phrase *insha Allah*, "by the will of Allah." Yoruba Christians will say "DV" ("God willing"), though few can tell you its Latin equivalent, and the Akan will convince you that all is "by the grace of God." Nothing and no situation is without God. The Akan of Ghana say *Nsem nyina ne Onyame* ("all things/affairs pertain to God"). That Africans maintain an integrated view of the world has been expressed by many.[20]

This African theology of grace pervades womanist theology and is the reason why womanists believe that God makes a way out of no way for them, their communities, and all people. This knowledge enables womanists to resist injustice in all its forms and to partner with God in promoting God's kindom.

Born a decade after Karl Rahner, Flemish theologian Edward Schillebeeckx (1914–) wrote about New Testament theologies of grace in the second volume of his Christological trilogy. Mindful of the significance of the human person who is experiencing God through Jesus Christ, Schillebeeckx identified what he called, "anthropological constants." These tentative and expressive characteristics did not completely or adequately sum up the mystery of the human person, but they did provide important touchstones around which to talk about the human person. Schillebeeckx's seven constants are concrete and communal in tone, thereby showing what feminists of all stripes know all too well: context matters. The human person is not a monad. She is in relationship with her material environment, with other human beings, and with herself. She lives in community at a particular time and place. For all of these reasons, Schillebeeckx's anthropological constants speak to womanist (and other contextual) theologians, because in our work we are compelled to tell our stories and identify our social locations to shatter the illusion that white male humanity is normative. It is our job to indicate exactly why and how difference matters.

Since womanist theology is based on putting African American women's diverse experiences at the hermeneutical center of the theological project, what follows is an exercise in womanist theology. Schillebeeckx's anthropological constants are evident in striking ways in the lives and witness of African American women.

Schillebeeckx's first anthropological constant captures what enslaved African American women recognized: human beings have and are bodies, and their bodies are engaged with the natural and material world. Enslaved women of African ancestry in the Americas knew all sorts of sexual abuse and disregard. After emancipation and beyond, circumstances required that African American women farm the land in addition to caring for their families, thus making it impossible for them to fulfill the expectations of Victorian womanhood. Later, out of necessity, many black women became domestics, lending credence to the oft-quoted words of Janie Crawford's grandmother in *Their Eyes Were Watching God,* "De nigger woman is de mule uh de world so fur as Ah can see. Ah been prayin' fuh it tuh be different wid you."[21]

Although the African American female experience is not monolithic, far too many black women are forced to negotiate the shifting landscape of race, gender, and class oppression, and when these three categories of oppression exist concomitantly, their impact is multiplicative, not additive, thus compounding an already excessive load. Nevertheless, as embodied creatures of God, black women have striven to love their bodies into life. This is evident in the hush arbors as much as it is in the church pew, not to mention the many examples in history and literature of black women. Harlem Renaissance author, cultural anthropologist, and protowomanist Zora Neale Hurston is quoted as saying in response to professional pictures taken of her, "I love myself when I am laughing and then again when I am looking mean and impressive."[22] A womanist spirit is reflected in this type of self-love and sass.

The human person is an embodied creature who is in relationship with nature, the environment, and the entire material world. Critical reason necessitates the human person's discernment and accountability to God, the human community, and the environment. In a mysterious way, the cosmos is also a recipient of salvation, and this fact obliges human beings to steward lovingly all of God's creation. Agreed upon ethical norms are needed to prevent suffering and exploitation.

Schillebeeckx's second anthropological constant is that a life of human flourishing involves other human beings. African American women have found support and solace as they have supported each other informally and formally by forming alliances through clubs, sororities, religious congregations, and societies. Womanist purviews are broader still, embracing the entire community. African American women's journeys toward integration and personal identity are contingent upon relationships with other human beings. Schillebeeckx notes that "this lays upon [women and men] the task of accepting, in inter-subjectivity, the other in [her or his] otherness and in [her or his] freedom."[23] This spirit of acceptance is most fruitful if reciprocated. Failure to recognize all persons as fully human can spiral into sinful acts that cause suffering and weaken the bonds of human community. Herein lies the sin of chattel slavery and legalized segregation, not to mention all the transgressions against sisters and brothers that mar God's image in community.

Throughout history, African American women have experienced their immersion in and relatedness to social and institutional structures. This is the third anthropological constant. These structures are formative of an individual's personal identity and as such contribute to or detract from the possibility of full humanity. The extended and fluid family of slavocracy to the present is a foundational structure. For the African American community, the black church has played a central role in affirming black life. These and other structures in the wider society are mostly "contingent [and] changeable"[24] at the hands of women and men. Like the other anthropological constants, ethical norms are necessary, especially when changes are called for because evolving circumstances demand alteration or a complete overhaul due to the fact that these structures have the power to "enslave and debase [people] rather than liberate them and give them protection."[25] Much is at stake as African American women navigate in and out of social and institutional structures and have their say.

The fourth constant asserts that people and culture are influenced by time and space. African American women and their communities have been formed by the history and geography that make up their milieu. It is in this context that they come face-to-face with their limits and enacted strategies to deal with them in meaningful ways. Often, instead of being paralyzed, African American women engaged in all kinds of resistance that modeled for future generations their critical and free consciousness, while also creating legacies in word, craft, and edifice. Truly, their lives were a *"hermeneutical* undertaking, i.e. as a task of *understanding* [their] own situation and unmasking critically the meaninglessness that [human beings] bring about in history."[26]

There is a mutual relationship between theory and practice. Schillebeeckx provides the rationale for this fifth constant when he says, "It is a constant in so far as through this relationship human culture, as a hermeneutical undertaking or an understanding of meaning, and as an undertaking of changing meaning and improving the world, needs *permanence.*"[27] African American women and their communities have grappled with the cognitive dissonance that happens when Christian and/or democratic views of humanity conflicted with the reality on the ground. African American women, such as Ida B. Wells-Barnett and Henriette Delille, linked theory and practice and in so doing made inroads against lynching and founded a religious congregation for free women of color, respectively.[28] By supporting the mutual relationship of theory and practice, that which befits humanity can be insured and sustained and potentially "bring[s] [humanity] *salvation.*"[29]

The sixth anthropological constant is that the human person possesses a religious and parareligious consciousness. Throughout human history, right to the present, women and men have held a variety of conceptions about life's perplexities. African American women are no exception as they have embraced a variety of religious experiences in response to the transcendent "to make sense of contingency or finitude, impermanence and the problems of suffering, fiasco, failure and death which it presents, or to overcome them."[30] This is ultimately about black women's strivings to find meaning and purpose where there seems to be none. This is also about what can be an impetus for a better future or for continuing to remain hopeful about a better future. As long as human beings do not fall into the trap of nihilism, with its judgment of ultimate absurdity, a type of "'faith,' the ground for hope" remains as a constant, according to Schillebeeckx. For those who may be called religious, this ultimate hope for a fitting human future is the living God.

These six constants exist as an irreducible synthesis that can be considered a seventh constant. This synthesis is the person within human culture. Here lies "[t]he reality which heals [women and] men and brings them salvation." The norms mentioned above, which have been further developed with African American women in mind, reflect the pluralism of the human community. For Schillebeeckx, salvation has import for each of the anthropological constants as conceptualized as "the whole system of co-ordinates in which [human beings] can really be [human beings]."[31] Schillebeeckx's inclusion of anthropological constants in the midst of his Christological project suggests that theological anthropology is linked with all of Christianity's major doctrines. This is likewise evident in womanist theology where themes of the triune God overlap with salvation, Christology, theological anthropology, and ethics. Womanists' God-talk is interconnected.

WOMANIST CRITIQUE

The last section on traditional understandings of theological anthropology began with the nature-grace disputes and their implications for Christianity's view of God and the human being. Though not explicitly noted, one can be certain that the human being under consideration was the male human being because his humanity was deemed normative. This problematic assumption has fueled theological feminisms' agendas since their inceptions. The womanist critique of theologian M. Shawn Copeland does not merely decry such assumptions; rather, in her essay "The New Anthropological Subject in the Heart of the Mystical Body of Christ," she proposes and rehearses decentering the assumed anthropological subject, the bourgeois white male. In his place, she makes invisible and forgotten poor women of color the new anthropological subject, thus displaying a critical and compassionate historical consciousness. Since the 1960s, political and liberation theologies have likewise worked toward this decentering. Copeland affirms:

> These theologies turned the spotlight on God's invisible human creatures: the exploited, despised, marginalized, poor masses whom Fanon, so lovingly, called "le damnés de la terre," the wretched of the earth. . . .These wretched of our globe are the 1.3 billion people who live in absolute poverty, the 600 million who endure chronic malnutrition; they are the hundreds of thousands sick with AIDS and tuberculosis, sold or forced into prostitution, and murdered—simply because *their* embodiment, *their* difference is rejected as gift and offends.[32]

Deeply moved by a story about a disturbing instance of transgression against the *humanum*, Copeland expresses calculated and measured outrage in this essay. Fatima Yusif is an undocumented Somalian woman in Naples who unexpectedly begins to give birth to her son on the side of the road. The response of the crowd to this happening was incomprehensible, prompting a writer for the *London Times* to title his story "Racists Jeer at Roadside Birth." Ms. Yusif's labor and subsequent birth are marked by the judgmental gaze of spectators who stopped to take in the latest roadside occurrence. Ms. Yusif would later recall the words of a boy who snickered, "Look what the negress is doing." This young mother recounts that never will she forget the faces of those who watched as if they were "at the cinema."[33]

Copeland is compelled to analyze the bystanders' warped sense of Fatima Yusif's humanity. To them, she is "other," different, and despised. This state of consciousness of the bystanders is the result of long and complicated histories of colonialism, slavery, and the wholesale objectification of "others" whose arrival in so-called developed countries is marked by the embrace of their service labor, often devoid of rights. Fatima Yusif and other poor and exploited women of color ought to be our new anthropological subject because their vulnerable social location calls out for attention and compassion. Theologians' attention to the subjectivity of these most vulnerable women can help transform their status in the eyes of some from "others," to sisters made in God's image and likeness.

With this move, Copeland reveals and explores the true status of poor women of color in social majorities. Social majorities, or members of the so-called two-thirds world, "have no regular access to most of the goods and services defining the average 'standard of living' in the industrial countries. Their definitions of 'a good life,' shaped by their local traditions, reflect their capacities to flourish outside the 'help' offered by 'global forces.'"[34] Among social majorities are refugees who migrate to escape war and/or to seek basic staples of life. Such a move is in continuity with the Catholic

Church's option for the poor. It also reveals Copeland's compassion for crucified humanity. By changing the anthropological subject, Copeland prompts an altogether new discourse regarding what it means to be human for the least of our sisters and brothers.

WOMANIST WAYS OF BEING IN THE WORLD

For womanist biblical scholar Renita Weems and first-generation womanist theologian Delores S. Williams, the biblical Hagar, Sarah's maidservant, shows African American women how to be their womanist selves.[35] Forced to bear Abraham's firstborn son in place of Sarah, Hagar navigated precarious circumstances and took her rightful place in salvation history, but not before being cast out into the wilderness with her son, Ishmael, to endure the elements and entrust her son and herself to the God of her life. Gifted by God, Hagar saw anew resources that previously were not observed or did not exist. Hagar is our "sister in the wilderness"[36] whose life and spirit remind black women to recognize divine intervention and salvation where and how one least expects.

Womanist ways of being in the world are challenged by a call to honesty, integrity, and resonance. In *Black Sexual Politics: African Americans, Gender, and the New Racism*, sociologist Patricia Hill Collins writes about the need for black folks to have "honest bodies." She elaborates on this by saying:

> Honest bodies strive to treat the mental, spiritual, and physical aspects of being as interactive and synergistic. No one element becomes privileged over the other. Because honest bodies . . . rejoin the mind, soul, and body, they become in one sense free. Starting with the mind, by interrogating one's own individual consciousness, is essential. Individuals who reject dominant scripts of Black gender ideology by fully accepting their own bodies "as is" move toward achieving honest bodies.[37]

So, as mentioned earlier, not only do human beings have bodies, we are bodies, and our bodies encompass what and who we are. This invitation to integration militates against the dualisms of bodies/souls, secular/sacred, and black/white that historically have attempted to break black bodies mentally, spiritually, and physically. Honest bodies are integrated and marked by a resonance that frees because despite the prevalent ideologies of the day, these bodies engage in critical reasoning that ultimately thwart these heresies/falsehoods and engender personal and eventually communal acceptance.

Practically speaking, this goal of developing honest bodies is a matter of life and death for African American females whose present ways of being in the world can be risky and death-dealing. One need only consider two facts regarding the health, or lack thereof, of African American female bodies. Despite our roundness and calls to celebrate our unique African physical features, African American women face increased health risks because a large percentage of our population is overweight or obese. The U.S. Office of Minority Health of the Department of Human Services reports that more than any other group, African American women have the highest rates of being overweight or obese. In fact, four out of five African American women in the United States are overweight or obese.[38] Such statistics necessitate critical reasoning and a reminder of human beings' call to be stewards. In this case, we are to steward our bodies and maintain an ordered lifestyle that promotes our bodily health and does not put us at risk for a host of illnesses, from diabetes to heart disease to strokes. Any rhetoric that suggests that our large size is endemic of who we are is wrongheaded and must be challenged. African American women need to remind themselves that they are children of God, and while loving their black selves as they are, they need to strive toward greater health and wholeness in body and soul.

Honest bodies also integrate their sexuality into all that they are. Another startling statistic suggests a death-dealing disintegration.

The leading cause of death for African American women, ages twenty-five to thirty-four is AIDS.[39] How can it be that after decades of education, African American women do not care for themselves adequately? Our sexuality is one of God's many gifts to us to be treasured, enjoyed, and shared. African American women must love themselves: mind, body, and soul. Regardless! Their lives depend on it. When African American women rehearse and witness to their love for themselves, they will teach others how to treat them.

For African American women, choosing honest bodies is an affirmation of their graced humanity and God's never-ending love and care. Such knowledge will be central to their sense of self as God's image in black.[40] Womanist ways of being in the world are synonymous with well-being and salvation that strengthens them to decry all those who would dehumanize and commodify them. For the glory of God is the human being fully alive.[41]

THEOLOGICAL ANTHROPOLOGY ROUNDTABLE

Susan Abraham, Elizabeth Groppe, Rosemary Carbine

We relate to God as the specifically human creatures we are. This is the central intuition of the classical doctrine of the human being, called theological anthropology. The three essays on theological anthropology in this volume present constructive and far-reaching challenges to traditional theological anthropology by radicalizing the particularity of the historical, social, cultural, and political contexts in which feminist and womanist Catholic theology must reflect on the relational nature of the human person and subjectivity.

Michele Saracino, for example, argues that traditional categories, such as "nature" and "grace," in classical theology remain unusable for feminist purposes because these categories do not sufficiently take into account the plural and many-layered experiences of women. Thus, when traditional theology speaks of women and their nature qua woman, it often narrowly emphasizes biological and cultural characteristics, such as mothering, as ideal states in which women must realize their personhood. This is the essentialist move. The criticism of this move comes from feminist circles constantly on the watch for the ways in which women's experiences are circumscribed by authority and power in the Church and society. Saracino turns the tables on magisterial and societal authority and power by pointing out that instead of emphasizing the biological in relation to masculinist ideals, the biological experience of maternity provides feminists with a way to tell the story of plurality as it is played out in their bodily experience of pregnancy, lactation, and care for children. Feminist theological anthropology, in her view, challenges traditional theology precisely by recasting the Church hierarchy's essentialism through the constructive cultural concept of "hybridity." Embracing hybridity in theological anthropology means that women are narrated as more than mothers, eschewing the Church's one-size-fits-all gender stereotypes in which women are reduced to their sexual and reproductive roles. Plumbing women's experiences for insights into the human person shows that we are all hybrids, both natured and graced beings who cannot be reduced to one side of that dualistic dynamic. Although our identities are a hybrid of multiple stories, we often live in the sin of blindness both to the multiplicity of our own stories and to the reality of the stories of others, which, when recognized, can act as the grace that reminds us of our differentiated, yet interdependent humanity.

Feminists have also consistently pointed out how traditional essentialist theologies of women's nature are shored up by problematic theological and social norms of self-sacrifice and self-abuse to meet the needs—familial, economic, and sexual—of others. In this vein, Teresa Delgado points to the urgent crisis of sexual exploitation and HIV/AIDS among Latina women, a consequence of internalizing such theologies of self-sacrifice and disempowerment. In traditional theologies, these theological ideals of self-sacrifice are often used to reinforce a religiously based hierarchical ordering of heterosexual relations and thereby undermine the ability of women to be justly relational. Delgado's critique of the traditional ideas of nature and grace Latina/mente argues that they do not go far enough to guarantee justice to women by overemphasizing the interdependency motif to disadvantage women. As in Saracino's essay, this essay picks up the thread of the body as the singular site of grace. A woman's body, as the site of graced gifting, frees theological anthropology from essentialist patriarchal concerns with domesticated motherhood, self-sacrificial interdependency, and sexual exploitation. The graced gifting of the body occurs in the sexual exchange of bodies that love themselves and others, not in the sexual exchange of global capitalist systems that commodifies bodies as goods to be bought or sold, or in a theological economy that values its patriarchal and masculinist ideals over the health and well-being of women.

The final essay in this section points to one of the most disgraced and demeaning contexts for theology, namely, the racialized body as the constructive challenge for ongoing feminist and womanist reflections on anthropology. LaReine Mosely replaces theological anthropologies built on racist ideals of humanity (at the basis of slavery, legalized segregation, and racism in the United States) with a renewed theological anthropology grounded in black women's experiences of not succumbing to the dehumanizing effects of racism. Rooted in a womanist method and ethos, Mosely examines the Catholic theological tradition for voices that did not ignore the lived reality of human life when speaking of nature and grace. Both Rahner and Schillebeeckx, therefore, engaged the material world in order to speak of a differentiated, rather than singular, economy of nature and grace. Differentiated human existence is thus a gift of God, a sacrament of God's gratuity. Nothing that dehumanized was part of the subtle and intricate relationship between nature and grace. Consequently, those structures and regimes of thought that enslaved and exploited human beings are judged to exist in defiance of divine grace, which flowed and continues to do so precisely in and through the victim-survivors of such dehumanization. The fact that black women survived to tell of their faith, hope, and strength in God is ample evidence of grace in their lives. What a human being is can only be found in those stories of dignity and graced existence, which black bodies and black women have refused to concede to the dis-grace of racism and its multiple interlocking oppressions. Such a responsive and dignified assent to black women's humanity is precisely the locus of a feminist theological anthropology today.

This roundtable was convened by feminist theologians writing on ecclesiology in this volume. As such, therefore, we read the essays through the lens of ecclesiology. A central idea that all three sections of this volume has worked with has been that the three loci have a perichoretic relationship; that is, they interweave, interrupt, and intensify each other. In our discussions of the three contributions here, it was clear to us that our vision of who we are as feminists, theologians, and Catholics cannot but take into account the responsibility we have to construct theologies of hope and justice. We cannot, therefore, despair that the Catholic *magisterium* seems to colonize consistently the experience of human motherhood to emphasize the highly celebrated "receptivity" and "sacrificial" nature of women. We cannot give in to the idea that our bodies only have functional uses for sex and procreation when they are ours to share, to give, and take pleasure in. In fact, since many of us are mothers and lovers, it seems to us to be anti-Christian to deny the tremendous gifts that arise from the giving of self for love and pleasure instead of for security and money. Finally, we cannot give in to the idea that racialized and sexualized bodies are simply victims of dehumanizing structures. We do suffer and are victimized, and we acknowledge that racism, sexism, and misogyny are alive and well in Catholic theology and institutions. But we are more than that; we are brilliant examples of hope, dignity, and care of self. As such, we are aware of our capacity to rehumanize those systems that have only recognized us as objects and things. The vision of the human community under God that emerges through this picture of what it means to be human is one of freedom in grace with the responsibility to speak, do, and live from that central understanding.

As teachers of Catholic theology, we see a number of ways these essays might enhance classroom discussions of what it means to be human and the implications of these constructive perspectives on Christology and ecclesiology. Saracino, for example, argues that the "one story" model cannot do justice to the complex interwoven stories of women and their experiences. In arguing for hybridity as a theological starting point for anthropology (and thus releasing the concept from its cultural moorings), she presents Jesus as a hybrid. If hybridity is an existential and anthropological condition to be located in the entire event of the incarnation, then women need not be held hostage to any one story or script to live their lives. Grace frees both Christology and women from the grip of static and singular theological stories about God and about being human in the image of God. Difference, therefore, can be accommodated within a narrativized framework in which Christology reveals to us what is most human about us. Communities of faith can coalesce around such narrative truths instead of simplistic biological and cultural essentialisms. Far from a politically correct postmodern theology, difference aptly characterizes what it means to be and become fully human in relation to our multistoried selves and others.

Similarly, Delgado's essay challenges traditional masculinist Christology by refusing to internalize gendered ideals of self-sacrifice that militarize self-sacrifice (machismo) for men on the one hand and sexualize it for women (marianismo) on the other. Instead, Delgado asks us to look beyond self-sacrifice and to retrieve the Christological imperative to re-member the broken body into the community for the sake of the community. This does not mean that we have to deliberately set out to break our bodies. Rather, her call is to recognize the brokenness that exists in our contemporary time and to incorporate those broken bodies back into the corporate and corporeal context of lived Christianity—a significant idea for feminist ecclesiology. Acknowledging that we exist in broken relations through our bodies reminds us to attend to the particular dis-graced experiences of all bodies. Such embodied experiences of consciousness raising about the broken body of Christ enables black women to seek what Patricia Hill Collins calls "honest bodies," and energizes the Church to resist personal and institutional structures of racism so that we shape a more honest church and body politic. Living in and into the *imago Dei* in an ecclesiological way means looking critically and constructively at what we create religiously and politically in reference to that image. Mosely's reflections on Fatima Yusif invites further feminist theological reflection on what it means to be church in a world marked by a broken body politic in globalized economies. Assisting in, rather than gawking at, Yusif's unexpected roadside childbirth would mean bringing to birth a new humanity, as well as a new way of being church. Like the Samaritan in the parable of the good neighbor (Luke 10:25–37), assisting at Yusif's childbirth serves as a postmodern parable for bringing to birth a new life, that is, creating more inclusive religious and political spaces of justice and peace.

Other strands of discussion that generated conversation in the roundtable centered first on the visual mechanics of racist, cultural, and sexual stereotyping that arose in the three essays. When difference is cinematized as a spectacle, it results in the gut-wrenching disgust engendered by the story of Fatima Yusif. Women's racialized and sexualized bodies are spectacularly disciplined, and each essay has attempted to contravene these disciplinary bonds. The implications of a methodology that attempts to examine and undermine the spectacular construction of gender, race, culture, and class are many. For example, we think that the negative effects of a pervasive media culture that purveys images of femininity and masculinity, sex and aggression, beauty and beastliness ought to be examined in relation to theological anthropology. As documented in Sut Jhally's *Dreamworlds 3: Desire, Sex and Power in Music Video* (MEF, 2007), popular music video culture reduces women to fragmented and disconnected body parts that passively await purchase, possession, and all manner of abuse by men. Such a media culture is directly responsible for creating the spectacle of an ideal, passive sexualized femininity that can entail lifelong sexual trauma for women and men. Second, any reflection on theological anthropology cannot ignore the anthropological assumptions of the globalized economy and the despair it has sown the world over. Who or what is a human being in such a system? Third, and most importantly, the constructive proposals in theological anthropology all point to the necessity to reflect on the human being as *imago Dei*. Traditionally, the recipient of grace in Catholic theology is precisely the *imago Dei*. As our ever-complex reality unfolds before us, we remain committed to each other, to our children, to our students, to our world, and to the Divine in speaking of a renewed iconography of this graced existence. These essays are a testament to that commitment precisely because the authors show us that everything that we are—as women, as mothers, lovers, friends, teachers, and theologians—is touched by hope, dignity, justice, and love.

QUESTIONS FOR DISCUSSION AND REFLECTION

1. What stories inform your identity? Are some of your stories more shameful than others? How might the stories of another compel you to retell and renegotiate your own stories in relation to the needs, memories, and stories of another?
2. What are some experiences, ideas, and institutions that have contributed to how African American Christian women understand themselves? What experiences, ideas, and institutions have influenced you?
3. Each of these chapters in the anthropology section has dealt implicitly with the notions of body and embodiment. Why might feminist catholic theologians be so concerned with the body? Should all Catholics be concerned? If so, why?

4. Why do you think that themes of embodiment play such a central role in feminist, womanist, and *mujerista* theological anthropologies?
5. The image of Mary as virgin mother has both perpetuated and challenged the ways women are treated sexually and otherwise. How has the image of Mary informed your self-understanding as a woman, particularly in relation to your sexuality?
6. Why do you think there exists so much controversy and disagreement around the role of sex and sexuality in the context of religious/spiritual experience? Why is sex such a contested battleground on which the claims of human morality/immorality are fought?

FOR FURTHER READING

Marcella Althaus-Reid, *From Feminist Theology to Indecent Theology: Readings on Poverty, Sexual Identity and God* (London: SCM Press, 2004). Althaus-Reid offers a new theological approach that examines liberation theology and feminist theology and marks a shift from these traditional critiques, resulting in what the author refers to as "indecent theology," using queer theory and postcolonial analysis to show more clearly how the shift from gender to sexuality has occurred in the context of globalization.

Tina Beattie, *New Catholic Feminism: Theology and Theory* (London, Routledge, 2006). This work provides a comprehensive critique of Hans Urs von Balthasar's Marian theology, including his understanding of sexual difference, which is integral to issues of identity and power in catholic feminist theology today.

Homi K. Bhabha, *The Location of Culture* (London: Routledge, 1994). This collection of essays from the legendary postcolonialist thinker provides an overview of the significance of hybridity or the "in-between spaces" of identity in literature, semiotics, and culture.

M. Shawn Copeland, *Enfleshing Freedom: Body, Race, and Being* (Minneapolis: Fortress Press, 2009). This groundbreaking work from the distinguished Catholic womanist theologian understands the complexity of being human, relative to questions of power and oppression, from the starting point of black female embodied experience.

Diana L. Hayes, *And Still We Rise: An Introduction to Black Liberation Theology* (New York: Paulist Press, 1996). This book provides an excellent overview of the emergence of black, womanist, and black Catholic theologies.

Dwight Hopkins, *Being Human: Race, Culture, and Religion* (Minneapolis: Fortress Press, 2005). This innovative book on theological anthropology takes seriously the categories of race and culture.

Elizabeth A. Johnson, *Truly Our Sister: A Theology of Mary in the Communion of Saints* (New York, N.Y.: Continuum, 2006). Johnson offers an interpretation of Mary as a blessing rather than a blight for women's lives in both religious and political terms—a view that must be reexamined in light of the lived experiences of Latin American women and Latinas.

Catherine Keller, Michael Nausner, and Mayra Rivera, eds., *Postcolonial Theologies: Divinity and Empire* (St. Louis: Chalice Press, 2004). This text brings together a wide diversity of authors whose essays are theologically constructive, not merely deconstructive or critical, in their visions for Christianity, under the themes of theological anthropology shaped by ethnicity, class, and privilege. It also addresses a Christology that intersects the claims of Christ and empire and a cosmology that imagines a postcolonial world.

Stephanie Y. Mitchem, *Introducing Womanist Theology* (Maryknoll, N.Y.: Orbis, 2002). This book is a helpful addition for those beginning to learn about womanist theology.

James B. Nelson, *Body Theology* (Louisville: Westminster John Knox Press, 1992). Nelson offers an incarnational theology that takes body and sexuality seriously as a locus of divine revelation, and human growth that seeks to overcome dualism of soul and body, and views sexuality as central to the mystery of human experience and to the human relationship with God.

Adrienne Rich, *Of Woman Born: Motherhood as Experience and Institution* (New York: W. W. Norton, 1995). This classic feminist work continues to be revolutionary as it reveals the ambiguity of motherhood relative to issues of identity, power, and authority.

Emilie M. Townes, ed., *A Troubling in My Soul: Womanist Perspectives on Evil and Suffering* (Maryknoll, N.Y.: Orbis, 1993). This important collection of essays draws from historical and contemporary contexts to show African American women's survival in the midst of suffering and oppression.

Part Two

CHRISTOLOGY

Chapter 4

CHRISTOLOGY BETWEEN IDENTITY AND DIFFERENCE: ON BEHALF OF A WORLD IN NEED

Jeannine Hill Fletcher

Christology, like all theology, is a profoundly human enterprise. At the intersection of the human and the divine, Jesus Christ stands as symbol through which Christians have affirmed their most intimate intuitions of God and insights into their own human existence. The ways Christians have thought about the person of Christ have been influenced by the wider social context and location of the individuals from whom the theological thinking emerged. Recognizing Christology as an ongoing process, Christians today are invited to return to the person of Jesus and find resources for human living. In the words of Kwok Pui-lan, Jesus Christ is the locus of a

> "contact zone" or "borderland" between the human and the divine, the one and the many, the historical and the cosmological. . . . Jesus' question, "Who do you say that I am?" is an invitation for every Christian and local faith community to infuse that contact zone with new meanings, insights and possibilities.[1]

In the project of Christology, Christians articulate anew an understanding of their identity in and through Christ.

Accepting the invitation to Christology and striving toward relevance for today, Christians must approach the biblical text and tradition with an awareness that this identity in Christ is situated in a complex world. Our current condition is constituted by globalization, where systems of travel, information, migration, and economics (among others) have compressed our world to make it "a single place."[2] These technologies and systems bring us into ever-greater contact with difference—different ideas, different worldviews, different ways of being human, and different religions. But the systems of globalization also diversely impact human beings, heightening conditions of inequality and injustice. Our world is in need of healing, a healing that must not be confined by the borders of identity. While Christians will look to the person of Christ as the symbolic identity marker under which they might bring forth a new humanity, the salvation found in Christ must transgress the boundaries of difference. With the biblical witness of the book of Revelation, "salvation is only possible after all dehumanizing powers are overcome and a 'new heaven and a new earth' has come into being, because salvation means not only the salvation of the soul but of the whole person."[3] Carrying on the Christian vision for a world in need, we might seek a Christology that enables care and concern across boundaries of difference. We need a Christology that recognizes that humans do not exist in individual isolation; we need a Christology that reflects and encourages our human relatedness. Such a Christology, for many theologians, is at the heart of the Christian vision. In the words of Tina Beattie:

> Christianity is essentially relational both in its proclamation of a Trinitarian God and in its celebration of the incarnation as an event that continuously reveals itself in the space of creative symbolic encounter between God, Mary, Christ and the Church. So the story of Christ is the story of Mary is the story of the Church is the story of humanity is the story of God, and the prismatic vision thus revealed cannot be adequately expressed by any one symbol in isolation from the rest. To recognize this means

developing a theological perspective that goes beyond the narrow Christological focus, to a more encompassing vision of incarnation that incorporates all of creation, including the male and female bodies and the natural world.[4]

From out of the creative symbolic encounter of God, Mary, Christ, and Church, a Christology of relationality might emerge.

CHRISTOLOGY OF RELATIONALITY

A Christology of relationality might begin from current insights into the human condition. From the perspective of psychoanalysis, relationality is evidenced as a fundamental characteristic of our humanity from the earliest forms of human development. We enter this world dependent upon those who have preceded us, and we walk through this world in complex networks of care, dependence, and fragile solidarity. We learn our first patterns of relationality in relation to the one(s) who will serve as "mother" (whether this is a biological mother or another mother). The 'm/other' (whether mothers, or father, or fathers, or caregiver, or grandparent, or sibling) calls the child forth into being through relationship. While the child's individuality emerges from the simultaneous identification with the other/mother and the recognition of a "separate" self,[5] some psychoanalysts posit that the act of individuation is never complete separation. Instead, separation includes the internalization of that first m/other relationship as well: "The loss of the other whom one desires and loves is overcome through a specific act of identification that seeks to harbor the other within the very structure of the self."[6] In this visioning of human development, the self is never alone, but internalizes the relationships that are formative. Such suggestions about the nature of human selfhood returns Christians to the story of scripture to recognize a new importance to Mary of Nazareth. Far from a mere conduit for bringing a savior into the world,[7] as the first primary relationship for the one who will come to be identified as savior, she constitutes his very self. In the Gospel accounts, she is the one who cradles and shelters the helpless newborn (Luke 2:7) and who very soon after introduces him to Jewish sacred ritual in his presentation in the temple (Luke 2:21-39). Along with Joseph, she continues his religious education, for example, marking together the feast of Passover by journeying to Jerusalem (Luke 2:41). While an important role is played in the early years of life, Mary's role in helping to shape Jesus' self-understanding is implicit throughout in her role in the Gospel accounts and continuing influence on his ministry. It is Mary who calls Jesus into public ministry in John's account of the wedding at Cana (John 2:1-11). Was it perhaps Mary who instilled in Jesus a love for the weakest, the child, as she had once given her promise of a life of care in her response to the annunciation? Was it she who shaped him to experience outrage at the misuse of monies in their exchange at the temple? Did he draw strength in his trust of God's promised reign as, at the crucifixion, he encountered his mother who stood by her commitment to God throughout her life? A Christology rooted in relationality recognizes Jesus' self-giving pattern fostered by those closest to him, and in this, Mary is key.

But since the self is not a static entity moving through the world from childhood onward, this dynamic development of the self is constituted not by the primary relationship alone, but through a wide variety of relationships. The ties we have with others "constitute a sense of self, compose who we are."[8] As feminist theologian Catherine Keller has articulated, "For if 'I' am partially constituted by you even as you partially constitute me, for better or for worse, that is if I flow into, in-fluence you as you in-fluence me, then my subjectivity describes itself as radically open-ended in time as well as space."[9] If what it means to be human is to be constituted by relationships, and we are in multiple relationships, a sense of the self in multiplicity emerges. In the words of Morwenna Griffiths,

"Identity [is] constructed, reconstructed and negotiated in relation-ships of love, resistance, acceptance and rejection."[10] Using this lens to understand the narrative of the Gospels, Jesus' self emerges in relation to friends, strangers, and even adversaries. For example, Jesus is called into a sense of self through his relationships with Martha and Mary of Bethany (Matt. 26:6-13; Mark 14:3-9; Luke 7:36-50; 10:38-42; John 11:1-4; 12:1-8). In an interreligious exchange with the Gentile woman of Syraphoenician origin, Jesus' mind is changed in the theological engagement through which she lays claim on him (Matt. 15:21-28; Mark 7:24-30). In looking at the sto-ries of Jesus through the lens of dynamic identity, we can imagine the way that his own understanding of himself and his mission was constituted by his own "creative, agential negotiation of the intersecting currents and competing loyalties" that ran through him.[11] Even one's adversaries call forth the development of one's own identity as a self. For example, it is when a lawyer challenges Jesus, interrogating him on the necessary requirements for a life of wholeness and eternal life, that Jesus indicates the heart of his teaching: Love God with all your heart, mind, and soul; and your neighbor as yourself (Luke 10:25-37). The entire persona, mission, and ministry of Jesus seems to embrace the communal nature of what it means to be human—embedded in relationships, called in care for the least, and fulfilled a vision of human being and becoming *together*.

As those around him call Jesus forth into new enactments of himself and his mission, he simultaneously transforms and empow-ers those who follow him. The very calling of disciples to follow indicates that his mission was not solitary. His teachings engaged his hearers in creative revisioning that drew them into the parables he used as vehicles. Jesus' vision of a reign of God had in mind not the well-being of an individual before God, but a holistic well-being for all. And he called his disciples into a relationality that empowered them as well: they were constituted and empowered by their encounter with him and with one another. In Jesus' presence, the broken are made whole, and in the dynamic exchange of the community, those who follow Jesus are empowered to do likewise, as the Acts of the Apostles is full of stories of those who carried on Jesus' mission, as they continued to share in his life-restoring power. The salvation that is announced in Jesus of Nazareth is not a singular salvation resting on one individual. The salvific vision of Jesus of Nazareth is enacted in his life and in the lives of those who follow him. The transformation of the world toward its fullness in justice and relationship is a process that discipleship enables in the many and diverse human beings who seek it. As Schüssler Fiorenza has reconstructed, "Sophia, the God of Jesus, wills the wholeness and humanity of everyone and therefore enables the Jesus movement to become a 'discipleship of equals.'"[12]

Portrayed as an adult in the Gospel accounts, Jesus has longed for such a community embodying the vision of wholeness, response, and responsibility, and he sees himself in the role of mother: informing and being mutually informed by the community in which he is embedded. In the Gospel of Luke, the words put on Jesus' lips envision him in the role of mother hen, longing to gather her children together as "a hen gathers her brood under her wings" (Luke 13:34). Jesus is shaped by those who mother him into being, *and* he himself takes on the role of mother. As he steps into the subject-position of "mother," he is not suddenly entering relationality; rather, the relationships with family, friends, and the wider social networks continue to impact his subjectivity. Yet, in mothering, one takes on a new pattern of relationality, learning new ways of being in the world and realizing new dimensions of the self as one takes on responsibility for another. Stepping into the mother role, what did Jesus learn about himself from those to whom he extended care? Perhaps the most powerful experience he claimed in adopting the subject-position "mother" is that he understood that what it means to be human is not, in fact, to be autonomous, self-directed, and free, but rather, to be willingly restrained by those relationships to which one has committed—to be willing to embrace one's own vulnerability in care for the vulnerable other. In the ultimate act of vulnerability, Jesus responds with his very life, refusing to compromise his countercultural vision, and being murdered at the hands of those who found such a vision threatening.

Continuing the pattern of mother care, early Christian writings envision Jesus' self-giving modeled on a lactating mother where the "milk of Christ" is spiritual nourishment.[13] This symbolism was taken up with enthusiasm during the Middle Ages as Caroline Walker Bynum introduces us to the little known medieval devotion to Jesus our Mother. Anselm of Canterbury (d. 1109) points to the image of Jesus as mother hen, confessing, "Truly, master, you are a mother."[14] And Bernard of Clairvaux (d. 1153) entreats his readers to seek in Christ's breasts the milk of healing, when he writes, "If you feel the sting of temptation . . . suck not so much the wounds as the breasts of the Crucified. He will be your mother, and you will be his son."[15]

Aelred of Rievaulx (d. 1167) similarly draws on the lactating imagery when he writes,

> On your altar let it be enough for you to have a representation of our Savior hanging on the cross; that will bring before your mind his Passion for you to imitate, his outspread arms will invite you to embrace him, his naked breasts will feed you with the milk of sweetness to console you.[16]

The image of Christ as breastfeeding mother draws in his own maternal relationship (and painted images of Mary breastfeeding will become popular a few centuries later).[17] Popular imagery of Christ employed this physical nurturance as metaphor for the divine self-giving that sustains humanity. Humanity suckles at the breasts of Christ as Christ gives himself for the lives of many, and

TYPES OF FEMINISM IN THE U.S.

Within the three historical waves of feminism in the U.S. thus far, different types of feminisms have emerged in U.S. politics, such as liberal, cultural, socialist, radical, ecological, postcolonial, and many others, based on differing feminist definitions of equality and justice. Liberal feminism lobbies for women's equal legal, political, economic, educational, and other rights. Cultural or romantic feminism emphasizes gender complementarity, or the definition of women in relation to men, and trades on a "cult of true womanhood," in which the moral superiority of women linked to women's maternal roles suits them to reform and uplift domestic, social, and public life. Socialist or Marxist feminism uses gender, economic, and race analysis to expose and challenge gendered and raced theories of work that value public waged work over private, unpaid, reproductive work. Radical feminism goes beyond lobbying for women's equality in political or economic life, and goes beyond liberal and other feminist efforts to establish equality by simply adding women to traditionally male-dominant arenas of life. Rather, radical feminism analyzes and seeks to overcome patriarchy as the root of most sociopolitical injustices. Ecofeminism analyzes multiple interconnections between the domination of the earth and the domination of women. Post-colonial feminism focuses on the plurality of non-white, non-Western women's voices and experiences, in which gender is complicated by multiple factors, including but not limited to race, class, sexuality, language, culture, and so on. It does so to raise questions about and ultimately to resist the alleged superiority of elite white Western norms of politics, personhood and in this case, womanhood, feminism, justice, and so on. As this all-too-brief typology demonstrates, feminism in the U.S. and global political context is far from monolithic, but rather is an elastic, complex phenomenon that is loosely unified around the empowerment and liberation of women.

Christians are called to carry on that mother role for a world in need. While an increasingly androcentric Christian tradition wrests the image of nursing away from the embodied experience of women as breast-feeders, it is only with the help of actual women's experiences of breast-feeding that the insight into Christ's mother role can be illuminated.[18]

RECOGNIZING CHRIST'S MOTHER-LOVE AS SACRIFICE

Self-giving love in the pattern of a breast-feeding mother can be understood at three o'clock in the morning, when for the 180th night in a row a mother stumbles from her sleep to answer the call of her crying child. There is little romance in this sleep-deprived selflessness. It is night after night after night after night after night after night. Around the globe, in every culture, at every moment in time, women emerge from their sleep—interrupted and silent—and care for a crying child. And, to be purposefully colloquial, it sucks. The theological language of self-sacrifice can glamorize the process of self-giving through an image of actions satisfying in themselves, or be glorified under the banner of the ultimacy of the giving in light of a supra-human ideal, or be constructed romantically in a mutual interdependence that is of benefit even to the one who sacrifices. But, self-giving at three in the morning is none of these: it is not glamorous, self-satisfying, supra-human, or rooted in mutuality. It is a plain old exhausting pattern of being depended upon. And the self-giving in history of breast-feeding women does not end when the sun comes up. It requires commitment all night and all day to giving of the self to the needs of the other. It is an impossible balance, but one which women who have chosen this (or economically are required to) find themselves pursuing. They stop what they are doing, bare their breast, and give of themselves. Or, sometimes, they simultaneously complete the tasks at hand with baby on breast. There are times, however, when the needs of the child demand more than a woman can give. She has given all that she has and is literally emptied. Giving of herself when the child wants more, she continues to offer comfort and suckle even when she has nothing left to give. And when her breasts are broken from the constant sucking, the child takes from her both blood and milk at the same time. Having committed to this course of action, she continues . . . a life depends upon it. The woman who has committed herself to nurturing her child in this way must follow through on the giving. And she herself is the gift. All that sustains the child has been produced within her, and all that can satisfy the needs of the other must come from within. There is no other real alternative. This is sacrifice. It is self-giving that empties the self with no necessary return.

This is the pattern of self-giving that is the choice of many women, but it is also a pattern that has enslaved women as wet nurses in countless contexts. Also, it is a pattern required for women in families where economic resources are scarce. Further, when women who can choose whether or not to breast-feed make the choice to do so, they can become trapped in a process of unequal caregiving, when partners or others in the community relinquish responsibilities under the presumption of it being the breast-feeding woman's responsibility to care for the child. There is danger, clearly, in holding up breast-feeding as yet another ideal to which women must adhere. And yet, my aim here is not to set up breast-feeding as the only option or the only manner of nurturing.[19] Rather, I'd like to use the experience of breast-feeding as one lens through which to understand the depth of theological meaning communicated in the images of Christ as nurturing mother. If Christ is imagined as a nursing mother, his style of giving is what hers is: it is day after day, every two or three hours—sometimes more frequently—being asked again to give even when it hurts and sometimes when there is nothing left to give. If Christians desire a world reconciled to God that reflects ideals of justice, the restoration of creation requires this kind of sacrifice. It requires self-giving that is not easy, that is not glamorous, that offers few immediate rewards and, at times, little satisfaction. When theologians describe Christians patterning their actions on Jesus' self-giving love, they sound the prophetic call of patterning ourselves toward this restoration of justice. When coupled with the imagery of humanity feeding from the divine breasts, we are offered a physical experience of what that sacrificial pattern entails. It entails round-the-clock attentiveness to the needs of the other. It requires self-giving that is self-emptying in a real sense. It demands a pattern of self-denial that puts the needs of the other before one's own. But just as the lactating mother requires nourishment to produce milk, so too must care be taken for one's own well-being. The pattern of self-giving love that is *Christa Lactans* consists of a lifestyle of giving, not in discrete acts of charity, but in the self-giving that nurtures others to become fully human themselves. That's what Christians are called to in the pattern of Jesus' self-giving love.

Framing Christ in the role of breast-feeding mother must also be joined with the remembered rejection of a narrowly constituted motherly role. While breast-feeding may give insight into the motherly care necessary for healing a broken world, it is the healing that is important, with breasts as illuminative, although not exclusive, vehicles.

> While he was saying this, a woman in the crowd raised her voice and said to him, "Blessed is the womb that bore you and the breasts that nursed you!" But he said, "Blessed rather are those who hear the word of God and obey it!" (Luke 11:27-28)

In contemplating the mother role of Jesus, the early communities also were critical of the socially constructed mother role in its limitations. For example, in the story of Jesus' response to the approach of his mother and his brothers, we see a concern for the narrow mother care that social constructions enable.

> Then his mother and his brothers came; and standing outside, they sent to him and called him. A crowd was sitting around him; and they said to him, "Your mother and your brothers and sisters are outside, asking for you." And he replied, "Who are my mother and my brothers?" And looking at those who sat around him, he said, "Here are my mother and my brothers! Whoever does the will of God is my brother and sister and mother." (Mark 3:31-35; see also Luke 8:19-20)

What appears to be an affront to the mother love of Jesus' own mother is a reminder that it is not mothers who bring about the healing of the world, but *mothering.* And this mothering must extend beyond the bounds of familial care: "Whoever loves son or daughter more than me is not worthy of me" (Matt. 10:37). The transformative healing of the reign of God announced by Jesus is not available through the narrow confines of family-first relationships. Rather, the mother-love care for children and others must extend out into the community, the wider community, the global community.

The reclaiming of sacrifice for a world in need runs the danger long identified by feminist theology of patterns of a patriarchal outlook that demands the sacrifice of women to the detriment of self.[20] Certainly, this remains a live concern. But the mother care to which we are called is not about biology—whether the biology of she or he who is mother or the biology of the one receiving the care. The mother care of Christ expands beyond the bounds of biology to pour forth for a world in need. That is, it is not biological mothers who are called to sacrifice; we are all called to sacrifice. To operate as if the transformation of a world in need will come without cost is to ignore the material realities of an embodied condition in a globalized world. For Christians to be willing to participate in the sacrifice that hurts is to embrace the human condition of our own vulnerability. In the words of Judith Butler:

> We come into the world unknowing and dependent, and, to a certain degree, we remain that way. . . . [I]nfancy con- stitutes a necessary dependency, one that we never fully leave behind. Bodies still must be apprehended as given over. Part of understanding the oppression of lives is pre- cisely to understand that there is no way to argue away this condition of a primary vulnerability, of being given over to the touch of the other, even if, or precisely when, there is no other there, and no support for our lives. To counter oppression requires that one understand that lives are supported and maintained differentially, that there are radically different ways in which human physi- cal vulnerability is distributed across the globe.[21]

The acceptance of the human condition of vulnerability and the recognition of the differential experience of this vulnerability calls forth a response of the Christian mother love across boundar- ies for a world in need.

CHRISTOLOGY FOR A WORLD IN NEED: INTERRELIGIOUS SOLIDARITIES

In our global age, the mother love of Christians mothered by Christ must extend to the global community and be willing to cross reli- gious borders. A story from a young Muslim woman engaged in interfaith solidarity resonates with the mother care of Jesus and the necessity for envisioning affinities that arise from our human condi- tion, despite cultural and religious differences. This young Muslim was a resident of Jerusalem, and her outlook had been structured by the media's portrayal of Jews in the conflict of the Middle East, which grew to a hatred of Jews and a general distrust of any non-Muslims in her community. Although she lived and worked side-by-side with Jews, Christians, and people of the Druze faith, she described these working relationships as distant and filled with distrust. It was not until she found herself in the maternity ward's common nursery shortly after having given birth to her daughter that her experience of her neighbors of other faiths shifted from seeing them as "the enemy" to recognizing their common humanity. For around the room were new mothers of every religion represented in the region—women whose backgrounds placed them on opposing sides of the conflict, women from families who were enemies divided by their faiths. But as she sat in this nursery, exhausted from the pains of childbirth, holding her daughter in her arms while her daughter nursed at empty breasts, she had an insight.

She had just lived through months of physical transformation and physical sacrifice, through sickness and change in her public persona. After months of anticipation and preparation, and after hours of agony and pushing and pain, somehow she had brought a small new life into the world. This new life was utterly dependent upon her, completely vulnerable. And the young mother was vulnerable too, dependent upon some reality beyond herself as she waited for her milk to come in. Having chosen to breast-feed her newborn, in the first days of the baby's life she was helpless until the milk began to flow. She waited, as her child sometimes wailed, as her daughter lost ounces that felt like pounds. The new mother was exhausted, helpless, and vulnerable, as she could do nothing but wait.

For this young Muslim mother, this experience of her own vulnerable humanity—dependent on a force, a reality greater than herself—provided a foundation for recognizing the humanity of the other. And this young woman had the powerful realization that she shared with every single mother who surrounded her—the Christian, the Jew, the Druze—the desperate experience of waiting for her milk to come in. It was at this moment of profound

realization of what connected this group as new mothers, a connection that was physical and embodied, that she recognized the
common humanity of her neighbors of other faiths. This experience
of connection with other new mothers transcended the boundaries
of religion that had so long distanced her from her coworkers and
neighbors in the conflict. It was this recognition of shared humanity
through the particularity of being vulnerable as a new mother that
led her to take part in an interreligious dialogue circle of women
concerned for peacemaking in their city.

The subsequent dialogue among this young mother and her
neighbors was not focused on "how rationally to convince someone from another tradition that yours is true."[22] Rather, their conversations developed out of a keen sense of the necessity to work
together to protect the bodies of their sons and daughters, their
husbands and parents. They talked about how each of them was
vulnerable and how neighbors of diverse religious backgrounds
might share the same physical space in a way that allowed for the
fullest human flourishing. In the process, they drew on their religions to envision a way forward, but their primary focus was not
to compare and contrast the diverse details of doctrine, but rather
to preserve the integrity of vulnerable bodies in a location where
human well-being was threatened daily.

In telling her story, the young woman provided a metaphor for
the desperate search for a common foundation for peace refracted
through the lens of motherhood. She closed her reflection with the
following words:

We feed them milk, we feed them love,
We feed them hatred,
Whatever we feed them they will eat
And they will become.

In these words, we are broadened out from the circumscribed experience of women in the nursing ward to a symbolic

representation of how each of us feeds the other, with maternal relationality as metaphor for the ongoing actions of women and men as we bring one another into being. We are all waiting for our milk to come in. We are all seeking the resources and the strength to sustain our world, our children, and future generations, in contexts divided by religious differences. Desperation arises from the sense of urgency that the earth and its inhabitants face in our times of limited resources, corporate greed, and national distrust. The metaphor of waiting for our milk to come in derives from one woman's embodied experience and is offered as a powerful metaphor through which women and men might share the experience of desperately wanting to be agents of sustenance and change in our religiously plural world.

If the Christian is fashioned on Christ as breast-feeding mother, s/he too is waiting for her milk to come in. As the twelfth-century vision held, "nothing is better fitted to serve as our mother than charity. These cherish and make us advance, feed us and nourish us, and refresh us with the milk of twofold affection: love, that is, for God and for neighbor."[23] And in our interreligious and globalized world, the neighbor to whom our care extends stands in need across religious boundaries. A Christology sufficient for a globalized world increasingly interconnected with religious difference and increasingly aware of the pervasiveness of injustice is a Christology that must stand on behalf of those in need. I am thinking with a hybridized Christ, a Christ-Christa who, having been nurtured by her mother emerges from out of embodied experiences of sacrifice and relationship to nurture the other. Such a Christ-Christa stands on behalf of a broken world. But standing on behalf of the other must not be a patronizing gesture. Rather, it must be understood in the way that Homi Bhabha envisions, where speaking on behalf means being willing to "half" oneself, to restructure one's interests and privileges in solidarity with the other.[24] As a mother, I act on behalf all the time. And while I first feared that this meant the loss of me, it is an invitation to a dynamic evolvement of myself. In the parallel language of Christian theology, God was not fearful of becoming less in the person of Jesus, but lives in and through Jesus of Nazareth as a way of dynamically involving Godself in the world, because behalfing/halfing does not diminish, but calls something particular into being.

In this age of interreligious awareness, I am also willing to share the divinity of God with other persons, figures, and events that emerge from a wide variety of religious realities. In a sense, I am willing to halve Christ, because God is infinite.

> "The *Divine Mother* exists in everything, animate and inanimate, in the form of power or energy. It is that power that sustains us through our lives and ultimately guides us to our respective destination," quotes Swarupa Ghose, a housewife with a newborn baby in her lap.[25]

As this mother, Swarupa Ghose, reminds us, the visions of God and the experiences of being human illumined in various religions are multiple. But this is also reflected in motherhood. Far from a unitary or universal experience, motherhood is a site of radical multiplicity. The subject-position "mother" is a most hybrid one. First, this is seen in the way that motherhood varies across cultures, historical contexts, and social locations. Motherhood could be the constricting limitations of raising seven children that propels one into advocacy for women's greater social and political freedoms, as was the case with Elizabeth Cady Stanton, who, no doubt, had all kinds of help in the child-rearing duties that enabled her to take on such an active political role.[26] Motherhood could be the surrogate role forced on slave women as mammy to white households in the American South.[27] Egyptian mothers created women's space and women's culture separated from the male-ordered public sphere, fostering essential family networks and becoming the transmitters of a living Islam, as the memoir of Leila Ahmed recounts.[28] The mother role could be identified with the soccer mom who juggles multiple responsibilities in North American comfort, or it could be identified with the immigrant mother who has left her own children behind to care for someone else's family in the affluence of a North American suburb. Mothers have borne their babies on their backs as they work the fields of China; and mothers have borne the symbol of the nation on their bodies as they struggled for independence under the sign of "Mother India."[29] The subject position "mother" is a hybrid one, not only in light of the cultural, geographic, and economic differences that infuse the experiences within "motherhood" as a category, but also in that any particular subject in the position of mother is multiple, as mother is called into a variety of roles, responsibilities, and relationships, none of which quite capture the whole.[30]

In this constructive revisioning of Christ that is in continuity with the creative process of all Christologies down through the ages, the hybridity of motherhood reminds us of the finally unpindownable nature of Christological reflection itself. It invites a consideration of Christ through this particular fashioning of motherhood as metaphor and a particular form of motherhood as a lens through which to vision the story of Christian identity amid difference. But it invites the multiplicity of meanings that might come forth in Christological reflection from a wide variety of subject-positions—of mothers and others—that will continue to unfold the mystery of Christ meaningfully today.

Chapter 5

LIBERATING JESUS: CHRISTIAN FEMINISM AND ANTI-JUDAISM

Elena Procario-Foley

What does Judaism have to do with Christian feminist theology? The reflections of this chapter begin from the reality that Christianity shares a relationship with Judaism that it has with no other religion. For instance, Christian scripture inherits thirty-nine books of sacred writing from Judaism. The person who stands at the center of Christianity, Jesus of Nazareth, prayed to the God of Israel using the sacred Jewish texts of his time. Christianity's unique relationship to Judaism, however, has been tragically characterized by Christian imperialism, which stems in part from misunderstanding and misusing Jesus. Judaism and Christian feminist theology intersect at the point of misunderstanding Jesus.

To set up the conversation, let us begin with a dialogue between a college student, his tutor, and another professional in the academic services office.

> **Student:** I have this religion class and I just don't get it. What does my professor mean that Jesus was a feminist?[1]
>
> **Tutor:** Your professor is probably pointing to the new life in God that Jesus preached in his lifetime and that we learn about in the Gospels.

Student: But how could Jesus be a feminist? I'm a Christian, not a feminist!

Tutor: By the way, those two identifications are not as contradictory as you think! Your professor wants you to understand that Jesus included all sorts of outcasts in his ministry who were excluded from Jewish life and observance. Liberation theologians sometimes call this Jesus' preferential option for the poor. And women were included in that category of the poor.

Student: I still don't understand. Could you give me an example?

Tutor: Jesus allowed women disciples—look at the story of Mary and Martha in Luke 10:38-42. Also, in Judaism, it is men who are given the sign of the covenant with male circumcision, and women just cannot participate as fully. But Jesus allows full participation for women in his community. St. Paul declares that in Christ there is no Jew or Greek, slave or free, male or female. (See Gal. 3:28)

Student: I get it now, thanks.

The student leaves, and around the corner of the makeshift wall divider appears a reading specialist who asks to speak with the tutor.

Specialist: I overheard you speaking to that student, and as a Jewish woman, I am offended by what you said.

Tutor: I'm sorry—I don't know what you mean.

Specialist: You are completely wrong in your description of Jewish women's involvement in covenantal life. Jesus could not have meant to denigrate Jewish faith in that way.

Tutor: I do not think it is a matter of Jesus denigrating Jewish faith, but of Christian feminists highlighting the complete inclusion of women in Jesus' ministry and the early church.

Specialist: You should not do that by demeaning Jewish women.

Tutor: *(stammering now)* But I did not think I was doing that; it is what I learned; it's what I was taught; I don't know what to say.

The specialist leaves, and the tutor feels profoundly confused and off-balance. Something feels quite correct about the specialist's comments, but it does not immediately cohere with what the tutor understands about Catholic feminist perspectives.

This is a true story. I was the tutor, a graduate student just about to begin dissertation research. It does not matter that the recorded dialogue is not a complete verbatim. I remember vividly, though, the anger of the reading specialist and the sting of the shame I felt for offending her. Though my offense was completely unintentional, the encounter revealed to me a set of blinders that I had appropriated from my Christian theological education.

ANTI-JUDAISM: REPREHENSIBLE CHRISTIAN POLEMICS

My long-ago responses to the student have coded within them a history of anti-Jewish Christian theology. "New life," "women as outcasts," "preferential option for the poor," "women's exclusion from the practice of Judaism," and the triumphal slogan of Galatians 3:28 all point in some manner to a Christian theological vision with a truncated understanding of Judaism at best and an imperialist view of Christianity at worst. Jewish scholars Amy-Jill Levine and Paula Fredriksen frequently warn us that bad history does not make good theology. It is incumbent, therefore, upon the Christian feminist theologian to be able to recognize anti-Judaism when it infects the good and necessary project of feminist theology in all of its different formulations. Jesus the Jew needs to be liberated from theology that denigrates Judaism—feminist or otherwise—or else Christology will be hopelessly anti-Jewish.[2]

Defining anti-Judaism is itself a difficult affair.[3] Some commentators do not wish to distinguish between anti-Judaism and antisemitism because they think that doing so allows Christians to avoid responsibility for the many atrocities committed by putative Christians against the Jewish people throughout history and especially during the *Shoah* (the Hebrew term for the period commonly known as the Holocaust). Mindful of this danger, many scholars maintain the distinction between the two terms because it allows us to identify theological attitudes that attack Jewish faith (anti-Judaism) from racist, social, and pseudo-scientific theories that attack Jewish people themselves apart from a concern for religion (antisemitism). Admittedly, too often the line between the two terms blurs easily, and anti-Jewish motifs have certainly fed the fires of antisemitism throughout history.

Nonetheless, identifying the broad features of anti-Jewish theology is important to be able to locate it within Christian feminist theology. Prior to the Second Vatican Council (1962–1965), French historian Jules Isaac (1877–1963) coined the term the *teaching of contempt* to refer to anti-Jewish thinking. He famously articulated it in a book of the same name through a series of ten propositions.[4] Isaac lost his family to the *Shoah* and dedicated the rest of his life to researching the origins of antisemitism. In brief, the teaching of contempt is a phrase that intends to refer to all Christian writing, legislation, and violence that has been directed against the Jews throughout Christian history. While Pope John XXIII was preparing for Vatican II, he invited Isaac to the Vatican to educate him about the Catholic Church's history with Judaism. Isaac presented the pope with materials that helped the council fathers to write the conciliar document that has subsequently revolutionized the relationship between the Catholic Church and the Jewish religion: *Nostra Aetate: Decree on the Church's Relationship to Non-Christian Religions.*

Over time, various lists and devices have been created to summarize Isaac's insights and his articulation of the teaching of contempt. One such tool is known as the "five Ds," which helps to frame the concepts needed to identify anti-Jewish themes or tendencies in Christian feminist (and other liberationist) theology. The five Ds are identified as: dispersal, dismissal, deicide, degenerate, and demonic. At this point we must be absolutely clear: the five Ds are false and defamatory claims about Judaism and the Jewish people generated by Christians over the centuries.

A key erroneous claim that developed very early within Christianity was that Jews are *dispersed* from the land. In 70 CE the Roman occupiers of Israel destroyed the Temple in Jerusalem, which was the focal point of ancient Jewish religious practice from approximately the tenth century BCE to 70 CE. The Romans razed the city, slaughtered thousands, and forced the Jews from their homeland. The thoroughgoing victory of the Romans and the subsequent *diaspora* (scattering) of the Jews was interpreted by Christians as evidence that God had rejected the Jewish people. As the diaspora continued and Christianity became the state religion of the Roman Empire (circa fourth century CE), the perception that God had forsaken the Jews as the chosen people hardened within Christianity. The Jews, according to this line of thinking, could no longer lay claim to the land. Since the land was one of the three promises God made to Abraham, and the Jewish people no longer held claim to the land, Christian anti-Jewish theology taught that God revoked God's promises to the Jewish people. The Catholic Church formally renounced its despicable theology that God withdrew the promises from Israel when *Nostra Aetate* referred to St. Paul's letter to the Romans 11:29, "For the gifts and the call of God are irrevocable."

Dispersal is closely linked to the next grossly false accusation: Jews are *dismissed* from revelation. Christians followed a mistaken logic that said that since God had rejected the Jews and dispersed them from the land, they no longer had a role in proclaiming God.

The Jewish people are thus superseded. Supersessionism is the idea that Christianity replaces Judaism in God's plan of salvation; they have no part in revelation. Interestingly, however, the Jewish people are not cast entirely away. In other words, it was not a religious goal to eradicate the Jewish people. Christian theology created dangerous conditions for Jewish life to greater and lesser extents at different times in history, but it was not genocidal. Christians recognized that the Jews gave the world God's word, God's testament (for Christians, the "Old" testament). For this achievement, Christians accorded the Jewish people some minimal theological recognition (and occasional civil and ecclesiastical protections). Even though Jewish scripture was "old" and superseded by the "new" testament, God and God's Word were first introduced to the world by the Jews. Moreover, Christians understood from St. Paul's letter to the Romans (chap. 11) that God mysteriously prevents Jews from recognizing salvation in Christ so that "the full number of the Gentiles" can come to salvation. Thus, though dismissed from revelation, the Jews play a role in the salvation of the world. And indeed, St. Paul proclaims "all Israel will be saved" (Rom. 11:26). Nonetheless, dismissal from revelation and dispersal from the land become deeply entrenched anti-Jewish Christian assumptions that haunt the history of the Jewish-Christian relationship.

Looming large in the difficult history that Jews and Christians share is the further odious accusation that Jews are a *deicide* people. Traditional anti-Jewish Christian belief has taught that Jews are cursed because they killed God. They killed Jesus and did not recognize him as the Messiah. Therefore, according to the teaching of contempt, it is right that all manner of evil befall the Christ-killers. Christian tradition made no distinctions and charged all Jews in all times and places with deicide. This sanctioned all manner of hateful actions toward the Jewish community. The anti-Jewish, Christ-killer, and deicide charges fueled rabid antisemitism over the centuries. Good Friday liturgies, for example, would spark spontaneous violence against Jews. *Nostra Aetate* repudiated the teaching of deicide.

Given the teaching of Jews as a "deicide people" who are "dispersed" and "dismissed," it is no surprise that Judaism was also unfairly characterized by Christianity as a *degenerate* religion. The clearest illustration of this charge comes in the exaggerated and erroneous polar description of Christianity as love and Judaism as law. This view depicts Jews as guardians of and slaves to the letter of a useless law. With this perspective, Judaism is viewed as a burdensome dead letter, a lifeless faith whose followers must be freed by the gospel. In the teaching of contempt, Christian love supersedes a moribund, degenerate religion.

Finally, the accusation that the Jews are *demonic* completes this summary of the teaching of contempt. The characterization of the Jewish people as demonic readily found artistic expression. One need only glance at medieval art to find ample examples of Jewish people represented in such grotesque manners as horned devils or as half human and half pig.[5] In the medieval period, Christians developed the hideous idea that Jewish families would find and murder Christian babies. Many reasons were purported to explain this behavior, but a popular explanation for such a calumnious charge was that the murdered body was used to make the Passover dinner. This is known as the Blood Libel, and it contributed deeply to the teaching that the Jews were demonic.

In one way or another, the teaching of contempt summarized by the five-Ds teaches a theology that Jews are an object lesson in divine justice. This compilation of false accusations creates an anti-Jewish theology of supersessionism that can take many forms. The Roman Catholic Church repudiated an anti-Jewish, supersessionist approach to Judaism with *Nostra Aetate,* the Second Vatican Council, and the subsequent documents from the Vatican Commission on Religious Relations with the Jews.[6] Official statements alone, however, cannot eradicate a long Christian history of anti-Jewish theology characterized by a pernicious and persistent teaching of contempt for Jews and Judaism.

TEACHING RESPECT: 6 RS

Mary C. Boys, Skinner and McAlpin Professor of Practical Theology at Union Theological Seminary in New York City, proposes that Six Rs emerge from the new teaching of respect in Christianity that developed in the denominations following the Shoah. The beginning of the documentary history of the teaching of respect is often dated to the Seelisberg Conference of 1947 and its declaration of the "Ten Points of Seelisberg." An extremely talented teacher, Boys has synthesized sixty years of the Christian rethinking of its relationship to Judaism into the following:

Refutation of the charge of deicide

Repudiation of antisemitism

Repentance in regard to the Shoah

Rejection of proselytizing

Review of teaching about Jews and Judaism

Recognition of Israel

The six Rs can lead Christians away from their traditional triumphal, supersessionist, and dehumanizing treatment of the Jewish people and toward a renewed relationship of equals based on respect and reverence.

See Mary C. Boys, *Has God Only One Blessing? Judaism as a Source of Christian Self-Understanding* (Mahwah, N.J.: Paulist, 2000) and specifically chapter 14 for the six Rs.

MISUNDERSTANDING JESUS AT THE INTERSECTION OF JUDAISM AND CHRISTIAN FEMINISM

One would not expect a theology crafted along the lines of feminist theology sketched in the introduction to include anti-Jewish themes. In a post–Vatican II era, a theology of contempt enters feminist theology (in fact, all Christian theology) when it attempts to articulate and validate Christian identity in superlative terms through an implicit or explicit contrast with Judaism. Jesus usually stands at the focal point of such a contrast. This type of comparison is a setup, and Judaism always loses.

For instance, the example of my infelicitous explanation of the significance of Jesus for women to my student was blatantly anti-Jewish because it implied or stated Jesus' superiority over and abrogation of the Jewish Law. Such an interpretation of Jesus' attitude toward Torah (which is better translated as instruction or teaching rather than "Law") is simply wrong on the facts and is not supported by a sober reading of the available texts. Two related things happen by fostering this errant view of Jesus' position toward ancient Jewish teaching. It creates an illusory perspective that Jesus, and by extension Christianity, allowed for women's full participation in religious life, whereas Judaism did not, and that Christianity offers life, justice, and love, whereas Judaism, by contrast, did not. Second, incorrectly stretching the limited available evidence for Jesus' attitude toward women creates a caricature of Jewish women during the time of Jesus. My youthful response, sparked by enthusiastic hope for a complete inclusion of women in the Catholic Church, unintentionally created just such a caricature for my tutee. Both Christianity and Judaism are misrepresented, but the problem is that Judaism is unfairly and unnecessarily denigrated in the comparison, while Christianity is artificially praised.

Far from explaining a theology based in relationality, equality, and community in diversity, my responses to my student repeated age-old patterns of hierarchical domination (in this case of Christianity over Judaism instead of men over women). Moreover, I cast a false impression of Judaism by not acknowledging the variety within late Second Temple Judaism and by not distinguishing it from the many forms of Judaism today. Methodologically, my recovery of the sources was left wanting, and my answers suffered therefore from poor historical research. My explanation of Jesus' relationship toward women created an impression of Judaism as a degenerate and repressive religion that Jesus was rejecting, just as God dismissed and rejected the Jews. This certainly reads distressingly like the proclamations of the old teaching of contempt. About such an explanation, Jewish feminist theologian Judith Plaskow states, "Feminists should know better!"[7] The ire of Plaskow's exclamation reflects the reality that feminists—whether Christian or Jewish—do not always agree, but the passion of the statement also implies that some misunderstandings are entirely avoidable. Indeed, Christian feminists should know better than to dehumanize a people in order to define their own. Such methodology is exactly opposite the feminist criterion that what is dehumanizing of any group of people is not of God, and it undercuts feminist efforts to promote the values of mutuality, equality, and community in diversity.

COVERT BUT UNINTENTIONAL ANTI-JEWISH THEMES IN CHRISTIAN FEMINIST THEOLOGY

Authors such as Amy-Jill Levine, Judith Plaskow, Susannah Heschel, Katharina von Kellenbach, and Mary Boys, among others, have identified a number of anti-Jewish themes that tend to appear in feminist writing. Before examining a few of the main motifs, however, we must note that the distinction between anti-Judaism and antisemitism becomes quite important at this juncture of the discussion. Both Catholic and Jewish scholars who have analyzed the dynamics of anti-Judaism and Christian feminism are quick to point out that they are generally quite sympathetic to the goals of feminist theology. When they critique a part of someone's work as anti-Jewish, they are not accusing the writer of antisemitism, but of not recognizing how persistently anti-Jewish elements creep into portions of the theology. Mary Boys, for example, explains that "Because anti-Judaism has replicated itself in many dimensions of Christian theological thinking for nearly 2000 years, it will be neither neatly nor quickly extricated. . . . Thus, in criticizing the theological perspectives of various feminist theologians, I am not accusing them of antisemitism. I am, however, questioning whether they have done justice to the complex relationship of Judaism to Christianity."[8] Keeping in mind that analyzing feminist theology for anti-Jewish themes is not a dismissal of feminist theology but actually coheres with the methods and norms of feminist theology, we will move to a discussion of three areas of concern that tend to appear in Christian feminist theology: Goddess religion and patriarchy, the characterization of Jewish women at the time of Jesus, and the Christian feminist appropriation of Jesus.

Jewish feminists, for example, indict Christian feminists for erroneously blaming Judaism for the death of the Goddess. The argument for the death of the Goddess begins with an idyllic depiction of the early millennia of recorded history or of prehistory. Gods and goddesses cooperated in a coequal sharing of responsibility for the care of the earth and its peoples, following a calendar determined by the cycles of the natural world. To be female, to be male, to be of the body, to be of the sky, or to be of the earth were all accorded similar value in a human community of equals who cherished their natural environment. In "Motherearth and the Megamachine," an essay that significantly influenced the first wave of Catholic feminist theologians and their students, Rosemary Radford Ruether describes a set of dualities that subjugate women to men. Identifying men with the mind and women with the changeable (read: unreliable) body, opposing objectivity to subjectivity, and setting spirit against nature all derive from Christianity's mixing of a Jewish male warrior God with a neo-Platonic preference for spirit over matter, according to Ruether.[9]

Ruether maintains that ancient Judaism's appropriation of land from the Canaanite natives involved a process of negating the land and suppressing religious observances based on cycles of fertility. It set up a male God as the supreme and sole ruler and in so doing killed the Goddess; or, in Ruether's words, "Yahwism repressed the feminine divine role."

At this point, lest I confuse the reader, I must be quite explicit about the explanation above. Even though Rosemary Radford Ruether is rightfully revered as a pioneering superforce in Catholic feminist theology (and is acknowledged as such elsewhere in this volume), her explanation of the death of the Goddess demonstrates how easily undercurrents of supersessionism can creep into feminist discourse. To be fair, Ruether's later, important study *Faith and Fratricide* makes abundantly clear that she is cognizant of the damaging effects of Christian anti-Judaism. Simply put, however, the example of the death of the Goddess, whether in the work of Ruether or others, serves as an example of anti-Judaism slipping into Christian feminist theology.

The deicide principle is repeated in feminist writing. Now, instead of killing Christ, Judaism is accused of killing the Goddess. Moreover, as a necessary corollary to charging Judaism with the death of the Goddess, Christian feminism blames Judaism for patriarchy. The dualisms of mind and body, objectivity and subjectivity, and spirit and nature that Ruether enumerated support the hegemony of male over female and of an eschatologically oriented history ruled by a father-God who negates the cycles of natural renewal.[10] Susannah Heschel notes that along with charging Judaism with the ascendancy of patriarchy, feminists claim that "the male religion described in the Hebrew Bible is said to legitimate violence and destruction."[11]

Working to demonstrate that Christianity need not be hopelessly patriarchal and sexist, Christian feminists have adopted the view of ancient Judaism as the originator of patriarchy and the murderer of the Goddess. Though not identical to the much more explicit traditional canard that "the Jews killed Jesus and are therefore forsaken by God," the charges of introducing patriarchy into human communities and killing the Goddess foster an equivalent negative and supersessionist attitude toward Jews and Judaism. Patriarchy in Christianity, within this construction of history, is understood as an evil import from Judaism and not an endemic characteristic of Christianity. Feminists then reason that Christianity can be reformed.

A second way in which anti-Jewish themes of contempt slip into Christian feminist theology is through an inaccurate presentation of the social location of Jewish women during the time of Jesus. Simply put, feminist theologians fall into the trap of portraying the situation of Jewish women at the time of Jesus as an extremely difficult life, characterized by being pushed to the margins of—if not explicitly excluded from—social and religious life. Again, when such errors occur, commentators do not usually impute anti-Jewish intention to the author. Some of the misrepresentations, especially in the early work of feminists in the 1970s and 1980s, are understood as a consequence of the available research, or lack thereof, on women in late Second Temple Judaism.

When inaccuracies occur, however, they are often closely linked to a third area important to this conversation: the feminist presentation of Jesus of Nazareth. Demonstrating that Jesus was qualitatively different from his time, and that "his time" was overtly and inordinately hostile to women, allows feminist theologians to present Jesus and Christianity as a haven for women. The underlying problem with this approach is that one has to ask the question: from what did women need a haven? And the answer returns inevitably: from Jewish sexism and patriarchy. Misrepresenting the plight of Jewish women and Jesus' relations with women are tactics that correlate closely with the teaching of contempt that Judaism is a degenerate and corrupt religion.

How does the presentation of late Second Temple period Jewish women and Jesus proceed? To answer this question, the following section will draw heavily from "Lilies of the Field and Wandering Jews: Biblical Scholarship, Women's Roles, and Social Location" and "Second Temple Judaism, Jesus, and Women: Yeast of Eden."[12] In these essays, Jewish scholar Amy-Jill Levine expertly synthesizes a great deal of detailed research concerning feminist scholarship and anti-Judaism into several errors, assumptions, or explanations present in feminist theology that contribute in small or more significant ways to perpetuating anti-Jewish perspectives.

Levine alerts us first to deceptively simple summary statements that are easily overlooked but frequently repeated (as in my dialogue at the beginning of this essay). In one fell swoop, a seemingly innocuous sentence, such as "Jesus liberated the outcasts of his day, including women" lifts up Jesus as better than his contemporary coreligionists and condemns the status of women. Judaism suffers in such a comparison to Jesus. *More importantly,* Jesus is deftly separated, bit by bit, from his Jewish reality. If he "saved women" from their Jewish plight, then he is rejecting his religion. Subtle supersessionism is at work.

One of the aspects of Jewish life from which Jesus presumably rescued women concerns obedience to so-called "oppressive purity legislation" (a second area of concern for Levine). Feminist theologians refer to women's presumed oppression under such regulations as a shorthand way of describing the difficulties of women's

lives at the time of Jesus. This is a subject prone to great misunderstanding, and therefore, some basic information is in order. The
Torah established sets of rules governing states of ritual purity and
impurity. The operative word here is *ritual*. Many activities at the
temple in Jerusalem required a state of ritual purity as eligibility for
participation. Discussion of ritual purity or impurity, however, is
not equivalent to a discussion of morality and sin. Naturally occur-
ring events in life affect one's ritual purity or impurity. Commonly
cited examples of contracting ritual impurity include coming into
the presence of a corpse, ejaculation, and menstruation. For every
ritual impurity there was a prescribed "cure" that varied according
to the impurity but consisted simply of a system of water immersion and waiting—"wash and wait," as it is often described.[13]

Women were not, therefore, automatically marginalized or
excluded from religious life because of monthly menstruation or
other ritual impurities. Such ritual purity was primarily a matter
for the temple and did not apply to synagogue activity or many
aspects of daily life. Thus, if a woman did not live in Jerusalem or
was not making a pilgrimage to Jerusalem for the festivals, many
of the purity laws simply did not, in practice, affect her daily life
(though applied in theory). This is in stark contrast to an attitude
that assumes that Jewish law denigrated women and prevented
them from participation in religious life. In "Lilies of the Field,"
Amy-Jill Levine marshals a host of examples to demonstrate the
prevalence of the notion among feminists that purity legislation
oppressed Jewish women, as well as to make the case that there is
much misunderstanding of the role of such legislation in the lives
of Jewish women at the time of Jesus.[14] Significantly, Levine quotes
several times from one author who explicitly cites the need to avoid
Christian antisemitism yet notes more than once that "women were
considered less clean than men and constituted a perennial threat
of pollution to men."[15] In this example, women are considered less
clean or pure than men in general (Levine notes that there is often no

distinguishing between cleanliness, purity, or pollution) and then become even more impure based on circumstances that arise. Little if any consideration is given to the dynamics of ritual impurity for men, thus leaving the impression that women are oppressed by an arbitrary, patriarchal system. Little if any consideration is given to the idea that Jewish women might have taken pride in their fulfill-ment of their tasks as prescribed by scripture. Far from preventing women's participation in religious life, following the way of life designated in scripture was a way for women as well as men to participate in relationship with God.

Misunderstandings surrounding the complexities of the purity regulations as they apply to women lead directly into a third impor-tant mode of anti-Judaism in feminist theology. The feminist assess-ment of Jesus' treatment of women is closely allied to the feminist presentation of the status of women. Levine states the problem well: "Whatever Second Temple Judaism may have been in terms of theology, politics, economics, or aesthetics, it was, according to this construct, generally bad for women. And, whatever the Jesus movement was, it was good for women."[16] The healing of the woman with the hemorrhage and the related story of the raising of Jairus's deceased daughter (Mark 5:21-43//Matt. 9:18-26 and Luke 8:40-56) are commonly used to depict the doubly outcast status of women qua women and as impure (from a flow of blood or other-wise), and to depict Jesus' rejection of the Jewish system of purity observances. About these New Testament stories, one writer notes, "The Markan Jesus creates a Jewish community that understands the realm of God as whole, inclusive, and without boundaries, not as the exclusive and separated realm protected by the Jewish officials. Since women were considered dangerously impure, their inclusion is a prime example of the Markan Jesus' inclusiveness."[17] Another avers, "The women lay claim to no rights. It is Jesus who sovereignly acknowledges that they have rights, and this is accom-panied by a dramatic, healing alteration in their lives."[18]

Both assessments continue to portray a negative view of Jewish women's lives at the time of Jesus and a positive attitude toward women that is attributed uniquely to Jesus. It is inaccurate to represent Jewish women as having no social or religious rights or as being marginalized because their impurity is dangerous to men; Jewish men also became regularly ritually impure as a result of their own activities. Emphasizing an image of Jesus as liberated from the confines of his religion and as liberating others into his new vision of the reign of God is easier if women are portrayed as hopelessly oppressed by a misogynist religion. Feminists who wish to reform patriarchal structures within Christianity reasonably look to Jesus for a vision of healing, inclusion, and liberation. The liberation won by Jesus on the cross for women and men does not, however, have to be established by denigrating Judaism. When examples such as the above are multiplied, one discovers a pattern of exaggerating both the situation of women and Jesus' response to women that bespeaks a triumphal supersessionism. On the one hand, Judaism slowly becomes associated solely with "Jewish officials" or "legalistic Pharisees," and the rich diversity of legitimate ways of being Jewish at the time of Jesus is lost. The Pharisees, for example, are routinely caricatured as legalists, instead of exploring their role as reformers calling people to holiness. Jesus, on the other hand, is represented as the radical reformer who breaks away from a corrupt and irredeemable religion and who inaugurates a new, inclusive community in loving relationship with God.

Recent research, by contrast, emphasizes details in the New Testament that support an interpretation of Jesus as a son of his religion, as an observant Jew of his time. Feminists need to account for Jesus as such. In the Lucan and Matthean accounts of the woman with the flow of blood, the Gospel writers note that the woman touched the "fringe" of Jesus' garment. Paula Fredriksen, for one, draws our attention to the fact that this "fringe" refers to the ritual dress *(tzitzit)* required by scripture (see Num. 15:38-39).[19]

Also, since men and women contracted ritual impurity on a regular basis, Jesus' contact with those in a state of ritual impurity (whether a bleeding woman or a leper, for instance) would not cause alarm. As an observant Jewish man, Jesus would simply follow the "wash and wait" protocols for returning to a state of ritual purity.

Fredriksen points to other details that get overlooked when we search the Gospels for support for our modern liberationist ideals. Among others, she explains that when Jesus tells the leper to present himself to the priest (Mark 1:44), or when Jesus enters the temple to pray, or when Jesus eats the Passover meal with his companions, the text demonstrates Jesus as an observant Jew, not as one who flagrantly abrogates the dictates of Jewish scripture. In all three examples, a state of purity is assumed as part of Jewish life (the leper needed to be certified as ritually pure by the priest, and presence at the temple or a Passover meal required ritual purity). Losing Jesus the Jew in favor of Jesus the proto-Christian feminist does not enhance the laudable goals of the feminist project. It weakens it by slipping into a teaching of contempt that does not exemplify the feminist values of radical equality, mutuality, and diversity in community. Fredriksen reminds her readers that ethics and ritual were two sides of a coin in ancient Judaism. Representing Jesus as flagrantly disregarding purity legislation, therefore, to emphasize his ethic of inclusiveness is incoherent. For Fredriksen, "we must begin from the premise that Jesus was truly a Jew of his own time. . . . Absent specific instructions on purity in what we can reconstruct of his teaching, we should assume *not* that Jesus ignored or opposed Jewish purity codes, but rather that he took them for granted as fundamental to the worship of the God who had revealed them, uniquely, to Israel."[20]

CONSEQUENCES FOR CHRISTOLOGY

Various authors have incisively labeled the failures of Christian feminism to avoid anti-Jewish traps as a repetition of the errors of the ancient Marcionite and Docetic heresies. Maricon, who died in the latter half of the second century CE, rejected the books that Christians understand as the Old Testament and advocated a truncated New Testament. Marcion set up a dualism of the God of the Old Testament versus Jesus' God of the New Testament. According to Marcion, the Old Testament God was a god of violence and war in contrast to Jesus' God of peace. Though Marcion's views were condemned as heretical, the teaching of contempt kept them alive in its espousal of the antitheses of law and love, letter and spirit, and old covenant and new covenant. Christian feminist theology repackages these offensive and misleading dualisms by "taking an old characterization of Judaism as a religion of law and labeling it male, in opposition to Christianity, a religion of love, which is labeled female."[21] One can recognize the deicide charge in the parallel of Marcion's God of Jesus defeating the God of the Old Testament, with Jesus the loving feminist overcoming the God of law.

Docetism, also an intellectual current of the late second century CE, rejects the full humanity of Jesus. According to this heresy, Jesus was only apparently human and thus did not truly die a human death, because he was truly spirit and God, divine not flesh. Of course mainstream Christianity rejected docetism because it contradicted the belief in the Incarnation and questioned the value of the material world. Christian feminism can tilt docetic, though, when it neglects, distorts, or rejects Jesus' Jewish context. Freed from his moorings in late Second Temple period culture, Jesus can be the pure spirit of feminist yearnings for equality and mutual relation, unencumbered by the historical messiness of being a Jewish man. The problem is that the feminist version of docetic Christology replicates various aspects of the teaching of contempt. As with the Marcionite dualisms, it sets up a God foreign to Jesus' historical Judaism, thus mimicking God's purported dispersing of the Jews from their land and dismissal from revelation. A docetic feminist Christology easily views the ancient Jewish system of sacrificial and purity observances as degenerate and demonic. Levine notes that little thought is given "to the idea that Jesus' own mission is embedded within formative Judaism, rather than external to it."[22]

Feminist Christology must consciously avoid the traps of anti-Judaism in order to liberate Jesus Christ to be a source of renewed life that vivifies communities of equals who live in mutual relation, celebrating diverse gifts from the Holy One of the universe.

CLAIMING IDENTITY AND RESOLVING ANTI-JUDAISM IN CHRISTIAN FEMINISM

Accusing Judaism of killing the goddess and contributing patriarchy to human culture, representing the plight of Second Temple Jewish women as worse than it actually was, and representing Jesus as disconnected from his Jewish milieu weakens the feminist project. Judith Plaskow specifies the core miscarriage of Christian feminism in this regard as repeating the mistake of patriarchy that feminism was supposed to have cured: projection of unwanted identity onto the vilified other.[23] The so-called "female" side of the dualisms of male/female, mind/body, objectivity/subjectivity, rationality/emotionability, reviewed earlier in this essay, are rejected and projected by patriarchal systems onto women. Similarly, Plaskow declares that Christian feminists have projected that part of their identity that they do not want to own—male-dominated structures, limited roles for women—onto the demonized other, Judaism. Plaskow writes, "Feminist research projects onto Judaism the failure of the Christian tradition unambiguously to renounce sexism."[24] Functioning on an alienating projection obstructs the possibility of successfully implementing a feminist worldview of equality, mutuality, and community in diversity.

Resolving anti-Jewish tendencies in Christian feminism requires, then, that Christian feminists stop projecting the failures of institutional Christianity to incarnate the vision of liberating wholeness that they see in Jesus onto a view of Judaism made distorted and hollow by their projection. The point of critiquing Christian feminism through the lens of anti-Judaism is not to vilify Christian feminist theologians, and far less to defend Second Temple Judaism or later rabbinic Judaism as more sensitive to feminist concerns. Rather, once aware of the traps, Christian feminists will readily find that they can and should partner with Jewish feminists to the benefit of both groups.

A brief return to the three main areas discussed in this essay will begin to disclose the potentially productive dynamics of an alliance of Jewish and Christian feminists. In dialogue together, Jewish and Christian feminists can critique the patriarchy in ancient Paganism, Graeco-Roman culture, formative Judaism, and early Christianity, instead of projecting responsibility for patriarchy onto one tradition or another and assuming that goddess worship will eliminate violence. Judaism does not have to be the foil against which Christian feminism succeeds as a noble and more egalitarian enterprise. Christian feminism should not repackage the deicide/Christ-killer charge. Instead, as Susannah Heschel suggests, Jewish and Christian feminists can address together the feelings of conflicted identity that come from being both alienated from a religious tradition that is oppressively patriarchal and hierarchical and simultaneously attracted to the deep truths and beauty available in the tradition. In the same vein, Plaskow argues that Christian feminism "ought to provide the opportunity for transcending ancient differences in the common battle against sexism."[25]

Second, when patriarchy is addressed as a common enemy, feminists can relinquish the need—unconscious though it may be—to vilify Jewish religious practice as degenerate and demeaning of women. Christian feminists can utilize the wealth of studies now available to explore the complexity and range of Jewish

women's lives in antiquity from peasant to patroness of syna-
gogues.[26] Instead of portraying Jewish religious practices (especially as they pertain to ritual purity) as oppressive, degenerate,
and demonic, Christian feminism can come to understand and
celebrate Jewish women's faithfulness to the covenant with God.
Such an understanding should develop in dialogue with Jewish
feminists who can describe the ambiguities attendant to Jewish
women's lives in the covenant.[27] Christian feminists with sympathetic ears should be able to receive such ambiguities in solidarity
and compassion.

Third, Jewish feminists can help Christian feminists locate
Jesus in his time as an observant Jew. Only subsequent to accepting
Jesus as a practicing Jew can we wrestle together with the implications of this reality for Christianity in general and feminism and
Christology in particular. The rejection of the Jewishness of Jesus
(as evidenced, for example, in feminist readings of the Gospels that
interpret Jesus as jettisoning ritual purity laws) is a form of supersessionism. Rejecting Jesus' Jewish context is akin to the teaching
of contempt that God rejected and dispersed the Jews for lack of
faithfulness to the covenant. To view Jesus as the creator of a new
egalitarian religion in which women will be welcomed and whole
at the expense of Jesus' Judaism, and a fair understanding of the
roles of women in Judaism, does violence to the feminist effort to
generate communities of equality and diversity. To allow Jesus'
actions toward women to be understood within the religious and
social categories of his time is to open the door to genuine relationship between Jewish and Christian feminists.

Resolving anti-Jewish tendencies in Christian feminist theology will liberate Jesus for constructive Christologies of relation,
which will bring us closer to the divine. Finally, allowing Jesus to
be Jesus instead of a projection of our current ideals will allow us,
as Christian feminists, to account authentically for the hope that is
in us.[28]

Chapter 6

REDEEMING CHRIST: IMITATION OR (RE)CITATION?

Laura M. Taylor

Several years ago, I received a framed cartoon from a friend. At first glance, the image resembled a traditional nativity scene: Mary, Joseph, and the three wise men were gathered around the manger admiring the baby Jesus. Yet, unlike more traditional portrayals, this one featured a speech bubble over the head of one of the magi, who mischievously proclaimed, "It's a girl!"

This provocative proclamation packs a powerful theological punch. By depicting the infant Jesus as a girl, the artist playfully disrupts the viewer's proclivity to see the Christ child as male. This perception has been key to androcentric theological discussions identifying Jesus' maleness as central to his person and saving work. Because these discussions have marginalized the roles and experiences of women in the Church,[1] the cartoon's depiction of the newborn Jesus as female unmasks the narrow-mindedness of Christological interpretations that focus exclusively on the *man*, Jesus Christ. But is this comedic Christological sex change powerful enough to challenge the negative situation of patriarchy in the church?

This essay explores the tension between feminist theology, which takes seriously the experiences of women and the flourishing of all persons, and androcentric interpretations of Christ that have contributed to human indignities around the globe. Focusing on the marginal experiences of women in the Church, I consider the ways in which faith in Jesus Christ has been troublesome for feminist theologians, particularly the interrelated issues of incarnation, ordination, and salvation. Although a guiding question in this essay is what the doctrine of Christ must accomplish for feminist theologians, I also address the ways in which feminist responses to this query have been problematic. Finally, in order to carve out a space for feminist belief in Christ, I challenge feminist thinkers to move beyond imitation Christologies toward more performative ones, as proposed in the work of Karen Trimble Alliaume.

FEMINIST CHRISTOLOGY: THE MALE PROBLEM

Nearly two thousand years ago, Jesus asked his disciples: "Who do you say that I am?" (Matt. 16:15). This question remains at the heart of Christology today. From Peter's pre-Easter confession—"You are the Christ, the Son of the living God" (Matt. 16:16)—to the early church fathers' understanding of Christ's death as a ransom paid for the debt of human sin, to Mercy Amba Oduyoye's recent imagery of Christ as an African midwife who brings life out of death, there have been myriad answers to Jesus' query. The multiple and oftentimes conflicting responses illustrate the various political, historical, and cultural contexts that have shaped Christological thought. Further, this ambiguity points toward experiences of God, who, although God became flesh, nevertheless remains a mystery.

The encounter of God in and through Jesus of Nazareth, who was crucified, resurrected, and professed as the Christ, is central to feminist Christology. As early feminist theologians sought to understand the marginalization of women in church practice and theological reflection, they realized that distorted understandings of Jesus Christ played a pivotal role in this exclusion. They claimed that sexist readings of the narratives, symbols, and doctrines of Jesus skewed the liberating gospel message for women and were complicit in determining their marginal status in both the church and society.

For Catholic feminist theologians, one of the greatest obstacles has been the long-standing ecclesial emphasis on the maleness of Jesus. By associating maleness with divinity, the *magisterium* has increasingly relegated women to second-class citizenship and prevented them from understanding themselves as created in the image of God. As Elizabeth Johnson observes, the issue for feminist thinkers is *not* that Jesus was born a male, but rather the ways in which his maleness has been construed in the official language, theology, and practices of the Church.[2] At stake are three interrelated issues—incarnation, ordination, and salvation.

INCARNATION

The incarnation, or the Word made flesh, is the event that brings salvation to the world for Christians. Yet, for many feminist theologians, this event is the scandal of the gospel in so far as androcentric logic has consistently privileged the manner in which the incarnation occurred, namely, in the male body of Jesus of Nazareth. The results of this androcentrism have been twofold. First, because Jesus is confessed by Christians to be the revelation of God, the idea that God became man (rather than woman) is thought to point to maleness as an essential characteristic of divine being. Second, and not unrelated, because the male body of Jesus Christ has been interpreted as the favored site of God's revelation, maleness has been perceived as the standard for both humanity and divinity. According to Sandra Schneiders, "If any of these ideas are true, the incarnation can only be seen as an unmitigated disaster for women."[3]

Feminist histories of theology have shown that this androcentric line of reasoning can be traced back as far as the early Church, when the Greek term "logos," or "word," was used to describe the historical presence of God in Jesus. For instance, the prologue to the Gospel of John begins: "In the beginning was the Word, and the Word was with God, and the Word was God" (John 1:1); "And the Word became flesh and lived among us" (John 1:14). This terminology, found in Greek philosophy, was intimately tied to the male principle and in particular the qualities of rationality, sovereignty, and divinity that were associated exclusively with the male sex. Rosemary Radford Ruether judges that the coupling of a male-principled, logos Christology with the man Jesus of Nazareth brings about the unwarranted idea of a necessary connection between the maleness of Jesus, the incarnation of the male Logos, and the revelation of a male God. In other words, this correlation suggests that the human Christ must be male in order to reveal the male God.[4]

Over time, this patriarchal framework has been naturalized by the repetition of the Father/Son metaphors used to interpret Jesus' relationship to God. As a result, the incarnation, although a decisive event for Christians, has functioned to the detriment of women. It has been used as a lynchpin in arguments that uphold the essential maleness of God and the necessary maleness of Jesus and, in so doing, has construed the male sex as normative of both humanity and divinity. Furthermore, these androcentric interpretations of the incarnation have suggested that women are incapable of imaging the Divine and have therefore functioned to justify the unequal status and role of women in the Church.

ORDINATION

A second way in which the maleness of Jesus has been an obstacle for feminist theologians is in discussions on the Roman Catholic sacrament of priestly ordination. According to Vatican teachings, women cannot be admitted to the priesthood. The magisterium's reasons for this include the belief that Jesus chose only men to become part of the twelve apostles, whom he established as the foundation of his Church; the notion that the apostles did not ordain women to succeed them in their ministry, out of loyalty to the example set by Jesus Christ; the perceived need to protect the Church's tradition of reserving the priesthood for men alone, so as to theoretically act in accordance with God's plan for the Church; and the premise that the sacrament of priestly ministry cannot adequately reflect the mystery of Christ unless assumed by a man, because Christ himself was a man.[5]

In each of these arguments against the ordination of women, "maleness" (or lack thereof) plays a key role. Although the magisterium proclaims that women are "necessary" and "irreplaceable" in the life and mission of the Church, it also insists that women are unsuited for priestly ministry due to their femaleness, understood as nonmaleness. It is the magisterium's theological identification of maleness with the mystery of Christ, however, that ultimately determines the marginal role of women in the Church. This identification has reinforced the idea that the incarnation of Jesus as a man (instead of a woman) was not a matter of chance, but rather a decisive moment in the life of the Church. For example, *Inter Insigniores*, or the "Declaration on the Question of Admission of Women to the Ministerial Priesthood," written by the Sacred Congregation for the Doctrine of Faith (CDF) in 1976, declares that the maleness of Christ was a fundamental part of God's plan. The document states:

> The incarnation of the Word took place according to the male sex; this is indeed a question of fact, and this fact, while not implying an alleged natural superiority of man over woman, cannot be disassociated from the economy of salvation; it is indeed in harmony with the entirety of God's plan as God himself has revealed it, and of which the mystery of the Covenant is the nucleus.[6]

This passage draws on Church teachings and scriptural imagery that interpret the salvation offered by God to humankind as a nuptial mystery, or covenant. Here, God is portrayed as the divine Bridegroom and the Church as his beloved bride. The nuptial mystery comes to fruition when the Word takes on flesh in order to seal and establish the new and eternal covenant by shedding his blood so that sins may be forgiven.

As stated by the CDF, this scriptural language and symbolism reveal the ultimate mystery of God and Christ. Because Christ is understood to be the Bridegroom, and therefore the head of the Church (his bride), the CDF contends that we cannot ignore the fact that Christ is a man. To do so, they argue, would contradict the importance of this symbolism for the economy of salvation, as well as the sexual differences created by God for the communion of persons and the generation of human beings. In effect, the magisterium maintains that marriage must always occur between a man and a woman, even in analogies of faith.

In creating a theological association between the maleness of Jesus and the mystery of Christ, the magisterium is able to restrict the priesthood to men. Just as it is thought that Christ necessarily became male, so too, they argue, can men alone represent Jesus. According to Church teachings, the priest does not act in his own name (in persona propria) during the exercise of his ministry, but rather he represents Christ (in persona Christi), who acts through him. This representation finds its supreme expression in the celebration of the Eucharist, in which the priest takes on the image and role of Christ, who accomplishes the sacrifice of the covenant. Since the Church teaches that sacramental symbols must naturally resemble that which they signify, the CDF specifies that role of Christ must be taken by a man; otherwise the natural resemblance between the minister and Christ could not occur.[7]

As feminist theologians have observed, the magisterium's focus on the maleness of Christ is more than just a matter of sexual difference; it is a case of radical exclusion and hyper-separation that has functioned to secure and conserve elite, male ecclesial power. Here, the dividing line between those who are able to act in persona Christi and those who are not is a single, physical characteristic possessed by one group and not the other: the male genitalia. Due to this essentialist categorization of the sexes, men are thought to enjoy a closer identification with Christ via their natural bodily resemblance, and women are excluded from leadership roles in the Church. This intense notion of separate natures is used to justify not only the wildly different privileges of men and women in the Church, but also, as is explored in the next section, their prejudicially different fates.

SALVATION

A third area in which the maleness of Jesus has been a stumbling block for feminist theologians is the doctrine of salvation. In her 1983 work *Sexism and God-Talk*, Rosemary Radford Ruether poses a question that has influenced the field of feminist Christology for several decades. Noting the ways in which androcentric interpretations of Christ had marginalized the voices and experiences of women in the Church, she asks, "Can a male Savior save women?"[8]

For Ruether, the ecclesial emphasis on the maleness of Christ places the salvation of women in danger. To make her point, she draws on the work of Gregory of Nazianzus. Bishop of Constantinople from 379–381, Gregory was forced to confront the various understandings of Christ that divided the community. Of particular concern was the belief espoused by Apollinarius and his followers, who argued that Christ's divinity eclipsed his humanity in the incarnation. Although Apollinarius believed that the divine Logos became flesh, he denied that Jesus had a human intellect or a rational soul, fearing that the acquisition of such things would jeopardize or taint the true and direct incarnation of the Word.

Gregory, however, argued that Apollinarius's attempt to preserve the divinity of Christ at the expense of his humanity undermined the saving act of the incarnation. Because the Word became human in order to save lost humanity, Gregory held that Christ had to become like us in all things but sin, which included the assumption of a human mind, will, and soul. Were this not to have happened, he reasoned, the Covenant initiated by God could not have been accomplished. In a letter against Apollinarius, Gregory wrote, "For that which [Christ] has not assumed He has not healed; but that which is united to the Godhead is also saved."[9] Put differently, what is not taken on by Jesus in the incarnation cannot be saved by Jesus because it remains estranged from God.

Ruether's question draws on this logic. She notes that if what is not assumed is not saved, then the salvation of women is theoretically in danger. As per Church teachings, the incarnation of the Word necessarily took place according to the male sex, and as a result, women are considered incapable of resembling Christ. Thus, Ruether surmises that one might logically ask to what degree (if any) can a male Savior represent women in the salvific event?

Ruether's cunning inquiry illustrates the way in which the maleness of Jesus has been naturalized in official theological discourse and praxis. His sex has been interpreted as essential to both his identity and saving work, and this, alongside the Church's dualistic framework that constructs men and women as polar opposites, has marginalized women, even in terms of salvation. Consciously or unconsciously, the Church, which declares that women are equal members in the Body of Christ, has prevented women from participating in the fullness of this image by virtue of their differently sexed bodies. As Lisa Isherwood notes, "When feminists consider whether or not a male savior can save women, the question goes beyond the maleness of the man and embraces the male who has been created by generations of fathers and sons in an attempt to gain a firmer hold on power in the world."[10]

FEMINIST CHRISTOLOGY AT AN IMPASSE

Given the ways in which the maleness of Christ has been used to legitimate male ecclesial power and prevent women's flourishing in the Church, some feminist thinkers have found the Christ symbol to be irredeemably patriarchal. Daphne Hampson, for example, claims that Christology and feminism are irreconcilable. She has therefore abandoned Christianity as a masculinist religion.[11] Likewise, Mary Daly and Naomi Goldenberg have argued that in order to develop a true theology of women's liberation, feminists must leave male-dominated symbols, such as Christ and the Bible, behind.[12]

For most feminist theologians, however, the contention that Christology is inherently sexist represents the undoing of what has traditionally been claimed of Christ. Thus, they have sought to extricate the liberating and inclusive aspects of Jesus' life and message from patriarchal control. Early feminist efforts to reconstruct the Christ symbol for women can be roughly divided into two camps: those who focused on the historical Jesus as the leader of an egalitarian sociopolitical movement and the embodiment of female-identified traits such as relationality and connectedness, and those who focused on the Christ-symbol as Sophia, or the female personification of divine wisdom. In addition to the images of Jesus as liberating prophet and Christ-Sophia, the next several decades of feminist Christology witnessed the emergence of the embodied Christ, the queer Christ, the ecological Christ, the black Christ, the suffering Christ, the mujerista Christ, and other images engendered by diverse experiences of women around the globe.[13]

Despite the wealth of new images, I suggest that the field of feminist Christology is at an impasse. As I have illustrated throughout this chapter, sex and gender matter Christologically, especially for the magisterium. Yet for the most part, feminist Christologies have been unable to challenge effectively this gender essentialism. The impasse is due, in part, to what I refer to as the Vatican's "body politic." The expression *body politic,* drawn from political thought, refers to the analogous relation between a corporate structure (that is, society or the state) and the citizen, where the structural body is thought to represent the human body in terms of both organization and polity. In Catholic teachings, this correspondence functions to denote the Church as the Body of Christ. One of the most recognized instances of this can be found in Paul's first letter to the Corinthians, where he describes the Church as a human body incorporating different parts. Paul writes: "For just as the body is one and has many members, and all the members of the body, though many, are one body, so it is with Christ. . . . Now you are the body of Christ, and individually members of it" (1 Cor. 12:12-27).

Yet, as feminist theologies have shown, when the magisterium refers to the Body of Christ—whether physically or metaphorically—it is to the male body. Consequently, those bodies that naturally resemble Jesus' body are accorded power within the semidivine politic, while those incapable of this resemblance (for example, females) are marked as inappropriate analogues and thereby excluded from political participation (such as the sacrament of priestly ministry). This sexually differentiated notion of citizenship classifies members of the Church according to their sex and invests them with fundamentally different values and roles, which are thought to stem from the ground of their being.

As Pope John Paul II illustrates in his apostolic letter *Mulieris Dignitatem*, "On the Dignity and Vocation of Women," the Church holds that human nature is embodied in two distinct but equal forms—male and female.[14] In turn, the male and the female are called to integrate what is masculine and what is feminine into a relationship of complementarity. This idea can be seen in the Church's teaching on marriage, which claims that the innate structure of human sexuality makes a man and a woman "natural" partners for the creation of new life. In the sacrament of holy matrimony, the woman and the man are to give themselves totally over to each other in their femininity and their masculinity. They are equal as human beings but different as man and woman (par. 7). Likewise, the Church teaches that a woman reaches the fullness and originality intended by God through the gender-complementary roles of mother and virgin, in which the woman gives herself to her husband and to God through the feminine markers of relationality, empathy, generativity, and intuition (par. 17–21).

This gender essentialism wielded by the Vatican makes the equality of women in the Church literally unthinkable. Because women are unable to resemble the physical body of Christ, they have no place within the corporate Body of Christ, except to serve at its most basic maternal and generative levels. Moreover, Vatican teachings declare that the disparate roles allotted to men and women stem from the mystery of Christ in relation to the Church and are therefore impervious to the equal opportunities granted to individuals in modern democracies. Thus, it is not that women are biologically unsuited for full ecclesial participation, but rather that the Vatican's body politic is structured and defined in a manner that includes women only in very particular ways. If this is true, then fighting to have women included in the present politic is counterproductive unless the opposition between the body politic and women's bodies is rethought.

Karen Trimble Alliaume claims that insofar as feminist theologians continue to assert that women must resemble Christ in order to be saved, they remain indebted to the body politic of the Vatican, which she terms the "economy of imitation." This system declares that Jesus is the norm that individuals must imitate in order to achieve salvation. Although women are able to resemble Jesus in terms of their everyday ethical behavior, she notes that they are precluded from imitating him in those functions that pertain to his divinity, such as the administration of sacraments. As a result, she contends that feminist Christologies, which focus on the salient aspects of Jesus' life and message as the key features that women resemble, remain beholden to the Vatican's imitative economy. By focusing exclusively on Jesus' humanity, she argues, these Christologies are unable to break the link between Jesus' maleness and the redemptive powers associated by the magisterium with his divinity. [15]

To illustrate her point, Alliume draws primarily on the feminist Christology developed by Ruether in *Sexism and God-Talk*. Here Ruether presents Jesus as the paradigm of liberated humanity, whose redemptive power stems not from maleness, but from a prophetic call to action that challenges others to participate in the struggle against injustice. In this interpretation, Jesus initiates a new community committed to sociopolitical action and right relations that propels one toward Christ. Accordingly, it is the community that imitates Christ's redemptive humanity, rather than specific individuals, and Jesus' maleness is significant only to the extent that he renounces patriarchy as a wrongful situation that must be redressed.[16]

For Alliaume, Ruether's attempt to downplay the significance of Jesus' maleness by focusing on his exemplary humanity inevitably backfires. First, in order for Jesus' rejection of the privileges associated with maleness to be efficacious for the contemporary reception of his message, he had to be a male. Therefore, Alliaume points out that Ruether's claim inadvertently reinscribes the historical maleness of Jesus as theologically necessary for her liberating conclusion. Second, Alliaume asserts that despite Ruether's best efforts to disavow the magisterium's hold over Jesus' maleness, her Christology ultimately remains beholden to its economy of imitation. In her redefinition of Jesus' liberated humanity as right relation, Alliaume notes that Ruether essentializes women as "relaters" and therefore better able to "resemble" Jesus. Because relationality is one of the stereotypically feminine markers that the Vatican associates with women, Alliaume claims the Ruether Christology reinforces, rather than undercuts, the magisterium's gender essentialism. In other words, Ruether's Christology suggests that women are able to resemble Jesus according to the Vatican-sanctioned, feminine gifts of right relation, whereas men inexorably maintain the stronghold over representations of Jesus' divine nature. Finally, Alliaume concludes that Ruether's account of the ways in which Jesus is more like women than men potentially implements a reverse form of essentialism, in which women, but not men, are able to resemble Jesus.[17]

Like Alliaume, I contend that the imitative body politic constructed by official Church teachings and practices presents a serious obstacle for feminist Christologies. Its gendered understanding of bodies and identities makes it nearly impossible to raise Christological questions that articulate bodily differences. In effect, the Church excludes a created reality that ultimately bears the imprint of the divine. It establishes women as members *of* but not full participants *in* the Body of Christ. Consequently, women who are unable to represent Christ in priestly ministry and who do not wish to be confined to the roles of mother or virgin need alternatives.[18] But, what are these alternatives? And how can feminist Christologies move beyond this impasse?

WHAT'S A "GIRL" TO DO?

At stake for feminist theologians in such questions is an inclusive understanding of Christ that is able to overcome the gender essentialism of the Vatican and assume *all* of humanity. In order to counter the Vatican's link between maleness and Christology, I propose that feminist thinkers need a new perspective from which to think about and live out liberating representations of Christ. Drawing on Alliaume's reading of Judith Butler, I suggest a performative framework as one such alternative. This framework does not reduce identities to reified categories measured by markers such as "male" and "female," but rather assumes that one's identity is ambivalent, in process, and open to reinscription. Such an approach, I hope, will enable feminists to dismantle the magisterium's monopoly on salvation and create a space for feminist belief in Christ.

Alliaume's essay, "Disturbingly Catholic: Thinking the Inordinate Body," uses the work of Butler to counter the gender construction found in official Church teachings and practices.

Butler, a feminist theorist, is known for her revolutionary understanding of identity, which claims that the categories of sex and
gender are constituted through language and discourse and are
therefore neither "naturally" nor "causally" related. She argues that
people commonly thought of as biologically female are not born
with feminine-identified traits, but are "gendered" over time by
enacting a received set of norms that prescribe how women should
or should not behave. According to Butler, this process begins at
birth (or during an ultrasound), when a doctor announces, "It's a
girl!" By assigning the baby a sex and a gender, the doctor's performative statement constitutes the baby as a particular kind of
subject. In other words, one is not born a girl, but is "girled" by
discourses that associate a specific set of meanings with the female
genitalia. Over the course of her lifetime, these discourses will
compel the "girl" to cite and recite (read: perform and re-perform)
the gender norms associated with her sex, such as playing with
dolls, wearing dresses, and so forth. This sequence of repeated acts
eventually produces the appearance of sex and gender as natural
or God-given.[19]

   Butler points out, however, that if the appearance of "natu-
ralness" is sustained only through dutiful repetition of specific
gender norms, then the categories of sex and gender are subject
to slippage if these norms are repeated differently (or not at all).
As she notes in her work *Gender Trouble,* the instability of gender
and other identity categories mean that one's performance of the
associated norms can never be exact and is therefore best understood as parody. Like all citations, parodic acts never exactly perform what they name. They thus lend themselves to processes of
resignification, or responses that undermine the original category
being enacted. Take, for example, cross-dressing or dressing in
drag. Butler illustrates that this act involves the appropriation of
a gender norm traditionally associated with one sex by a member
of the opposite sex.[20] A man in drag inevitably draws attention to

the disjunction between his "male" body and the "female" gender he is performing, particularly when "he" makes a better "she" than most biologically identified females.[21] The shock associated with such realizations sheds light on the ways in which the relations between sex, gender, and desire are naturalized in a heterosexually oriented society. A heterosexist society, such as the one authorized in Church teachings, establishes a linear connection between one's sex, one's gender, and one's sexuality. According to this system, femaleness is thought to give rise to femininity, which, in turn, is "naturally" expressed through the sexual desire for men, and vice versa. By subverting and "denaturalizing" these connections, cross-dressing exploits the instability of gender identities and calls into question the very assumptions on which this society operates.

Drawing on Butler's notion of gender identity as performative, Alliaume explains that Christian identity also materializes through the repetition of certain culturally intelligible norms. Just as becoming a woman entails the citation of the particular norms of womanhood, becoming a Christian involves the citation of specific Christian norms accepted by the Christian community, namely, Jesus Christ. Yet, as Alliaume observes, the canonical body of Jesus has been the site for patriarchal reifications of maleness. The discourse of the magisterium has repeatedly invested the body of Christ with certain meanings and associated it with certain practices based on a naturalized link between the maleness of Jesus and the sacrament of priestly ordination. Because the citation of Jesus is constitutive of Christian identity, and because the male Jesus is the standard assembled by the Vatican, women's bodies are unable to fit within the anatomically normative parameters and are, therefore, incapable of imitating Christ. Whereas men's bodies are considered "natural" vehicles for and culturally intelligible recipients of salvation, women's bodies are declared inordinate and fail to materialize within the Body of Christ, except as salvific beneficiaries, and even this is up for debate. If this is the case, then the identity categories of "Catholic" and "woman" seem mutually exclusive. [22] So, what are Catholic women to do?

It is at this juncture that I believe Alliaume's theological appropriation of Butler's work makes a significant contribution to the field of feminist Christology. By applying Butler's citational understanding of bodies and identities to Christological conversations, Alliaume dislodges "women" and "Jesus" from the relation of imitation and navigates the discourse beyond the threat of impasse in several important ways. First, drawing on Butler's deconstruction of the body, Alliaume reveals the "fictitious" nature of maleness as a foundational category for the body (and Body) of Christ. Her argument maintains that maleness, like all identity categories, does not exist prior to the magisterium's utterances, but is a performative product of them. Second, Butler's notion of cultural intelligibility allows Alliaume to demonstrate that what feminist Christologies are protesting is not the idea that Jesus was a man, but rather the way in which "maleness" has been used to construct an understanding of identity that forecloses on all differently sexed/gendered identities. This failure of women's bodies to matter, Alliaume argues, is not the result of misunderstood texts or doctrines, as feminist Christologies have traditionally claimed, but rather it stems from the community's inability to reconstruct the rules of recognition in ways that allow all bodies in the Body of Christ to matter.[23]

For this reason, Alliaume suggests that Butler's notion of gender performativity is an important framework for interpreting feminist Christologies. If to imitate means to resemble or to produce an exact copy, then women are doomed to failure when trying to replicate a male figure, such as Jesus. If to perform, on the other hand, means to act or to give a rendition of, then women are able to cite the body of Christ without having to duplicate it perfectly or entirely.[24] Alliaume explains:

A performative and citational reading is better able to account for the ways in which women already *do* "re(as) semble" Jesus. *Re(as)sembly* connotes an alternative to resemblance, since the latter is understood as imitation of or representation of Jesus, a representation from which women are liable to disqualification. Re(as)sembly of Christ denotes communal performances of Jesus rather than individual women's representations.[25]

Whereas feminist Christologies have traditionally remained beholden to the Vatican mandate that men and women must "match up" to a preexisting aspect of Jesus (that is, his right relationality or liberating humanity), she argues that Christologies read as performances of Jesus are able to illustrate the way in which bodies come to be in communal citational processes.[26] The agency for re(as)sembly, she states, is not located in either the Church hierarchy or resisting feminist subjects, but "in the interaction between them, in the moment when the very constraints of the 'norms' we cannot help but cite (like Jesus' maleness) allow the possibility of our citing them differently and thus reshaping them."[27] Thus, Alliaume shifts the notion of redemptive power from mere bodily resemblance to that which exists in and through our relationships with one another as they emerge out of our citations of Jesus.[28]

In sum, Alliaume's citational understanding of Jesus has liberating implications for feminist Christologies that help move it beyond impasse by enabling women's bodies to matter. It dismantles the magisterial Body of Christ that has haunted feminist theologians, and in so doing, empowers women, who find themselves somehow implicated in or accountable to the Catholic tradition, to re(as)semble the norms of Jesus in ways that undermine this hegemonic paradigm. These (re)citations, Alliaume argues, should not be read as uncovering women's essential resemblance to Jesus from the guise of patriarchy, but rather as performative claims made by women to (re)present Jesus. She states, "To 'cite' Jesus with one's own body refers to what appears to be a preexistent relationship of congruity between Jesus and women, a relationship that is actually *created* in the citation."[29] Let us turn to one such example.

PERFORMING CHRIST: A COMMUNAL NARRATIVE

If, as Alliaume suggests, the citation of Jesus' body is constitutive of Christian identity, then this body includes the stories and sayings of Jesus, as well as their repetition.[30] Elizabeth Conde-Frazier's article, "Latina Women and Immigration," looks at *testimonios,* or the faith stories of Latinas, that interweave biblical narratives with the narratives of women's everyday lives.[31] Like Alliaume, Conde-Frasier emphasizes that these stories, when shared publicly, both create and maintain communities. Moreover, she notes that for Latinas/Latinos, testimonios are a form of "doing theology." They include the voices and experiences of those who have been marginalized in traditional "academic" theology and are therefore transformative and life-giving.[32]

To illustrate her point, Conde-Frazier recounts a testimonio shared by a group of women at a retreat. This narrative weaves together the everyday struggle toward justice of women who have been sexually abused and the account of the hemorrhaging woman (Mark 5:21-34). After briefly summarizing this story, I conclude that it provides a powerful example of women (re)citing Christ.

As told by Conde-Frazier, the women's story begins in a Church bathroom one Sunday following services.[33] This bathroom had been the group's gathering place for many years, as it was one of the few places where the women felt unhindered by the male pastor and free to interpret the scripture as it spoke to them as women. On this particular Sunday, the women were discussing the Gospel story of the woman with a hemorrhage. According to the scripture, the woman had been bleeding for over twelve years and physicians had only made her condition worse. Having heard of Jesus' miracles, the woman believed that he had the power to heal her. One day she saw him in a crowd and came up behind him, placing her hands on his garment. Immediately, her hemorrhaging ceased. Jesus felt the power flow from him and turned around to see who had touched him. The woman knelt before him fearfully. He said to her, "Daughter, your faith has made you well; go in peace, and be healed of your suffering" (Mark 5:34).

That morning, from the safety of the bathroom, the women posed a series of questions: What would it feel like to have your period for twelve years? What might cause someone to bleed like that? What would it be like to be judged as unclean? Together, the women looked at this story from many different angles. Yet, two members of the group, Minerva and Ana, remained silent. Eventually, their silence filled the room, and Minerva spoke up. She said she knew why the woman was bleeding.

For Minerva, this story centered around "touch." She began to (re)cite the narrative from the perspective of a young woman who had been sexually abused. She spoke about the girl's body beginning to develop, of men starting to take notice, and of one man, in particular, who often touched her inappropriately. Through her tears, Minerva recounted the "infections" his touch brought— shame, fear, self-hatred, and paralysis. "The woman bled to protect herself," Minerva said. "He would not touch her if she was unclean. She bled each time she remembered what he had done to her." Minerva recalled the woman's many trips to the doctor, which only made her feel worse. She was mocked for being a twenty-four-year-old virgin, and the doctor told her just to get married and have sex.

"One day," Minerva continued, "the woman heard of a man who did not have an infectious touch. Instead, he had a healing light. But the woman could not bear the thought of being touched by a man, even one whose intentions were pure." Hearing these words, Ana fell to the floor and started sobbing. Betsaida tried to comfort her, but Ana screamed, "Don't touch me; don't touch me!" Minerva responded, "But what if I touch him? What if I touch him until the curse that was put on me is healed?" Taking the handkerchief from her Bible, Minerva tied it to the bottom of her skirt. She stood near Ana but turned away. "When the woman touched Jesus' garment," Minerva uttered, "her shame subsided. She was able to close her eyes and see a beautiful woman looking back at her. She was finally able to touch her breasts without fear." As Minerva continued her reenactment, Ana reached for the handkerchief tied to Minerva's skirt. She held on to it, and her crying grew softer. Minerva turned around and, remaining in character, asked who had touched her. Ana knelt before her and said it was she. Minerva then told Ana that she had been sexually molested by her uncle, and Ana told Minerva the story of her rape. While they told each other their secrets, the other women formed a circle around them and prayed silently.

Suddenly, Ana shouted, "Give me water to be cleaned!" Ana approached the sink and took off her shirt. Placing her hands under the running water, she poured it over herself. Minerva did the same. When they had finished, the rest of the women took the water and, without touching either Minerva or Ana, poured it on them from all directions. As the ritual drew to a close, Minerva proclaimed: "The woman knelt before Jesus and told him the truth. She told him her secret, and he drew out the woman's faith in herself: she was not a walking curse; she could have faith in her body again, in her own spirit, and in her womanhood."

This powerful testimonio recounted by Conde-Frazier exemplifies a lived theology among the disempowered. Through their (re) citation of the Gospel text and the sacrament of baptism, the women in the story reincarnate Christ in and for one another. This performative act opens up a path for women's struggle toward justice and converts nonsanctioned sexed/gendered identities into political agency. More than this, it illustrates the fluidity and vulnerability of *all* our representations of Christ. It demonstrates that re-citing Jesus is not simply about ordinate, ontological changes, but also about reenacting Jesus' ministry and performing God with us.

These themes of performativity and instability are well known in Christological thought. As Lisa Isherwood observes, Christianity inherently tells stories of "queer transformations, of unstable categories and bodies all enacted through the body of a man who proclaimed 'God with us.'"[34] Michael Himes notes that this incarnational event is *not* first and foremost the revelation of who God is, but rather the revelation of who we are. Quoting Irenaeus of Lyons, a second-century church father, Himes contends, "The glory of God is a human being fully alive."[35] To be fully human, I argue, is to contest the terms that allocate value to certain groups or individuals over others. It is to ask why certain bodies fail to matter and to reenact the ministry of Jesus in order to make political claims on behalf of these bodies.

The performative framework outlined throughout this essay challenges women to reinhabit their place *in,* but not *of,* the Body (and body) of Christ. Rather than letting ourselves be put into boxes meant to categorize and dismiss, we can use the complexities of our lives to challenge the belief that any person or group is more righteous or deserving of identification with Jesus. While women will never be included in the Vatican body politic as currently structured, they can certainly loosen its hold over women's bodies by changing the boundaries of the community and creating a space from which differently sexed subjects can speak and act.

Returning to my initial question, I conclude that the wise man's proclamation—"It's a girl!"—constitutes a challenge to the negative situation of patriarchy in the Church when read from a performative perspective. Rather than inserting a "girl" into a male-dominated role or altering the sex of Jesus without challenging the hegemonic norms of belonging and participation, a performative perspective opens up the doctrine of Christ in a way conducive to furthering the Body that performs him. Given this, I propose that Christologies should not be understood as hermetically sealed entities, but rather as historically constructed formations, cited, recited, transformed, and performed anew in the pluralized identities of the Christian people.

CHRISTOLOGY ROUNDTABLE

Michele Saracino, LaReine-Marie Mosely, Teresa Delgado

As feminist Christology continues to evolve, new questions and metaphors emerge, some of which seek to be faithful to past questions and promises and others that shake up the theological terrain altogether. Each of the contributors to this section beautifully balances both these challenges through three interconnected threads: the non-maleness of Christ, relationality, and religious pluralism. Each essay, moreover, underscores how the task of collaborating with scholars in a conversational venue such as this volume leads to other theological implications worthy of consideration.

Theologizing from the starting point of the non-maleness of Christ is not new. Few can forget when Rosemary Radford Ruether asked the life-changing question of whether a male savior can save women, breaking through ecclesial, commonsense logic that the maleness of Christ is the salvific dimension of Christ. Her work liberates the authors in this anthology to imagine and construct Christology in a way that breaks free not only of a male Christ, but also of a binary between a male and female Christ, consequently shattering other life-threatening binaries as well, including Christian versus Jew. The "aha" moment of this section is not that Christ is not male, but rather that while Christ's constructed gender can be read as a metaphor for understanding the person and work of Jesus Christ, it is always up for negotiation. No one "story" about Christ, including that of his "maleness," ought to dominate Christology, thus making room for Jeannine Hill Fletcher's lactating Christ and Laura Taylor's performative Jesus. While debating the maleness of Christ has been a liberating trajectory, at this point in history, such repartee has the potential to trap women and men inside and outside the church in binary configurations, thereby limiting their agency and voice. Resisting any binary thinking about Jesus also extends to Elena Procario-Foley's work as she asks readers to journey into her experience of violence against Jewish women, implicitly imploring every Christian to interrogate how the categories of Jew and Christian have been constructed in dichotomized ways at the expense of finding genuine, life-giving solidarity with all others.

As one grapples with problematic dichotomies in any context, the thread of a more complicated sense of relationality emerges. One of Hill Fletcher's sections in her essay is entitled "Christology and Relationality," but before she even delves into that, she writes about our present globalized world that receives the subdiscipline Christology in unique ways because of the changing context on the ground. This context has been influenced by technology, economy, and other factors in such a way that we really are one world; we are related. In thinking through Hill Fletcher's claims, we should be careful that we don't romanticize these notions of "one place" or "global village" at the expense of not recognizing and acknowledging the stark differences that characterize lifestyles in the two-thirds and one-third worlds and our complicity in maintaining those distinct worlds. Salvation can transcend these differences, but what role can individuals and groups play to promote this salvation or well-being?

Hill Fletcher speaks in a compelling way about the manner we "learn our first patterns of relationality" from our mothers or other mothers. This first m/other relationship is tremendously formative. We can surmise that this was also the case with the mother-son relationship of Mary and Jesus. Perhaps this insight will enable us to rescue Mary of Nazareth from weak and tepid representations that have plagued Christianity. Mary was not only "the reed of God"—she was her own person. This enabled her to bring forth the best and the true from her son Jesus.

Beyond Mary's relationship with her beloved son, how intriguing to learn about the medieval devotion to Jesus our mother! This image flies in the face of gender essentialism and suggests a fluidity regarding gendered identities, concretizing a complicated sense of relationality. This is reminiscent of Taylor's efforts to move beyond what she understands as feminist Christology's impasse. For her, performance trumps imitation, and the Jesus of this medieval devotion performs the role of maternal nurturer to the extent that *his* breasts bear "the milk of healing." Perhaps our transgendered and bisexual brothers and sisters might be able to give us some insight here. Hill Fletcher's inclusion of this devotion has the potential to spark one's imagination regarding the utter selflessness that characterizes breast-feeding. It is no surprise that it is the breasts of the Crucified that are to be suckled.

As stunning and counterintuitive as this image might sound to some, is it any more stunning than bringing together the ontologically different categories of creator and creature, that is, divinity and humanity? To speak of the incarnation is to speak of hybridity. This hybridity characterized Jesus and in different ways characterizes us. We are immersed in a world of grace, and we are made in God's image and likeness. This means something, and yet our embodiment as females is a deficit for us as Catholic Christians, giving way to Ruether's distinction between an egalitarian anthropology and a patriarchal anthropology, whereby the former is widely valued in secular society and the latter in the church hierarchy.[36] Patriarchal anthropology fuels the Church's understanding that because women do not have male bodies, they cannot image Christ. This is fallacious, because both women and men are made in God's image and likeness. The historical particularities of Jesus of Nazareth's gender, race, and ethnicity do not prevent him from being paradigmatic for all of humankind.

Like feminists before us, Taylor identifies the crux of many Christological problems: power. This is where these Christological essays complicate any commonsense notion of relationality. Taylor's quote from feminist theologian Lisa Isherwood says it well, "When feminists consider whether or not a male savior can save women, the question goes beyond the maleness of the man and embraces the male who has been created by generations of fathers and sons in an attempt to gain a firmer hold on power in the world." In this way, the church is clearly an institution of domination. This dimension must be dismantled. What's needed here is an ideological critique that will provide a forum to shed light on the problematic ways male superiority is maintained at the expense of all—a critique that aims at a more complicated relationality.

Collaboration with those deemed "others" and dialogue about complex issues of power and identity are important practices in moving toward a more complicated, and hence, life-giving sense of relationality. Wouldn't this be a great topic for collaboration and dialogue: Jewish and Christian feminist scholars discuss Jesus? Procario-Foley gets the ball rolling by showing us that Jesus needs to be liberated by our (Christian feminists') unintentional anti-Judaism. We need a crash course on Second Temple Judaism! Since the research is now out there, there are no excuses. Nonetheless, feminist Christology must negotiate a difficult balance between the historical datum of Jesus' Jewish reality and the theological claim that Jesus is constitutively different for Christians. Articulating a Christology that honors Jesus' own religious experience, as well as the Christian experience of Jesus, is necessary if we are committed to genuine relations of solidarity with our Jewish sisters and brothers.

Out of a complicated relationality flows the claim that one is hard-pressed today to theologize about the person and work of Jesus Christ in a way that refuses to allow for a genuine openness to other religions. Religious pluralism, therefore, is the third thread that surfaces among these three essays. Procario-Foley decenters traditional Christian feminist responses to Jesus' person and work to make room for what Jewish scholars argue about the New Testament period and, specifically, Jesus. This is not done to be politically correct, but out of a posture of hospitality for others that moves beyond tolerating another's person and perspective to embracing both in a way that changes one's own person and perspective. Her experience in graduate school, offending a Jewish woman, was a turning point in her life, in her conversion. When we meet someone face-to-face who challenges us, that is, when we have an embodied encounter with an "other," it is hard to ignore the gravity and the veracity of their stories. In many ways, this is a challenge of the roundtable discussion as well. It is one thing to encounter a theologian on paper, but when we sit down to discuss their work as we have as part of the roundtable process, we are all opened by the materiality of the other. They are not abstract disembodied ideas, but vulnerable, storied selves, many of whom are risking their theological/academic safety to tell their stories and open Catholic theological discourse to and for others.

This risk is reflected in interreligious theological pursuits. When Hill Fletcher writes: "We need a Christology that recognizes that humans do not exist in individual isolation; we need a Christology that reflects and encourages our human relatedness," she hopes for connections with others across religious boundaries and faiths. As she puts it, "In our global age, that mother-love of Christians mothered by Christ must extend to the global community and be willing to cross religious borders." Hill Fletcher gets to the heart of this when she reflects on the Muslim woman who is waiting for her milk to come in, bearing a universal experience that many other women feel. Sharing a common humanity opens the conversation for salvation for all—a willingness for her to "share the divinity of God with other persons, figures, events, that emerge from a wide variety of religious realities." And finally, by introducing the work of Alliaume into the conversation, Taylor challenges any normative Christology, and even opens up the possibility for a Christology devoid of a traditional ontology, in that anyone can perform "Christ," and in doing so opens Christologies to others, including those from other religions.

Religious pluralism is a hot button and an important buzz word in theological discourse—spanning across issues related to what Jesus means for non-Christians to how non-Christians experience salvation. Each of these essays leans toward the latter issues and is representative of a countermovement within the church. They do not argue that salvation through Jesus is possible for everyone, which in and of itself in today's religiocultural climate is quite radical; rather, they explicitly and implicitly claim that there is a new dawn for Christology in which everything about the subject-matter, Jesus Christ, is fluid, open, performative. They explode any self-contained or narcissistic understanding of what is salvation and for whom it belongs.

In reflecting on the state of Christology in a "post" context—for some postfeminist, for others post-Christian, and for many postmodern—as we approached this roundtable we questioned if theology can ever really be free from the patriarchal power structure of the Church fathers and mothers. Some contributors have referred to the process of writing here as painful, even traumatic, while others have called it self-revelatory, because they have learned much about themselves in the process. In writing for undergraduate readers, each one of us has a responsibility to acknowledge and demonstrate where traditional theological categories, the ones that have "authority," emerge from and how they have been interpreted. Yet, as Catholic feminist women, many of us resist the imposition of having to deal with the tradition, because we and others who are cast as "other" have been hurt by it. In bringing them up, we open old wounds, and even worse, give the most damaging theological claims authority. This has been a fundamental tension since this anthology's inception, which has continued throughout the writing process. At times, we feel foolish and even belittled that we have to go back to our theological fathers and mothers to prove that we have anything constructive to add to the theological project of the twenty-first century. Are we mere adolescents in an elongated ecclesial lifespan, or are we more fundamentally dealing with the age-old problem of others trying to claim a place in context, which traditionally has not been able or willing to accommodate them?

Each of the essays in the Christology section and in the anthology at large demonstrate this challenge of teaching students about theology, without recycling that which has already been rendered unusable or insufficient. Taylor's work gets to the heart of this issue when employing the work of Karen Trimble Alliaume; she posits the futility of imitation regarding questions of Jesus and ordination, and instead privileges the performance that resists any identification with institutionalized power and authority. Hill Fletcher's work on the "mother-role of Jesus" forcefully pushes against any normative, singular reading of Jesus, humanity, or mothering, and ultimately kicks traditional categories to the curb. Finally, in listening to the anger and frustration of Jewish feminists, Procario-Foley is converted and asks us to be open to thinking about Jesus outside any simple box that Christian "liberationists" want to put him in and reimagine him in light of solidarity with our Jewish sisters and brothers.

Dealing with traditional theological categories was not the only challenge in this collaborative Catholic feminist project. Another was adhering to distinctive theological loci. Each one of the Christologies in this section, and even throughout the other theologies of the anthology, is in and of itself hybrid. Hill Fletcher's work is more of a hybridized Christology-anthropology, and Procario-Foley's work is representative as much of ecclesiology as it is of Christology. Many of us were aware of that tension coming in and thought it was less of a problem than a product of where the field of theology is going. In our age of globalization, all boundaries are breaking down, even those between traditional theological loci. Yet, as we are continually pushed by the authority-seeking voice inside of ourselves or the public voice of the academy to ask, "How is this an anthropology, a Christology, or an ecclesiology?" some of those old wounds opened yet again.

We owe so much to all the theologians who came before us, as well as to the other feminist Catholic scholars with whom we struggle to stand shoulder to shoulder. But let there be no mistake— standing shoulder to shoulder is not easy. At times, our experiences, issues, and questions seem as if they are competing with one another—that we are all vying for the smallest piece of the pie. In those moments, it is difficult not to repeat exclusionary and hurtful patterns of relations. This is where each of the essays speaks to the ethical import of standing shoulder to shoulder. It is not enough to accept a person on paper or even in the every day, but if we take the lactating mother who shares my anxiety seriously, if we listen to the complaint of our sisters, how we hurt them, then maybe we can begin to perform a new solidarity, reimagining and recreating a new life-affirming way of living.

QUESTIONS FOR DISCUSSION AND REFLECTION

1. Think of the various ways you have seen Christ represented symbolically (as the Good Shepherd, as Fisherman, as King). Where do these images come from? What types of human experiences do they represent? Are there images of Christ that you can imagine that connect with women's experiences? Why do you think this is or is not the case? What does the image of

Christ as mother, or Christ as breast-feeding woman communicate? Is this an image that should be included in the tradition? Why or why not?

2. Hill Fletcher's essay argues for a new Christology attentive not only to women's experiences, but also to the reality of religious pluralism. It suggests that Christian theology needs to be in conversation with people of other faiths. Do you agree? Why or why not?

3. What are the consequences for Christianity for denigrating Judaism?

4. Do you think Christian and Jewish feminists have something in common?

5. Why and how are androcentric interpretations of Christ a problem for feminist theologians?

6. What is different about doing Christology from a feminist perspective?

FOR FURTHER READING

Mary Boys, *Has God Only One Blessing? Judaism as a Source of Christian Self-Understanding* (Mahwah, N.J.: Paulist, 2000). Boys presents a state-of-the-art analysis explaining how the Christian narrative can and must be reread with respect for Judaism.

Caroline Walker Bynum, *Jesus as Mother: Studies in the Spirituality of the High Middle Ages* (Berkeley: University of California Press, 1982). Bynum provides an overview of the many ways Jesus has been envisioned as mother in the history of the Christian tradition.

Elisabeth Schüssler Fiorenza, *In Memory of Her: A Feminist Theological Reconstruction of Christian Origins* (New York: Crossroad, 1992). This seminal text of feminist theology offers the outlines for a Christology of relationality rooted in biblical scholarship.

Edward H. Flannery, *The Anguish of the Jews: Twenty-Three Centuries of Anti-Semitism* (Mahwah, N.J.: Paulist, 1999). In this classic, Flannery, a Catholic priest, presents a historical account of antisemitism.

Jacquelyn Grant, *White Women's Christ, Black Women's Jesus: Feminist Christology and Womanist Response* (Atlanta: Scholars, 1989). In response to traditional feminist Christologies, which fail to speak to nonwhite and non-Western women, this book proposes a womanist theology that speaks to the reality of contemporary black women.

Lisa Isherwood, *Introducing Feminist Christologies* (Cleveland: Pilgrim, 2002). This book explores the wide range of feminist Christologies that have emerged from the experiences of women around the globe, including an overview of the past, present, and possibly future developments within the field.

Amy-Jill Levine, *The Misunderstood Jew: The Church and the Scandal of the Jewish Jesus* (New York: HarperOne, 2006). Levine, a Jewish scholar of the New Testament, argues for a reconciliation of church and synagogue while insisting on the reality of Jesus as a Jew.

Kwok Pui-lan, "Engendering Christ: Who Do You Say That I Am?" in *Postcolonial Imagination and Feminist Theology* (Louisville: Westminster John Knox, 2005). In this essay, Kwok introduces a variety of contemporary re-visions of the image of Christ.

Maryanne Stevens, ed., *Reconstructing the Christ Symbol: Essays in Feminist Christology* (New York: Paulist, 1993). This volume contains six feminist critiques of classical Christology, which attempt to overcome the various experiences of patriarchy within the Christian tradition.

Tatha Wiley, ed., *Thinking of Christ: Proclamation, Explanation, Meaning* (New York: Continuum, 2003). This work gives a historical and systematic overview of a broad range of contemporary Christological issues, including the nature of scripture, doctrinal development, anti-Judaism, religious pluralism, the religious legitimation of colonialism, and issues in spirituality and ethics.

Part Three

ECCLESIOLOGY

Chapter 7

WOMEN AND THE *PERSONA* OF CHRIST: ORDINATION IN THE ROMAN CATHOLIC CHURCH

Elizabeth Groppe

Krista brims with enthusiasm. Her passion for mission is palpable. "She is fired," one of her theology professors tells me, "with love for Christ and the church." Her spirit, no doubt, has been shaped by her upbringing in a family of very active and committed Catholics. Her mother and father served their parish in St. Louis as council members, lectors, and eucharistic ministers. They enrolled Krista and her brother in Catholic schools. Now a senior at Xavier University, Krista's time here has been marked by a variety of forms of service to Xavier and the broader Cincinnati community, including four years of leadership within campus ministry. Personable and outgoing, she is skilled at developing and nurturing the social relationships that are the bond of community life. "We are all instruments," she explains. "We are like flutes or clarinets, and God is the breath, flowing through us and making music with our gifts."

One August, while assisting with the orientation program for new students, she met a quiet and reserved young man who shared with the orientation group his call to the priesthood. Reflecting

153

on this encounter, Krista realized that her own passion for the faith community could be of service in an ordained ministry. As a laywoman, there are many ways in which she can contribute to the church. Yet, she noted, the people who give the church its direction, make decisions about faith and ethics, and represent the church to the world are ordained men. Her bright mind, communication ability, and relationship skills could "help transform the church in a way that it might become more faithful to its mission." Her gifts match those appropriate to ordained ministers, and she has a strong sense of vocation. Krista knows, however, that "at this time there is no place for me in the structure of the church because I am a woman." In contrast, the young man she met at orientation "will be greeted with open arms at the cathedral." She notes this without bitterness and wishes him well.

In Roman Catholicism, the priest stands at the head of the church *in persona Christi* (in the person of Christ), and historically, this position has been taken only by men. At the same time, conformity to Christ is the vocation of all the baptized. When I asked students enrolled in theology courses at Xavier, "Are there persons you believe represent Christ or act in Christ's image?" they responded to my questionnaire with stories about mothers, grandmothers, a nun in a parish, a priest, a friend named Courtney, a theology professor, Dorothy Day, Martin Luther King, and Mother Teresa. Some spoke in general terms of teachers, social workers, doctors, and friends, and many said that everyone has the potential to represent Christ. To live in the image of Christ, they explained, is to live out of love, to do God's will and follow God's commandments, to devote oneself to the underserved and overlooked, to fight for the poor and for justice, to be forgiving, to be selfless, and to live life to its fullest. To act as Christ, Krista told me in conversation, is to live with "unwavering compassion for everyone" and to "fearlessly point out the flaws in our social structures," like Jesus, who "turned society upside down."

Given that the vocation of all the baptized is to "clothe our-selves in Christ" (Gal. 3:27), and given that we can recognize the image of Christ in both male and female persons, why have women been proscribed from standing *in persona Christi* as a priest ordained to celebrate the Eucharistic liturgy and lead a Catholic ecclesial community in public witness to the compassion and justice of God? Should the requirements for ordination be adapted so that Krista too might be greeted with open arms at the cathedral? For the past fifty years, the Catholic Church has been grappling with this question. This chapter offers an overview of the theological debate and concludes with my own reflection on the priest as an instrument and sacramental sign of divine wisdom.

BIBLICAL PERSPECTIVES

The practice of Jesus and the apostolic church is central to discussions concerning the ordination of women. Yet the question, "Can women be ordained to the Roman Catholic priesthood?" is not directly addressed in the New Testament. The Pontifical Biblical Commission (PBC) is a group of Scripture scholars appointed by the Vatican to serve in a consultative capacity. Their 1976 report "Can Women Be Priests?" concludes that questions concerning the priesthood, the celebrant of the Eucharist, and the leadership of local communities imply "a way of looking at things which is somewhat foreign to the Bible" (par. 4).[1] Although the New Testament does describe the Christian assembly as a priestly people (1 Pet. 2:5, 9; Apoc. 1:6; 5:10), and speaks of a priestly and sacrificial ministry (Rom. 12:1, 15:16; Phil. 2:17; 1 Pet. 2:5, 12), "it never uses the technical term *hiereus* [priest] for the Christian ministry" (par. 5). It is Jesus Christ who is designated as the true high priest and the true Temple (John 2:21; par. 33).

In establishing the kingdom of God, the PBC continues, Jesus chose twelve men after the fashion of the twelve patriarchs of the Old Testament to serve as leaders of the renewed people of God

(Mark 3:14-19). After Christ's death and resurrection, the apostles were entrusted with the mission to evangelize all nations (Matt. 28:19; Mark 16:5), develop the kingdom of God, and govern the church. Elders, prophets, and teachers presided over the first communities established by the early missionary movement (par. 49).

According to the PBC, some women did collaborate in "properly apostolic work" (par. 41): Lydia, Prisca, and the mother of Mark offered their homes for meetings (Acts 16:14-15; Rom. 16:3; Acts 12:12); Euodia and Syntyche are described as collaborators of Paul (Phil. 4:2); and nine or ten of the twenty-seven persons whom Paul thanks or greets at the end of his epistle to the Romans are women. In several of these cases, the PBC notes, "Paul insists on specifying that they have tired themselves for the community, using a Greek verb (*kopian*) most often used for the work of evangelization properly so called" (par. 42). Paul also mentions a woman deacon (*diaconos*) of the church of Cenchreae who was a protectress for many, including Paul himself (Rom. 16:1-2). And "Junias" or "Junio" is placed in the rank of the apostles (Rom. 16:7); whether this figure is a man or a woman is a matter of debate (par. 44).

Despite the collaboration of women in apostolic work, the PBC determines that "all that we can know of those who held a role of leadership in the communities leads to the conclusion that this role was always held by men (in conformity with the Jewish custom)" and that "the masculine character of the hierarchical order which has structured the church since its beginning thus seems attested to by scripture in an undeniable way" (par. 53, 54). At the same time, the PBC emphasizes that the question of the historical practice of the first Christian communities and the normative value of this practice are two distinct matters. Over time, changing circumstances have, in fact, led to changes in some of the practices of the apostolic church. The administration of baptism, for example, was originally the charge of the apostles (Matt. 28:19; Mark 16:15ff.), but others (including women) were later entrusted with this responsibility (par. 64). In sum, the PBC concludes with respect to the debate about the ordination of women, "it does not seem that the New Testament by itself alone will permit us to settle in a clear way and once and for all the problem"(par. 66).

HISTORICAL PERSPECTIVES

If the New Testament does not definitely settle the question of the ordination of women, what light might be shed on the matter by the subsequent tradition of the church? In reviewing this historical record, one must be sensitive to the various ways in which the term *ordination* has been employed. In Roman Catholicism today, the term is used exclusively with reference to the sacrament of holy orders in which a man is ordained as a deacon, priest, or bishop. Prior to the twelfth century, however, the Latin terms *ordinare* and *ordinatio* had the broader meaning of the consecration and designation of someone to take up a specific function, or *ordo,* in service to the community.

There is incontrovertible evidence that in the first four centuries women were ordained as deacons.[2] The term *deacon* is used in the literature of this era in a manner that is most likely gender inclusive, and the feminine form *deaconess* also occurs. The ministry of the deaconess included assisting at baptisms of women, instructing the baptized, and visiting the sick. The *Didascalia Apostolorum* (a second-century document) states, "Let a woman rather be devoted to the ministry of women, and a male deacon to the ministry of men."[3] Women became deacons in a liturgical laying-on of hands accompanied by prayers nearly identical to those used for males. Use of both the female and male diaconate began to wane around the fifth century in the West and in the ninth century in the Greek-speaking Eastern church.

From the fifth through the twelfth century, according to Gary Macy, women were ordained to a number of offices within the

Catholic Church, including deaconess, widow, virgin, canoness, abbess, and nun. The Latin term *ordinatio* and its cognates are used with reference to women in both liturgical rites of ordination and in statements of popes and bishops. The same term is used of male priests and deacons. Although abbesses did not preside at the Eucharist, they did hear confessions, preach, baptize, excommunicate members of their communities, bless laypeople, and consecrate nuns. There were liturgical rites that designated women to distribute communion. There are even references in extant texts to women *presbyterae* and *episcopae*, although what precisely is intended by these terms is unclear. Scholars long assumed that these feminine forms of the Latin words *presbyter* (priest) and *episcopus* (bishop) referred to the spouse of a priest or bishop, but in some of the contexts in which these terms appear, this is an implausible interpretation.[4]

After the twelfth century, the meaning of ordination narrowed. Increasingly, the term was used primarily in reference to ordination to the priesthood, a sacrament conferred only on men. There is, however, at least one recent case in which the sacrament was administered to women. When Stalin occupied Czechoslovakia in 1948, he attempted to crush religion through the confiscation of church property and the internment of priests and members of religious orders. In this context, Fr. Felix Maria Davidek, himself a former political prisoner, became a bishop in the underground church. In prison, he had ministered to other interred men, and he had deep concern for those in the women's prison who had no access to the sacraments. Upon his release from prison, he led the underground church in study and discussion of the question of the ordination of women, and in 1970, he ordained Ludmila Javorova. She worked closely with Davidek at the risk of her own imprisonment. Her ministry consisted of visiting the sick and dying in hospitals and other places where it would have been difficult for a male priest to access. "I just wanted to serve," she reflected. "I only wanted to make the life of others lighter. . . . I know that I am only a means, that God works through me."[5] When Davidek could not carry out his promise to travel to Rome to tell the pope of Javorova's ordination, she took it upon herself to write John Paul II a letter, which she sent in 1983. She never received a reply. In 1996, when an Austrian magazine published an article about Javorova's ordination, she was immediately summoned to the bishop's office and prohibited from exercising priestly ministry. Her ordination and the sacramental ministry she had exercised were, she was told, invalid.

THE SECOND VATICAN COUNCIL AND ITS AFTERMATH

With the convocation of the Second Vatican Council (1963–1965), the ordination of women became a matter of concern not only to Czechoslovakia's underground church, but within Roman Catholicism at large. As the council opened in 1962, Gertrude Heinzleman, a Swiss attorney, presented a petition to the preparatory commission calling for women's ordination. The petition was not granted. Nonetheless, the council did articulate a biblical theology of the entire church as a priestly people consecrated by the Spirit and called to holiness, and it emphasized baptism as the sacrament of conformity to Christ.[6] The council also restored the diaconate as a proper and permanent ministry, and Phyllis Zagano subsequently made the case that women should again be ordained to this ministry in which we once served.[7] Over the course of the 1960s, scholarly articles and doctoral dissertations advanced theological arguments for the ordination of women to the priesthood.[8] In 1970, the National Coalition of American Nuns (USA) called for women's ordination. In 1971, the International Synod of Bishops recommended the creation of a global commission to study the issue (although the commission was never established). In 1974, the Leadership Conference of Women Religious (USA) resolved

that all ministries in the Roman Catholic Church should be open
to women, and in 1975, the Canon Law Society of America issued
a report stating that the "realization is growing that the view of
ministry as preeminently sacerdotal is not necessarily incompatible
with admitting a woman to the apostolic succession of order," and
that church tradition and canon law develop over time through both
continuity and change.[9] The first Women's Ordination Conference
was held in Detroit in 1975, concurrent with a meeting of the United
States Catholic Conference, at which the topic of the ordination of
women to the priesthood did arise.

Animated discussion of the issue within the Catholic Church
was kindled not only by the Second Vatican Council's ecclesial
renewal, but also by the decisions of other Christian denominations to include women in ministry. The Congregationalists
had begun ordaining women as early as 1853, and the Wesleyan
Methodist Church began the practice in 1891. The Northern Baptist
Convention ordained its first woman in 1907, and the Southern
Baptist Convention (USA) in 1964. The Presbyterian Church in
the USA (North and South) ordained women in 1958 and 1964,
respectively. The Methodist Church began ordaining women in
1956, the Church of the Brethren in 1958, and the African Methodist
Episcopal Church in 1960. In 1970, the Lutheran Church in America
and the American Lutheran Church revised their disciplinary rules
to allow for women's ordination. In 1976, the General Convention
of the Episcopal Church approved the practice of the ordination of
women, and in 1992, Anglican synods in England, Australia, and
Southern Africa followed suit. These developments were particularly significant, as the Anglican and Episcopal traditions share the
Roman's Catholic Church's theology of sacramental ordination and
apostolic succession.

Although ordination to both the deaconate and the priesthood
has remained closed to women in the Catholic Church, women have

been a vital force in postconciliar parish life. In 1986, according to a major Notre Dame study of the U.S. church, women predominated in many ecclesial roles. They constituted over 80 percent of Confraternity of Christian Doctrine teachers and sponsors for the catechumenate; over 75 percent of adult Bible study leaders and participants; over 80 percent of the membership of prayer groups; nearly 60 percent of those involved with youth groups; over 85 percent of those who lead or assist in ministries to the poor, the sick, the grieving and the handicapped; over 50 percent of parish council members; and over 50 percent of Eucharistic ministers.[10] Moreover, as the number of ordained priests has fallen well below the pastoral needs of the church, women with extensive theological and pastoral training have increasingly assumed pastoral positions in which they exercise all the same functions as a priest, with the exception of the administration of the sacraments.[11] This creates a problematic disjunction between the church's pastoral and sacramental ministry.

INTER INSIGNIORES: THE "DECLARATION ON THE ADMISSION OF WOMEN TO THE MINISTERIAL PRIESTHOOD"

In the decade after the Vatican Council, discussion of the ordination of women was gaining momentum. Then, in 1976, as the Vatican engaged the leadership of the Anglican Church in dialogue concerning their decision to ordain women, the Congregation for the Doctrine of the Faith (CDF), a branch of the Roman Curia, published *Inter Insigniores.*[12] In this "Declaration on the Admission of Women to the Ministerial Priesthood," published within the pontificate of Pope Paul VI, the CDF took the position that women cannot be ordained to the priesthood and outlined theological reasons to support this stance.

First, the CDF emphasized that a male priesthood is the church's constant tradition. Both the Roman Catholic Church and the Eastern Orthodox have unanimously held over the course of centuries that neither priestly nor episcopal ordination can be validly conferred on women. The CDF acknowledged that prejudices against women mar the Christian tradition, but in their judgment this prejudice is not determinative of the theology of ordination, which is rooted in the church's intention "to remain faithful to the type of ordained ministry willed by the Lord Jesus Christ and carefully maintained by the apostles" (par. 11).

Jesus spoke publicly with the Samaritan woman (John 4:27) and departed from Mosaic law to affirm the equality of marital rights and duties of women and men (Matt. 19:3-9; Mark 10:2-11) (par. 16). In his itinerant ministry, he was accompanied by a group of women, and although Jewish law of this period did not value women's testimony, the risen Lord appeared first to women charged to take the paschal message to the apostles, who then became the official witnesses to the resurrection (par. 17). Yet, the CDF emphasizes, despite this striking break with conventional attitudes toward women, Jesus did not call any woman to become one of the twelve apostles.

The apostolic church remained faithful to this example. The election to fill the place among the Twelve vacated by Judas resulted in the choice of Matthias, even though Mary was among those gathered in the upper room after the ascension (Acts 1:14). Some women did work with Paul for the gospel and even exercised an important influence on conversions. Yet, despite Paul's break with many Mosaic practices and the spread of Pauline communities within a Hellenistic world where pagan cults were entrusted to priestesses, the women who worked with Paul were not ordained (par. 25).

Inter Insigniores acknowledges that ecclesial practices develop historically and that the church today "is conscious of possessing a certain power over the sacraments, even though they were instituted by Christ" (par. 34). This power, however, is limited by the church's responsibility to preserve the sacraments' unchanging substance. Sacramental signs are not a matter of convention, but natural signs expressive of deep symbolisms and a means to link Christians of every era to the Christ event. When a priest or bishop exercises his sacramental ministry, he "does not act in his own name, *in persona propria*: he represents Christ, who acts through him" (par. 41). This ability to represent Christ takes supreme expression in the celebration of the Eucharist, in which the priest takes on "the role of Christ, to the point of being his very image, when he pronounces the words of consecration" (par. 42). Because the priest is a sacramental sign of Christ, there must be a natural resemblance between Christ and the minister that would be difficult to apprehend if the priest were not male (par. 45). Christ is truly the firstborn of a new humanity in whom there is no longer a distinction of Jew and Greek, slave and free, or male and female (Gal. 3:28), yet "the incarnation of the Word took place according to the male sex" in accordance with the mystery of the covenant (par. 46).

The covenant, the CDF continues, is a nuptial mystery of the love between God and his chosen people, sealed by the blood of the Word become flesh. In this covenant, Christ is the bridegroom and the church the bride (Matt. 22:1-14; Mark 2:19; John 3:29; 2 Cor. 11:2; Eph. 5:22-23; Rev. 19:7, 9). The church, *Inter Insigniores* concludes, is a society of a unique nature and structure, established not by human choice but by the mystery of Christ. Within this society there is indeed a universal calling to divine filiation (Gal. 3:28) and a real equality of all the baptized. Yet "equality is in no way identity, for the church is a differentiated body, in which each individual has his or her role" (par. 68). Although women may have a subjective desire for ordination, true vocation is conferred by Christ, who chose only "those he wanted" (Mark 3:13) for the priesthood (par. 65).

WRITINGS CONCERNING WOMEN AND THE POSSIBILITY—OR NOT—OF ORDINATION

From the Vatican:

Report of the Pontifical Biblical Commission: July 1976

Inter Insigniores: Declaration on the Admission of Women to the Ministerial Priesthood: October 1976 (from the Congregation for the Doctrine of the Faith)

A Commentary on the Declaration [Inter Insigniores]: January 1977 (from the CDF)

Responsum ad Dubium regarding Ordinatio Sacerdotalis: October 1995 (from the CDF)

From Pope John Paul II:

Mulieris Dignitatem (On the Dignity and Vocation of Women): August 1988

Ordinatio Sacerdotalis: On Reserving Priestly Ordination to Men Alone: May 1994

From the United States National Conference of Catholic Bishops:

Theological Reflections on the Ordination of Women: 1972

Strengthening the Bonds of Peace: A Pastoral Reflection on Women in the Church and in Society: November 1994

For a one-volume account of the discussion and documents since Vatican II, see Deborah Halter, *The Papal "No": A Comprehensive Guide to the Vatican's Rejection of Women's Ordination* (New York: Crossroad Publishing Company, 2004).

QUAESTIO DISPUTATA: THE RESPONSE TO *INTER INSIGNIORES*

In the medieval period, theological reflection sometimes took the form of a disputed question *(quaestio disputata)*, in which participants explored two sides of an issue. The promulgation of *Inter Insigniores* in 1976 was followed by such a spirited discussion. The debate ranged over a variety of issues, including biblical theology, the interpretation of tradition, nuptial theology, sacramental theology, and Christology.

In the area of biblical interpretation, for example, Albert Descamps affirmed *Inter Insigniores'* emphasis on the significance of Jesus' choice of twelve men as apostles. This was clearly a deliberate decision on Jesus' part, he wrote, not a reflection of cultural norms, for the apostles were an original messianic institution without parallel in the culture of that era and of great importance to the ministry of Jesus.[13] Elisabeth Schüssler Fiorenza, in contrast, critiqued what she saw as an assumption that the Twelve and the original apostles are one and the same group of persons. The New Testament, she explained, attests to various conceptions of apostleship. In the Pauline letters, the oldest writings in the New Testament, the term *apostle* is still very fluid and includes those who witnessed the resurrection (1 Cor. 15:7; Gal. 1:17-19), itinerant and charismatic missionaries (for example, Acts 14:4, 14; Rom. 16:7; 1 Thess. 2:6ff.), and emissaries of the churches (2 Cor. 8:23; Phil. 2:25)—some of whom are women. The apostles are not identified with the Twelve until the Lukan writings, several decades after Paul, and in Luke-Acts they have a very specific historical and eschatological function limited to the primitive church. They are not replaced when they die (Acts 12:2), and the elders and bishops in Acts are not identified as their successors. *Inter Insigniores'* position that the church cannot ordain women because Jesus included no women among the twelve apostles, Schüssler Fiorenza contends, is without basis in the New Testament.[14]

Yet Scripture, in Catholicism, is interpreted through the lens of the living tradition of the church. This tradition, *Inter Insigniores* had emphasized, has been constant in its practice of reserving priestly ordination for men. No one has disputed this point. Some scholars, however, did question the CDF's assumption that this tradition is rooted in an intention to be faithful to Christ. John Wright examined in full context sources from the church fathers cited in *Inter Insigniores* and concluded that the patristic opposition to women preachers, teachers, and priests stemmed from assumptions about the inferiority of the female nature, temperament, and social status. He found "meager support for the claim that the tradition of not ordaining women was motivated primarily by the church's intention to remain faithful to the will of Christ."[15] Dennis Michael Ferrara, in turn, examined the scholastic theologians cited by *Inter Insigniores*—St. Bonaventure, Duns Scotus, Richard of Middleton, and Durandus of Saint-Pourçain—and found that three of the four did speak of Christ's institution of a male priesthood. Yet, Ferrara notes, the reason they offered to account for Christ's action is women's natural state of subordination to men, an explanation that *Inter Insigniores* itself finds faulty.[16]

Some theologians did affirm *Inter Insigniores'* account of the male priest as a symbol of Christ the bridegroom. Hans Urs von Balthasar, for example, emphasized that the covenantal love of God and Israel reaches fulfillment in the incarnate Christ's nuptial bond with the church, personified as feminine in the New Testament. In the mystery of Christ-church, the natural sexual difference of male and female is charged with supernatural meaning and protected from the deformations of patriarchy, matriarchy, or the leveling of the sexes to which human society is prone.[17] The reservation of priesthood to men, he concluded, is essential to the symbolic expression of both God's intended sexual differentiation of the human family and the mystery of nuptial love of Christ the Bridegroom for his church. Carroll Stuhlmueller, in contrast, argues that the nuptial imagery of biblical covenantal theology is much more complex than *Inter Insigniores* allows. Isaiah speaks of Yahweh as the husband of Israel, who is full of *racham-im*, a term meaning tenderness, which is derived from the Hebrew word for the maternal womb (Isa. 54:7-8), and Jeremiah's covenantal theology portrays Israel as both masculine and feminine (Jer. 31:1-5). "Biblical symbols modulate with amazing versatility and at key moments break natural laws and resemblances," he concluded, and the rich nuances of this nuptial symbolism can best be expressed by a priesthood of both men and women.[18]

Inseparable from the nuptial theology of the Declaration is its position that the priest stands in the person of Christ *(in persona Christi)* and must therefore be male. This, *Inter Insigniores* explains, is consistent with the sacramental theology of Thomas Aquinas, which requires that a sacramental sign (in this case, the priest) must bear a natural resemblance to that which is signified (Christ). According to Dennis Ferrara, however, *Inter Insigniores* misrepresents the sacramental theology of Aquinas, who had disqualified women from ordination not because of their lack of a male physique, but because of their state of social subjection to men. It is in this sense that woman (and slaves) lack the natural resemblance to Christ necessary for exercise of the priesthood.[19] Sara Butler, in response, concludes from her own study that although "we rightly reject the hierarchical understanding of sexual differentiation Thomas appeals to, it is possible that we can imagine another, nonhierarchical, way of understanding the complementarity of the sexes that may illuminate the reasonableness of this determination."[20]

Another response to *Inter Insigniores'* theology of the priest as a sacramental sign of Christ came from theologians who emphasized that the resurrected Christ of Easter is not bound by the limitations of a historical male body. Christ, writes Sandra Schneiders, is not simply the historical Jesus of Nazareth, but "the glorified

Jesus animating his body which is the Church. Christ said to Paul, 'Why do you persecute *me?*' (Acts 9:4), because the literal fact is that the Christ is composed of all the baptized. This means that Christ, in contrast to Jesus, is not male, or more exactly not exclusively male."[21] Sara Butler, in counterpoint, emphasizes that although it is indeed true that all the baptized are members of Christ's Body, there is nonetheless a distinction to be made between the church and Christ, whose bodily resurrection did not abrogate his historical humanity.[22]

As evident in this theological interchange, the discussion sparked by *Inter Insigniores* in the pontificate of Pope Paul VI continued well into the pontificate of Pope John Paul II. Many scholars did not find the argumentation of *Inter Insigniores* persuasive, and a majority of Roman Catholics in the United States and Europe favored the ordination of women.[23] In 1994, Pope John Paul II issued the Apostolic Letter *Ordinatio Sacerdotalis*—"On Reserving Priestly Ordination to Men Alone"—which reiterated that a male priesthood was established by Christ. Accordingly, "the Church has no authority whatsoever to confer priestly ordination on women, and this judgment is to be definitively held by all the Church's faithful."[24] In the fall of 1995, the CDF declared that the teaching of *Ordinatio Sacerdotalis* belongs to the deposit of faith and requires definitive assent, having been set forth infallibly by the magisterium.[25] These statements provoked major public debate, which now expanded to include not just the question of the ordination of women, but also the invocation of infallibility. Cardinal Bernard Law believed that the 1995 CDF statement should end all disputation and that theological discussion should now be limited to exposition of the church's position. Canon lawyer Ladislas Orsy, however, noted that although the CDF is due the respect proper to the Roman Curia, it does not have the charism of infallibility. In 1997, a committee of theologians appointed by the Catholic Theological Society of America to study the matter concluded that *Ordinatio Sacerdotalis* does not meet the church's criteria for infallibility.[26] The ordination of women has continued to be a *quaestio disputata.*

IN PERSONA CHRISTI: THE PRIEST AS INSTRUMENT AND SACRAMENTAL SIGN OF THE WISDOM OF GOD

Having sketched some of the background to the discussion of the ordination of women in the Catholic Church, I will conclude with a reflection on the priest as an instrument and sacramental sign of Christ. This theology is part of a long tradition. Cyprian of Carthage (d. 258) described the celebrant of the Eucharist as standing in Christ's place *(vice Christi)*, Thomas Aquinas (1225–1274) stated that at key moments of sacramental ministry the priest acts in the person of Christ *(in persona Christi)*, and the 1994 Catechism of the Catholic Church describes the priest as Christ's icon (par. 1142).

Vatican II's renewed theology of the entire church as the body of Christ and a priestly people has restored Catholicism's sense of the vocation of all the baptized to "clothe ourselves in Christ" (Gal. 3:27). At the same time, the church maintains that within this common priesthood there is a distinct role for the ministerial priest who stands *in persona Christi Capitis*—in the person of Christ the Head. When, for example, the priest elevates the Eucharistic bread and states, "This is my body," the ordained minister acts in a unique way as an instrument of Christ. It is ultimately Christ who iterates these words, and the priest is simply the vehicle through whom they are spoken, like the flute through which music flows. As celebrant of the Eucharist, the priest simultaneously offers the prayers of the congregation standing *in persona ecclesia* (in the person of the church) and speaks the words "This is my body" standing *in persona Christi.*

Who is this *persona* or "person" of Christ? Xavier students believe they have glimpsed this *persona* in the love of mothers and grandmothers, in Dorothy Day's nonviolent witness for peace and justice, in the compassion of Mother Teresa, and in the fidelity of female friends. This person of Christ, according to the creedal and trinitarian tradition of the church, is in fact none other than the incarnate Word of the triune God. In 451 CE, the Council of Chalcedon determined that Jesus Christ is not a strange amalgam of two persons (one human, one divine), but rather the very person of the divine Word in whom a human and divine nature are united without confusion, change, division, or separation.[27] Aquinas's theology of hypostatic union is a classic formulation of this tradition. According to Aquinas, the person of Christ is the second person of the triune God—the divine Word (John 1:1-5) or Wisdom (1 Cor. 1:24)—who assumed a human nature in order to redeem humanity and lead us to eternal communion with God.[28] Christ, writes Elizabeth Johnson, is "Wisdom made flesh."[29]

As the very Wisdom of the incomprehensible God, the *persona* of Christ is neither male nor female in the constricted human sense of these terms. And, at the same time, as the divine Wisdom, the *persona* of Christ is the origin of the perfections of both male and female persons—whatever these may be—for it was through Wisdom that the cosmos was created.[30] Wisdom is the "fashioner of all things" who "pervades and penetrates all, for she is a breath of the power of God" (Wisd. Sol. 7:22, 25). Intelligent, holy, beneficent, steadfast, beautiful, and pure, she is "a reflection of the eternal light, a spotless mirror of the working of God, and an image of his goodness" (Wisd. Sol. 7:22-26).

The priest should be transparent to this divine Wisdom, of which the ordained minister is but an instrument. At the same time, the priest is also Wisdom's icon in the sacramental life of the church, which makes visible the mysteries of the faith. As *Inter Insigniores* affirms, the sacraments must bear reference to the essential "constitutive events of Christianity and to Christ" (par. 37). One of these constitutive events is the hypostatic union of the second person of the triune God—the divine Word or Wisdom—

with a human nature in Christ. Because this divine Wisdom is both beyond gender and the origin of the perfections of female as well as male persons, the mystery of Christ can best be sacramentally manifest by a Catholic priesthood in which both women and men stand *in persona Christi* and bear public witness to God's compassion.

Women standing together with men *in persona Christi* at the Eucharistic altar, at the side of those abandoned on city streets, and in public acts of nonviolent resistance to war and injustice will make visible the mystery that the Wisdom of God that is united to humanity in Christ transcends our categories of "male" and "female." This will challenge us to overcome any idolatrous assumptions we may harbor in our religious imaginations about the gender of God and invite us to enter more deeply into God's ineffable mystery. It will also invite us to recognize God's Wisdom in the perfections of both male and female persons and to approach men and women with respect for their dignity and vocation to holiness. In a culture that systematically denigrates, commodifies, and violates women's bodies in advertising, film, and pornography, it is imperative that the church bear public and symbolic witness to the mystery that women and men alike can serve as an icon of Wisdom made flesh.

In the compassion of Christ, the *persona* of the Wisdom of God, who is the origin of the perfections of male and female in a manner beyond all the limitations of human gender, took on our human condition to redeem us from sin and death. *Inter Insigniores'* position that it is the church's responsibility to "better proclaim the mystery of Christ and to safeguard and manifest the whole of its rich content" is a strong theological foundation for the ordination of both women and men to the priesthood. The church will better proclaim and manifest Christ's mystery on that day when Krista— like her male colleague—is greeted with open arms at the door of the cathedral.

Chapter 8

"ARTISANS OF A NEW HUMANITY:" RE-VISIONING THE PUBLIC CHURCH IN A FEMINIST PERSPECTIVE[1]

Rosemary P. Carbine

Feminist ecclesiology reflects on the mission and marks or features of the Christian church from the perspective of women's and worldly well-being. It ordinarily involves the reform and reimagination of the church's institutional as well as sacramental structures and practices based on women's differing experiences of oppression and empowerment in religion and society. Rather than focus on the inner ecclesial praxis of the church, this essay charts some new terrain in feminist ecclesiology by addressing the church's political praxis. This essay advances a feminist theology of the public church, or the church's political agency and actions in the U.S. context.[2] What is the public church in the Roman Catholic tradition? What does it mean to rethink it in the U.S. context in a feminist theological way?

Within the Roman Catholic tradition, the public church refers to the Catholic Church's attempt to shape U.S. public discourse, policy, and civic life regarding issues of major social and political import from a religious perspective on the common good. *Gaudium et Spes (GS)*, or the Pastoral Constitution on the Church in the Modern World, not only provides a concluding signature statement from Vatican II, but also offers a prominent theological understanding of the Church's political mission and ministry.[3] *GS* considers faith-based public engagement as integral to love of God and neighbor (pars. 24, 27), salvation (par. 43), and realizing the kingdom of God or its theological vision of society based on love, justice, and peace (pars. 39, 45). On these theological grounds, *GS* explicitly rejects any religious withdrawal from public life (par. 43). Instead, *GS* identifies the Church's central mission—to model and protect the equality and dignity of humanity even in modern public life (par. 73)—and extends that mission to articulate the Church's sociopolitical role as a critical advocate of basic human dignity and rights, justice, and the common good, thereby becoming in itself a sacrament or sign of that kingdom (pars. 40–42, 45).[4] Of course, the Church's advocacy for human rights, especially the right to political participation, contrasts sharply with its own institutional structures that lead to a less than fully participatory church for women and that more recently failed to protect men and women affected by the U.S. clergy sex abuse scandals.[5] The public church in the Catholic tradition, therefore, may be considered "public" because of its "convocative capability,"[6] or its ability to combine the resources of religion and politics in pursuit of a more ultimate public, that is, a more just and justice-oriented vision of common life that guides, but often goes beyond, the present unjust sociopolitical (and at times ecclesial) order. *GS* places an ultimate public or transcendent public good that presses beyond our familial, cultural, and national relationships, in an eschatological context of the future kingdom of God. That guiding future vision motivates the Church's public mission and ministry to work for this-worldly social justice (pars. 21, 39, 43, 57).

Although Catholic social teaching identifies political participation for all Catholics as a practical effect of the sacrament of baptism, women are not recognized as the public church (*GS*, par. 43). While women in recent twentieth- and twenty-first-century U.S. history participated in faith-based political activism on poverty, war, immigration, and many other pressing concerns for social justice, long-standing clerical and patriarchal assumptions about the Catholic Church's political actors (bishops, priests, official male spokespersons) do not allow women to be recognized as representatives of the church, broadly construed as the people of God, in U.S. public/political life. For example, recent histories of Catholic public engagement in the twentieth and twenty-first century recount a mainly clericalist tale of prominent U.S. bishops and their differing strategies to influence U.S. government officials and policies at the local, state, and national level.[7] A snapshot of the current U.S. immigration reform movement further illustrates that women galvanized the church's political engagement in the United States around immigration issues but are not regarded as the public church in their own right.

Women, especially undocumented Latina mothers, figure prominently in the Christian church's recent political engagement in the United States. Elvira Arellano and her U.S.-born son, Saul, sought sanctuary in Adalberto United Methodist Church in Chicago beginning in August 2006 to resist Elvira's deportation to Mexico. While in sanctuary, Elvira created La Familia Latina Unida, an organization that lobbied U.S. senators and representatives at the state and federal levels to sponsor a bill protecting her and other similar parents from displacement from their families. She was arrested and deported in August 2007 after she exited a mass and rally for immigrant civil rights at Our Lady Queen of Angels Catholic Church in Los Angeles. Women such as Elvira aimed to expose moral problems with the current U.S. immigration system, exemplified by the increased U.S. Immigration and Customs Enforcement raids from Boston to Los Angeles that detained and displaced parents, mainly mothers, from their families without respecting their legal rights.[8]

Grassroots (that is, nonelite) mothers such as Elvira have called Christian churches, as well as a range of religious groups, into political action on immigration reform, sparking the renewal of the sanctuary movement.[9] Tracing its heritage to activist Christian churches that sheltered and supported Central American refugees in the 1980s,[10] the New Sanctuary Movement (NSM) began in May 2007 to raise public awareness about immigration reform through prayer vigils and educational literature, as well as to provide legal, financial, food, clothing, and spiritual aid to undocumented families. Headed by Rev. Alexia Salvatierra of Clergy and Laity United for Economic Justice in Los Angeles, the NSM coordinates an interfaith network of religious organizations in Los Angeles, Chicago, New York, and a growing number of other U.S. cities that want to keep undocumented families together by advocating particularly for parents with U.S.-born, and therefore, citizen children, who have come to signify the nearly 12 million undocumented people in the United States.[11]

The NSM is positioned between a rock and a hard place with regard to politics, religion, and gender. Relative to politics and religion, the notion of any religious building (church, temple, or mosque) as a safe haven is not recognized under U.S. law, thereby putting religious organizations in the NSM at legal risk. United States' federal immigration officials fully respect the right of religious groups to practice civil disobedience or to break what such groups consider unjust laws, but nonetheless will prosecute any illegal assistance to undocumented residents.[12] Relative to gender, the NSM credits Los Angeles Catholic Cardinal Roger Mahony with serving as the nation's moral conscience on immigration issues, as well as stimulating this new movement (see inset box on page 177). Clearly, adding mothers, leading non-Catholic clergy women, and lay Catholic activist women (in parishes and other organizations affiliated with the NSM) into the mix of bishops and other official (often male) Catholic Church spokespersons does not sufficiently redress clerical and patriarchal presumptions about the Church's agents and actors in U.S. public life—presumptions that effectively exclude ordinary women from being the public church.

NEW SANCTUARY MOVEMENT—WHY NOW?

In March of 2006, Cardinal Roger Mahony of the Archdiocese of Los Angeles said he would instruct his priests and others working in the Archdiocese of Los Angeles to disregard provisions of House Bill HR4437 that would criminalize providing humanitarian aid to persons without first checking their legal status. Cardinal Mahony's statements were significant in awakening the general public and legislators to the moral and human dimensions of the question—effectively changing the terms of the public debate.

On March 27, 2006, hundreds of religious leaders gathered in Washington, D.C., to exercise their moral authority to seek to ensure that the deliberations of the Senate judiciary committee took into account the human and moral realities of immigrant families. The resulting legislative proposal was significantly more compassionate and inclusive than the House measures.

Since that date, faith leaders around the country have continued to work in their local areas to respond to the needs of immigrant workers and their families and to support coalitions working on comprehensive immigration reform. Over the months, key leaders have also sought to define the particular contributions that clergy and congregational leaders could make to the larger struggle. The crisis of ongoing raids and deportations as well as the opportunity offered by the push for federal legislation increased the urgency of creating an effective and prophetic national strategy. In November of 2006, through conversations between faith leaders across the country, these visions coalesced into a new national initiative—the New Sanctuary Movement.

Excerpted from http://www.newsanctuarymovement.org/why-now.htm.

This essay intends to offset such a dominant clerical and patriarchal understanding of the public church within the Catholic tradition by developing a more adequate feminist theology of the public church, which enables and empowers women to recover their rightful place as the Church's political actors and agents. To facilitate this goal, this essay engages with Catholic theological understandings of the presence and practice of the Church in U.S. public life, through the symbol of Christ and its underlying anthropology. It critically analyzes dominant Christic and related anthropological symbols in magisterial (that is, official church) theologies that limit women's active political presence, and then reconstructs those same symbols through a critical feminist interpretation of Wisdom Christology found in *Gaudium et Spes*, the Vatican II constitution on the Church's public role. As we will see, re-visioning the public church in a feminist perspective provides a meaningful theological way for women to reclaim being the public church, or a sacramental sign of the body of Christ in public, based on their political praxis, and not on their maternal or non/ordinate status.

CHRISTOLOGY: PATRIARCHAL SYMBOL OF THE PUBLIC CHURCH

Taking some philosophical, theological, and ethical reflections on Christian symbols as our starting point, religious symbols shape and sustain a worldview, as well as imbue religious adherents with a sense of identity and morality in that world.[13] That is, such symbols mediate our knowledge of God and the world. In addition, they provide a meaningful way for us to interpret and navigate the world so as to enhance our place and praxis in it with respect to divine, human, and earthly relations. Christian symbols of God, such as the Trinity in which three coequal persons of Father/Creator, Son/ Redeemer, and Spirit/Sustainer participate in nonhierarchical relations within the godhead, express and embody religious and political notions of egalitarian community, as well as educate us with a particular identity and sense of mutual responsibility in that community. Nevertheless, such symbols can also collude with dominant ideological worldviews in ways that reinforce oppression in personal, family, socioeconomic, and political life as well as reinscribe dehumanizing race, gender, class, and sexual norms, among others.[14] Sacred symbols, therefore, provide one potent theological locus for raising critical questions about the relationship between the Christian imagination and women's religiously based political agency and participation.

As demonstrated in Part 2 of this book, Christology can be used to legitimate and sustain patriarchal worldviews and norms; likewise, it can also be reconstructed to promote alternative liberating worldviews; rethink gender, race, class, sexual, and interreligious norms; and, ultimately, edge us toward more egalitarian and just relations. With regard to the public church in this essay, Christology serves as a particularly problematic theological symbol in dominant Christian theologies with respect to its implications for who and what constitute the Church's religious and public actors. As the following analysis will show, the symbol of Christ functions in a sample of magisterial writings—from John Paul II to Benedict XVI—in a fixed physicalist way that reduces the incarnation to Jesus' male or masculinized body, and consequently justifies patriarchal constructions of gender norms, roles, and relations in both religious and political life.

In the 1995 "Letter to Women," written for the United Nations conference on women in Beijing,[15] the late Pope John Paul II advocates for "real" gender equality, especially with regard to women's social, economic, and political rights (pars. 4, 6). Equal creation in the image of God (pars. 7–8) forms a theological basis for such gender equality. And yet claiming equal creation in the *imago Dei* need not subvert social inequalities in race, gender, class, sexual, and human-earthly relations. This papal letter proves no exception to this theological trend, as it elaborates a "different but equal" theological anthropology that, in fact, leads to a "different and unequal" status for women. The letter emphasizes gender complementarity, or defines women primarily in relation to men on the physical, psychological, and ontological grounds of women's capacity for self-gift. That is, women's capacity for self-gift, to give help to men (pars. 7, 10), in the letter is attributed to women's reproductive ability to mother. And, as the late pope argued, women's biological capacity to give life shapes and structures women's ways of knowing and of being human, such that all women express an "affective, cultural and spiritual motherhood" (par. 9).

Relevant to our theological reflection on the public church, the late pope regarded women's political engagement from a biologically essentialist perspective, which reduces women to their maternal body and elides or negates the plurality of their embodied experiences of race, gender, class, sexuality, and ability as they are shaped by varied social, cultural, and historical contexts. For example, in the letter, women's maternal nature or "genius" (pars. 9, 11, 12) fits all women—regardless of parental status or particular context—for reproducing a "civilization of love" (par. 4) and for rendering an altruistic "service of love" (par. 10) to others and society. Similar to what feminist theorists label romantic or cultural feminism, the late pope proposed that women participate in public life, because they apply and actualize their maternal genius to improve the public good.

Likewise, in the 2004 "Letter to Bishops,"[16] the current pope, Benedict XVI, previously Cardinal Joseph Ratzinger and the head of the Congregation for the Doctrine of the Faith, reasserts gender complementarity on the theological grounds of creation and Christology. Although upholding the Trinity as a model of egalitarian human relations (pars. 6, 7) and advocating for women's equal access to social, economic, and political life (pars. 13, 14), the letter argues for a creation-based account of physical, psychological, and ontological complementarity between men and women (pars. 5, 6, 8).

The current pope forwards a theology of creation rooted in Genesis 2, which structures women's identities according to their bodily (which in this case is reduced to biophysical) nature and sexual status (par. 13). Such a biological determinism shapes women with certain gendered "values" and "traits" (par. 14, 16) that orient them by their nature, in a submissive and subservient way, to and "for the other" (pars. 6, 14), that is, to and for men. While such patriarchally defined feminine traits as "listening, welcoming, humility, faithfulness, praise and waiting" are arguably open to and cultivated by all baptized members of the Church, women signify them ontologically, or by their very nature, "for all Christians [as examples] of how the Bride [the Church] is to respond in love to the love of the Bridegroom [Christ]" (par. 16).

Moreover, this letter gives theological legitimacy to the definition of women in relation to men through its interpretation of a divinely ordained marital metaphor for salvation in Christ. In Catholic theology, salvation is portrayed in the scriptures via spousal symbolism between Christ and the Church (Eph. 5:22–33), in which Christ the Bridegroom and head of the Church saves the bride and Body of the Church. In addition to reinforcing all sorts of hierarchical dualisms, this spousal symbolism is applied in this letter as a literal theological norm to prescribe "the very nature" of both divine-human relations in salvation (pars. 9–10), as well as gender roles and relations in the Church (pars. 11–12). These sexed and gendered symbols of soteriology certainly carry deep implications for dualistic sex and gender roles and relations that cannot be addressed here in great depth.[17] Let's look briefly, though, at how the current pope advances an "iconic complementarity" of gender roles in the Church and in society based on this nuptial ecclesiology.

When situated within such a literalized marital metaphor for soteriology, women cannot function as Christ the male head of the Church, and thereby cannot be ordained or participate in its leading decision-making roles. Only men, definitively, represent

Christ's active offer of salvation as the Bridegroom to the Church, who receives and responds to the offer as the Bride. Summarizing the institutional church's scriptural, historical, theological, and pastoral arguments on the non ordination of Catholic women,[18] women cannot serve as Christic icons in ordained ministry because they are not male; that is, they do not resignify the masculinized head of the Church that is derived from the male-sexed body of Jesus in the incarnation. Thus, this soteriological symbolism asserts a patriarchal Christology and anthropology in which most women, like the Church, are defined in submissive and responsive relations to some elite, ordained men who resignify Christ. Reinforcing that anthropology, both letters urge women to emulate Mary in her sexual roles as virgin, bride, and mother (Letter to Women, par. 11) and thereby "place themselves at the service of others in their everyday lives" (Letter to Women, par. 12). In an ecclesiological setting, this means that women, together with nonordained men, are actively "listening and receiving the Word of God" (Letter to Bishops, par. 15). This letter, then, frames women within a literalized spousal imagery for salvation, which in effect isolates women from imitating Christ, boxes women into modeling dominant anthropologies and ideologies of Mary,[19] and portrays women as passive recipients rather than active agents of the Church's mission and message in ecclesial and, by implication, public life.

In sum, both letters utilize theological symbols such as creation in the image of God, or the Trinity, to justify gender equality in the Catholic tradition. Nonetheless, both letters ultimately undermine that equality with a physicalist anthropology and static symbol of the *imago Christi*, which in turn alienates women from leadership roles in the Church's ordained and public ministry. In both letters, dominant theological constructions of anthropology and Christology prove problematic for women, theologically and politically. Theologically, women's political agency and activism in both letters are situated within patriarchal images and norms of motherhood, such that women embody service to the common good via their biological nature and its associated traits, rather than their political praxis. The call to pattern Christian life on the Christ event—when modified particularly for women through the magisterium's Mariology—raises the danger of identifying women not only with self-gift, but with self-sacrifice, or a kenotic kind of self-giving that leads to submissive self-abnegation.[20] Politically, both letters advance highly romanticized, patriarchal feminine roles for women as mothers that restrict women's ability to stand *in persona Christi*, whether in ecclesial or public ministry. Excluded from sacramental ministry on the anthropological and Christological grounds that they are not men and, therefore, cannot resignify the Church's salvific mission, women are also barred from public ministry, from being the public church, or actualizing the Church's mission to protect human rights and the common good in public life.

FREEING THE CHRIST SYMBOL
FOR A FEMINIST PUBLIC CHURCH

Christology, in conjunction with an anthropology of complementarity, blocks women from leading church positions (both in ecclesiastical ministry and structures of governance) and serves to limit women's religiopolitical agency and activism, effectively shaping a primarily clericalist face and voice of the public church. Nevertheless, Christology still matters for feminist theological reflection on the Church's public engagement, for elaborating a feminist theology of the public church. Rather than judged totally bankrupt for its apparent lack of emancipatory religiopolitical implications, Christology can be reconstructed in a feminist perspective to eschew essentialism or biological determinism found within patriarchal theologies, as well as to edge toward a more just theology of political participation, so that women are viewed as active agents of the public church. Such an alternative theological symbolic for the public church may be advanced through a feminist reinterpretation of *Gaudium et Spes*. A reading of *GS* from a feminist perspective reveals its heretofore neglected Christology that restores theological significance and visibility to women's religiopolitical action for the common good.

READING CHRISTOLOGY IN *GAUDIUM ET SPES*

The Catholic Church's religiopolitical activism in the U.S. context is often narrowed to single issues (such as abortion) or to so-called nonnegotiable issues advocated by some U.S. bishops in the 2004 U.S. presidential election (for example, abortion, embryonic stem cell research, euthanasia, human cloning, and same-sex marriage). By contrast, the public church envisioned in *Gaudium et Spes* endorses a broader social justice agenda that seeks to subvert the institutionalization of injustice and inequality in all facets of life, whether personal or political (pars. 27–29). In keeping with Vatican II's method to read the signs of the times in light of the gospel, *GS* portrays the common good in modern life as fractured by structural sin (pars. 13, 37), which is manifested in domination and discrimination along gender, race, class, sociopolitical, religious, and inter/national lines (pars. 4, 8, 29).[21] Particularly, in public/political life, the common good—or the totality of conditions that advance personal and social fulfillment and flourishing (pars. 26, 74)—is undermined by the sociopolitical disempowerment of citizens (pars. 73, 75), exemplified by voter disenfranchisement in the 2000 and 2004 U.S. presidential elections.[22] From a theological perspective, such denial of public participation amounts to a denial of full human dignity. *GS* represents the Catholic Church's first attempt in conciliar statements to outline a theological anthropology based on relationality (pars. 12, 24, 25)—with God (par. 19), with ourselves (pars. 24–25), and with others in society (pars. 42–43). Such a relational anthropology sheds light on both our increasing interdependence (pars. 5, 23) and complex conflicts (pars. 10, 25).[23] In this relational anthropology, human beings are created for sociality in all dimensions of life, moral, religious, and political, and are called to realize that relationality by contributing to the common good (pars. 26, 30), social justice (par. 29), and public life (par. 31).

GS addresses the Church's mission to realize the common good in public/political life via theological anthropology and Christology.[24] In GS, the fracture of common good is connected to many "imbalances" that distort humanity, personally and collectively (pars. 8, 10, 13), but which are ultimately healed in Christ, the paradigmatic model of redeemed humanity (pars. 10, 22, 24, 38, 45). Thus, making a just sense of self is reciprocally linked to making a just social order via Christology (pars. 3, 22, 41). According to David Hollenbach, Christology in GS proffers "a sharper theological focus on how the gospel points toward the kind of world that Christians should be helping to build."[25]

On my reading, different Christologies in GS correspond with different ways of transforming our selves and our society for justice. On the one hand, the "unchanging" incarnate union of divine and human natures in Christ (par. 10) implies a too irenic integration of religious and public life. That is, such a static Christology presumes already reconciled relations within humanity itself and between humanity and God, expressed in the events of the incarnation, crucifixion, and resurrection of Jesus (pars. 2, 22, 45). Modeled on this Christology, Christians are "made a partner in the paschal mystery" and hope in an other-worldly, resurrected life after death (par. 22). While addressing humanity's existential anxieties about death (pars. 18, 22), this Christology does not sufficiently grapple with substantial sociocultural, economic, and political barriers to participating in and benefiting from U.S. common life, which are mentioned elsewhere in this pastoral constitution (pars. 4, 27, 73, 75). On the other hand, a dynamic Christology—rooted in the prophetic life-ministry of Jesus for building the kingdom or family of God—illustrates a broader notion of the "work of Jesus Christ" beyond the cross for salvation (par. 32; cf. 3). It invites all people to imitate a "craftsman" Christ (pars. 32, 43) and join in his life-long work for spiritual and social renewal as "molders [artisans] of a new humanity" (par. 30; cf. 43, 55). The common good in this Christology is not yet achieved, but must be continually envisioned and enacted based on an "incarnational solidarity,"[26] or a Christic praxis of social justice that emulates the life and ministry of Jesus for the kingdom of God. Such praxis anticipates and partially reflects a more just sense of self and common life that ultimately awaits a future eschatological fulfillment (pars. 38–40).[27]

Rather than competing Christologies, these two theological understandings of Jesus in GS recall a creative eschatological tension between the already, the reconciliation of all things symbolized in the unity of divine and human in Jesus, and the not yet, the active antici-pation of that reconciliation via Christic solidarity and praxis. Yet, which Christology better assists women in being the public church? If the renewal of self and society mutually depend on discipleship, on imitating Christ, then feminist theologians point out that the for-mer, static Christology in GS, rooted in a fixed incarnate identity of divine and human natures in the historical male person of Jesus, proves problematic for women, both theologically and politically. As Elizabeth Johnson argues, the myopic focus on the maleness of Jesus within dominant Christologies carries an "effective history" that raises questions about women's theomorphic, Christomorphic, and salvific capacities, thereby relegating women to second-class citizens in the body of Christ and, by implication, in the body politic. Women cannot be construed as representatives of the public church, of the body of Christ in public, under a static incarnationalism that stresses the necessity of Jesus' maleness to know God, imitate Jesus, and be saved.[28] However, the latter Christology in GS—associated with Jesus' life-ministry for the coming kingdom of God and with becoming "artisans of a new humanity"—holds much untapped theo-political potential for women to reclaim in being the public church. Nevertheless, this latter Christology must be critically reap-propriated from a feminist perspective. Although Vatican II paral-leled U.S. second wave feminist movements, *GS* attends primarily to human rights, civil rights, antiwar, and postcolonial movements rather than to gender justice in its pursuit of social renewal.[29] Building on an insight from Mary Catherine Hilkert, I propose to critically retrieve and recuperate such a dynamic, performative Christology in *GS* through the Wisdom tradition.[30]

RECONSTRUCTING CHRISTOLOGY THROUGH THE WISDOM TRADITION

The links between Christology and the Wisdom tradition are implic-itly embedded in *GS*. Passages that serve as the interpretive key to the entire constitution (pars. 10, 22)[31] demonstrate, but do not forge, those links between its Christology and the Wisdom tradition. These passages refer to Jesus as "the image of the invisible God, the first-born of all creation," from Colossians 1:15 (par. 10, cf. 22), which belongs within the Wisdom literature of Jewish scriptures.

The Wisdom tradition describes a female personification of the divine who participates in creating, redeeming, and sustaining everyday life, especially by acting as prophetic street preacher and banquet host of justice and peace. As Elizabeth Johnson and other feminist scholars have well documented, early Christian communi-ties borrowed from the Wisdom tradition to explain the divine iden-tity and soteriological significance of Jesus. What Jesus did in his prophetic life-ministry disclosed who Jesus was, namely, his identity as the earthly representative of divine Wisdom and the redeemer. Of significance to feminist theological reflection and praxis, portraying Jesus as Wisdom contests and counteracts solely masculinist symbols and language for the reality of God and the imitation of Jesus. That is to say, female language and metaphors for the divine open up theo-logical space for women to regain their theomorphic ability to iden-tify with and image God in Jesus, in both sacred and sociopolitical

times and places. Furthermore, a feminist critical appropriation of
the Wisdom tradition highlights the salvific significance of Jesus'
life-ministry for bringing about the kingdom of God, and thus coun-
terbalances a singular focus on Jesus' death and resurrection in dominant static Christology. Focusing on Wisdom's deeds shown in Jesus'
liberative preaching, healing, and inclusive eating practices (*GS*,
par. 32)—as well as in the similar deeds of his followers—enables
women and men to reclaim their Christomorphic capacity to emulate Jesus in their liberative praxis, not in their bodies.[32]

This shift in feminist Christology from the person to the
ministry of Jesus empowers women and men to identify with and
imitate Jesus by actively continuing his life-ministry, especially but
not only, in political praxis for justice. As *GS* states, "Conformed to
the image of the Son who is the firstborn of many brothers and sisters . . . the entire person is inwardly renewed, even to the 'redemption of the body' (Rom. 8:23)" (par. 22), which implies even to the
redemption of the body politic. Conformity to Christ (Gal. 3:26–28;
2 Cor. 3:18) consists of imitating Jesus' ministry, not his maleness
or any other physical feature of his historical identity. As Johnson
concludes, "Being christomorphic is not a sex distinctive gift. The
image of Christ does not lie in sexual similarity to the human man
Jesus but in coherence with the narrative shape of his compassionate liberating life in the world, through the power of the Spirit."[33]
Being Christomorphic involves political and performative—not
biological—solidarity with Jesus.

As demonstrated in the previous section of this essay, the ability to imitate Christ in dominant magisterial theologies is connected
to religious constructions of biologically based gender norms and
roles. Unable to stand *in persona Christi*, women's capacity to engage
in public life emerges from and is closely linked with their biological maternal genius. Based on the above critical feminist retrieval of
Wisdom Christology in *GS*, women imitate Christ by actively participating in his liberating ministry for creating community, and by

engaging in a political and praxical kind of discipleship based on living out major principles and patterns of Jesus' prophetic lifework for the kingdom of God. In feminist perspective, women's religio-political participation has more to do with their active agency for justice than with their maternal nature.

Feminist Wisdom Christology, thus, shifts the theological emphasis from the person to the ministry of Jesus, and in so doing enables women to reclaim their right to be the public church, to identify with and imitate Jesus' mission—to resignify Jesus—through their political praxis. As Hilkert rightly observes, "the reign of God is discovered among and entrusted to human persons and communities despite all of our limits. . . . Because Wisdom has pitched her tent among us and sent her Advocate to seal us in the truth, we have the power to enflesh the communion that is our final destiny—if only in fragmentary ways."[34] Enfleshing communion or striving for a more just community is performed, individually and collectively. By constructing such a praxically rather than biologically based Christology from the resources of Vatican II and feminist theology, the theological notion of the public church widens to incorporate any person or group (organization, social movement, and the like), including but not limited to the institutional Church, which serves as a Christological "harbinger" (*GS*, par. 92) or sacrament of the already begun but not yet fully realized kingdom of God.

WOMEN, SACRAMENTALITY, AND THE PRAXIS OF THE PUBLIC CHURCH

In sum, this essay critically reclaims key texts and insights from Vatican II to elaborate a feminist theology of the public church, in particular the Catholic Church's role and representatives in U.S. public life. A feminist rereading of *GS* through the lens of feminist Wisdom Christology sheds new theological light on the role of the public church, which is treated in *GS* as a sacrament or sign of an abiding, this-worldly divine presence that lures the world toward

greater justice, love, and peace. Further feminist reflection on sacramentality can assist in expanding on what and who constitutes the
Church's public agents and actors.

According to Susan Ross, sacramentality in its broadest meaning applies to the sacrality of the world and refers to discerning
the divine presence within (but not identical with) all human and
earthly life. In Catholic tradition, the divine presence is signified in
central communal celebrations such as the seven sacraments, and
encountered primarily in the event of the incarnation, of God taking
flesh in Jesus the Christ.[35] Consonant with a wider understanding
of the Church as sacrament in *GS*, a feminist theological perspective on sacramentality in public life—on what constitutes being a
sign of the transformative and just presence of God in the world—
highlights political praxis for justice as a means of embodying that
divine presence. And yet sacramentality suffers from ambiguity. We
cannot easily equate certain political actors or movements with the
good society, framed in theological terms as the kingdom of God
(*GS*, par. 39). Any religiopolitical activism—whether clerical or lay—
recalls or points toward, but is not equated with, that kingdom which
was inaugurated in the incarnation of the divine and of justice in
Jesus. Therefore, we can only propose some modest feminist theological criteria for discerning the presence of the kingdom in public life.

Being the public church entails a praxis of imagining and seeking to realize a more just, participatory common life as envisioned in
Jesus' ministry for the kingdom of God. That is to say, being the public
church in feminist perspective entails a hope-filled or eschatological
praxis for building the common good, for weaving and reweaving a
more just fabric of common life itself. When the ministry of Jesus serves
as a model for the Church's social and political engagement, when discipleship takes the form of social and political praxis for justice, then
all people—the institutional Church and everyday lay Catholics—can
emulate Jesus, can participate in the eschatological work of Christ, striving to re-imagine and at least partly realize a just and justice-oriented

common life. Most importantly for women, being the public church is associated with a performative imitation of the ministry of Christ for the kingdom, rather than an ontological signification or biological replication of the historical human nature of Jesus Christ. Based on their praxis of incarnational solidarity rather than their physical bodies and capacities, women—and all nonordained people for that theological matter—are viewed as disciples of Christ and potentially stand *in persona Christi*, thus offering a far more expansive, rather than mainly clerical and patriarchal, understanding of the Church's public agency.

A feminist theological understanding of the public church proposed in this essay empowers women to be the public church, as well as makes women's leading roles in the history of the Church's political participation more theologically and materially visible. A performative theology of discipleship grounded in working for the kingdom of God certainly resists dominant Christologies that limit the Church's political actors to ordained and other prominent male spokespersons, as well as magisterial theologies that frame women within motherhood. It is their praxis of justice, not their nonordained or maternal status, that makes women the public church. How this feminist theology of the public church concretely affects and transforms the Church's mostly intransigent theology of priesthood and of ordination lies beyond the scope of this essay. However, rather than altogether dismiss motherhood as a potential theological catalyst for reflecting on the public church, we can rely on feminist biblical interpretations of the family structure in the kingdom of God to broaden maternity beyond biology into a larger social-political notion of generativity. As long noted by feminist theologians and biblical scholars, the kingdom or family of God is defined in the Gospels and early Christian literature not by blood kinship and patriarchal structures of family relations, but by discipleship.[36] The new family of God, rephrased in some women's theological reflection as the kin-dom of God to avoid any imperialist meanings, includes women and men who not only "listen and receive," but also "hear and do" the

Word of God for justice (Matt.12:46–50; Mark 3:31–35; Luke 8:19–21). By elaborating a participatory and praxical Christology through the theological resources of feminist Wisdom Christology and gospel-based views of the family of God, a feminist perspective on the public church argued in this essay stresses generativity as a major feature of the Church's public engagement. Rather than limited to clerical or other institutional Church representatives who speak in public about pressing political concerns from a religious perspective, a feminist approach to the public church emphasizes the kind of society that is generated, that is, imagined, created, and sustained, through the Church's, that is, the whole Church's, political agency and action.[37]

Situated within a rich theological horizon of generativity that is not reduced to maternity, ordinary women can act as hearers and doers of the eschatological message and ministry of Jesus, signifying in their praxis the metaphorical birthpangs of the reign of God (for example, Rom. 8:18-23). As emphasized in feminist Wisdom Christology, women in the Gospels already engage in such praxis as Jesus' close friends and advisors, financial backers, evangelizers, and prophetic witnesses to the cross, resurrection, and earliest Christian communities. In the current U.S. context, women like Elvira involved in the New Sanctuary Movement exemplify such praxis by utilizing the church (both physically and symbolically) as a model of the public good rooted in love, justice, and peace—too long denied to immigrant workers under the United States' current legal system and labor markets, but mandated by scriptural ethics and parables about the reign of God (for example, Lev. 19:33–34; Matt. 25:34–36, 41–43). From a feminist theological perspective, the goal of the public church to create a more just common life, which we as artisans, according to GS, cocreate with God and with one another, now allows us to recognize and interpret all—men and women, clergy and laity, scholars and activists, single spokespersons and whole social movements—as siblings, interrelated in our efforts to bring to birth and nurture some of the political conditions of love, justice, and peace associated with being in and becoming the kin-dom or family of God.

Chapter 9

JUSTICE AS THE MARK OF CATHOLIC FEMINIST ECCLESIOLOGY

Susan Abraham

I was eight years old when I watched the ordination of a priest in my parish in Mumbai, India. I clearly remember the smell of the incense and the wonderful music provided by the church choir, particularly as they sang one of my favorite hymns, *Here I Am, Lord*. I also remember that it was the moment of my "first commitment" to God, for I, too, had clearly heard God's voice "calling in the night," as in the words of the hymn. I looked at my mother and said with conviction, "Ma, I know what I will be when I grow up. I am going to be a priest." My mother patted my head with a perplexed look. It was many years later that I understood some of the reasons for her perplexity. I was female in a culture where Christianity was a minority religion. As a minority religion, in the context of many other relativizing truth claims, gendered roles provided clarity and definite identity to mark religious boundaries. It took me years, also, to realize that the context of pluralism often solidifies gender roles, stifling what can be other ways of being for women and men. In other words, when there is a pluralism of religious and truth claims, gender roles can become rigid as a way to safeguard a particular identity. When I came into my own as a feminist theologian, I immediately recognized the obvious reaction to pluralism by

Roman Catholic ecclesial officials, who insist on constructing a sta-
ble identity for ecclesial structures in terms of gendered difference.
In this view, a "catholic, one, holy, and apostolic" church required
women and men to stick with traditional gender roles. In fact, these
capacious marks of holiness of the church[1] continue to be presented
in a narrow, masculinist perspective. The marks of the church have
also been the basis of the imperial face of the church. In the era of
colonialism, for example, catholicity has been interpreted to mean
that Christian churches anywhere in the world had to acknowledge
the primacy and superiority of the Roman Church. Or, apostolicity
has been narrowly interpreted from the perspective of Western elite
masculine leadership. As a feminist and Catholic theologian from
India, I am convinced that we have to challenge the narrow and
gendered interpretation of the marks of the church by infusing the
church's catholicity with justice through a more capacious theological imagination, in order to rethink the problem of gendered and
colonial ecclesiology. A capacious catholic imagination for feminist
theology, that is, an imagination for broadening and deepening the
claims of universality in Catholic theology, is a necessary element
of catholic feminist theology.

Ecclesiology is at the heart of the Catholic theological enterprise. Ecclesiastical patriarchy, however, employs the logic of domination and subordination to define the role of women in the church
solely in terms of the sex/gender division. The domination/subor-
dination model is not explicit in church teachings, because official
Catholic theology will argue positively for the equality of women
and men. Instead, the sex/gender divide in official Catholic theology results in the complementarity model in which the gendered
roles of women are sanctioned within a domination/subordination
framework. In doing so, it excludes women from the sacramental ministry of the Church. This essay is being written just as the
Vatican has issued the edict of excommunication for any women
and the bishops who will ordain them, citing that the Church has no

"authorization" to change the "will of its founder" in having chosen men as his apostles.[2] This is a literalist[3] and positivist[4] argument that must be challenged by invoking Catholic theology's potential to think symbolically. The possibility of a theology of symbol, informing our understanding of the meaning of the choice of the Twelve, helps us to escape the rigidly juridical framework underlying this edict.[5] Moreover, the narrow Christological emphasis on Jesus as communicator of divine truths, which are then mediated by the chosen few men, shores up the doctrinal and teaching power of the magisterium by presupposing a theological anthropology in which women and men are essentially different, though equal. Not only are theologies of the incarnation and creation compromised here, but our understanding of the nature and mission of the Church is seriously distorted by the triple sins of literalism, legalism, and juridicism. These three together seek to ignore the historicity of all human institutions, to argue that the first responsibility of institutional guardians is to be faithful to the rules and conventions of the tradition. Instead, this essay seeks to argue that the Catholic theological tradition also permits a larger and broader view than just the juridical or the literal. The first step in imagining a more just church is to grasp the potential of the grammar of Catholic theology, in order to move beyond a rigid legalism and work toward justice. The grammar of the Catholic tradition, explored below, can enable us to think of rules in view of justice. Justice, in the Catholic theological view, is the care and concern for community that arises from the sacramental basis of Catholic theology.

CATHOLIC GRAMMAR AND ECCLESIOLOGY

Catholic theology possesses a particular grammar that underlies its theological assertions. Richard McBrien, in *Catholicism*, asserts that there are three Catholic foci that comprehensively inform its theological enterprise. These are sacramentality, mediation, and communion, each of which upholds the particular tension between transcendence and immanence. It is the particular configuration of sacramentality, mediation, and communion that leads to Catholicism's vigorous theology of community under God, that is, its ecclesiology. On this view, "Catholic" is less an identity category arising out of membership. Catholic, rather, has to do with *being* a Catholic, that is, a particular religious way of being in the world. To be a Catholic is to have a sacramental view of the world, its capacity to mediate divine truths through material and created reality, and its view that all reality has its deepest meaning in being created by a loving God. Such a grammar allows Catholic people to speak of the divine spark in all of creation. If ecclesiology is at the heart of the Catholic theological enterprise, it cannot but be that a Catholic grammar underscores the manner in which Catholics imagine community and church.

The first idea, sacramentality, is the perspective that can apprehend "the divine in the human, the infinite in the finite, the spiritual in the material, the transcendent in the immanent, and the eternal in the historical."[6] One is catholic because one has such a sacramental vision. Sacramentality is a perspective, a way of apprehending creation as revealing of the divine, and the sacraments are exemplars of such a perspective. Of course, sacramentality can be carried too far. If all created reality is indeed sacramental, then anything and everything becomes divine. This is not a tenable position for Catholic believers, for our beliefs about God require us to maintain the critical distinction between immanence and transcendence. Sacramentality is the assertion that everything has the capacity to *reveal* the divine. The genius of the sacramental imagination however, maintains the transcendence of God by arguing that the sacramental vision is best understood when we see God's presence in the world in *relational* terms. That is, God's immanence and transcendence are not static and unchanging attributes; God's immanence and transcendence are ways in which God relates to the world. Thus, the theologies of creation and incarnation make sense when we grasp the active presence of the Divine in the world, which in its capacious goodness is poured out into every mote, speck, and particle of created reality (immanence) without exhausting itself in that reality (transcendence). Catholic ecclesiology attempts to enact the realization of such a relationship of the Divine to created reality.

If we imagine the Divine presence solely in static terms, and miss out on the relational basis of sacramentality, it can become idolatrous. Thus, it is not just the sacraments that are sacramental. Reality itself is sacramental because God chooses to relate to reality. Such a relational basis is often forgotten when official arguments are marshaled to exclude women from the priestly office of church. Official arguments against the ordination of women stress that women have "different" vocations, decreed by God, that have to do with women's capacity to reproduce. Note that such an emphasis places women in primary relationships to men, whereas clerical masculine reality is always placed in primary relationship to God. The Catholic sacramental focus demands that justice be served to women who are eminently able to have and sustain relationship with the divine on their own terms.

The second idea, mediation, is the perspective that all experience of God is primarily mediated and rooted in historical embodied experience. That is, no one has a "pure" experience of God. Mediation is a useful idea in that it reminds us to think of the Catholic perspective in relation to concrete historical realities of time and space. Carried too far, the principle of mediation cannot preserve the tension between transcendence and immanence and descends into magical thinking. The principle of mediation in Catholic theology is best seen in its commitment to the ordained ministry of the priest. While God is present in all that we do and is present everywhere, it is also true that there are some moments or places where such action can be focused with particular attention. Consequently, in its rituals and rites, for example, the priest functions as a mediator, not because he is possessed of magical powers or because he can limit the human and divine encounter, but because the priest as a mediator can help focus one's attention on the divine-human relationship *for the sake of the community*.[7] One's gendered reality is only accidental to the fulfillment of such a vision and is not the whole of embodied reality. Any gendered reality, in other words, can mediate the divine-human relationship. To insist that the mediator can mediate primarily because of his gendered reality is to impose a very human limit on the capacious promise of the principle of mediation. The only way to undercut the taint of magic in the work of the priest is to advance theological arguments for embodied, plural mediations of the divine. That is, the principle of mediation can bear the weight of the argument for multiple genders and their capacity to mediate the divine-human relationship. The principle of mediation reminds us that Catholic theology is primarily oriented toward the community of all and not just one type of historical reality. Plurality, as an inherent logic of creation, can be celebrated by feminist theologians interested in advancing catholic ecclesiology to be more inclusive, by emphasizing the symbolic role of the priest in the whole of ecclesiological practice and theology. Since the role of the priest is symbolic in essence, the accident of gender remains marginal to the enactment of such a role.

Finally, the principle of communion asserts that our experience of God is always mediated in community. One can indeed have a personal or individual relationship with God or with Jesus, but the coherence of the tradition obtains from its sacramental and mediated view. All experience of God is given life within the communal context of creation, incarnation, and salvation. In other words, Catholicism seeks to preserve the balance between immanence and transcendence in such a way as to bring all of life, history, and human experience within the ambit of communion under God. Communion, too, can be distorted; an overemphasis on the communal dimension will undercut individual conscience and ultimately freedom of thought and action. For example, many well-meaning

Catholics will argue that the communion of Catholics, the unity the Church has striven toward for centuries, would immediately fracture if women were to be ordained to the priesthood. Once again, a capacious imagination may be able to assist us. Our view of communion need not reflect homogeneity as the basis of unity; Catholic communion can be unity in a divinely ordained plurality. When justice becomes the mark of the communion of the church, the principle of Catholic communion could become a potent force for the Catholic community seeking full humanity under God. In this sense, the church becomes truly "Catholic," because its universality is not hobbled by a narrow theological imagination upholding the sex/gender division.

In order not to compromise the inherently capacious Catholic theological imagination, we have to rethink ecclesiology in broader terms. Even mainstream ecclesiology demonstrates the challenge of pluralism to institutional models of church. Thus, it is not just feminists who are presenting challenges from pluralism to the institutional church. Dean Hoge and Jacqueline Wenger, in their book *Evolving Visions of the Priesthood: Changes from Vatican II to the Turn of the New Century*,[8] point to the incredible changes that occurred in the 1960s as the reason for such conflict. The cultural and political maelstrom unleashed by the civil rights movement, the antiwar movement, the women's movement, and the sexual revolution all came on the heels of the changes inaugurated by Vatican II. Many younger priests felt that the atmosphere of change would introduce deeper institutional changes to priesthood, such as optional celibacy, for example.[9] What happened, instead, was a period of deep uncertainty. The pre–Vatican II model of priesthood, cultic priesthood, was severely challenged by these changes. This model placed a great deal of significance on worship and sacraments. In executing these responsibilities, the priest wore distinctive clothing, lived in a rectory, and maintained distance from ordinary social lives of people. As a "separate clerical caste," priests thought of themselves as "men set apart."[10] This model began to be challenged by the "servant-leader model" of priesthood after the council, emphasizing the shared human condition between priests and laypeople:

> The Church itself was now defined, following the council teaching, as the people of God, a community in which the clergy-laity distinction was much less important. A priest's distinctiveness now came from his spiritual and institutional leadership within the community, not just as a matter of ontological difference coming from holy orders. Moreover, the earlier concept of "ministry" as the domain solely of priests was now redefined as the work of all baptized Christians, both priests and lay. Now nobody had to become a priest to do ministry.[11]

Susan K. Wood, in her commentary in Hoge and Wenger's book, points out that the newest generation of priests today largely identify themselves with the cultic model, whereas priests fifty-five to sixty years of age and older identify themselves largely with the servant-leader model.[12] In the present context, hierarchical ecclesiology is favored over collegial ecclesiology. The rift seems particularly significant around discussion of the theology of (priestly) ontology. The theology of ontology asserts that ordination produces a permanent ontological change in the priest, making him different from laity. Ontology, or the study of being, refers to the understanding of the basic nature of person. In the cultic model, this difference is highlighted to the extent that priests look like a different caste within the church. In the servant-leader model of priesthood, such a theology of ontology is not abandoned, but its orientation shifts from the individual to the individual's relationality with others. Instead of an ontology of difference, the servant-leader model emphasizes an ontology of relationship. Neither model takes a close look at how the institutional church affirms the sex/gender division, thus compromising the capacious catholic theological imagination. Both models tend to favor a male elite caste of priests, though the servant-leader model demonstrates a better ability to accommodate the feminist emphasis on justice and inclusivity because of its emphasis on an ontology of relationality.

The emphasis on justice may seem to bring in a secular ideal to ecclesiology. For many, the word *justice* seems to imply "democracy," a secular concept. Feminist theology argues that justice is more than a secular democratic ideal; justice is at the very heart of the grammar and language of Catholic theology. Such justice means that the elitism and exceptionalism of the institutional priestly caste must give way to more of a capacious imagination of sacramentality, mediation, and communion. Justice in relation to ecclesiology is not just about the Church being an inclusive space of worship. Emphasizing justice transforms catholicity as a principle of openness and inclusivity for the whole of Catholic theology. It transforms holiness as the mark of being open to the work of the Spirit, which is new for every generation. Finally, it transforms apostolicity as a principle of close imitation of Jesus and the apostles who welcomed men and women to the table.

CHRISTOLOGY AND THE THEOLOGY OF SYMBOL

A theology of symbol safeguards the theological potential of the three main Catholic foci of sacramentality, mediation, and communion. A theology of symbol enables us to look at Catholic theology's capacity to accommodate the challenges from pluralism and ethics, in that it moves us away from thinking of theology as a set of propositions that require "belief," and more as a way to see the world and to trust the tradition to respond to the needs of the whole community. In a postenlightenment context, there is much suspicion of the word *symbol*, since it is simplistically opposed to authoritative truth. In our present cultural context, authoritative truth yearns to look very like its secular counterpart, scientific truth. Scientific truth seems to possess a particular sort of unquestionable authority, and its language is transparent and its meaning clear. This is called scientific positivism. When religious truths are asserted in such a cultural context, it is assumed that the language and meaning of such religious assertions are "objective" in the manner that scientific assertions are. However, theological speech has a symbolic character, precisely because it preserves the tension between immanence and transcendence. Not only is theological and religious speech symbolic; it is also not value-free, as many scientific statements are assumed to be. For feminist theologians, therefore, the task is complex. Not only do we have to insist on the symbolic nature of religious language, but we also cannot avoid the responsibility of pointing out how such language shores up elite masculinist power.

One of the best, if rather complex, proposals for a theology of symbol as the underlying basis of all Catholic theology is Roger Haight's *Jesus, Symbol of God*.[13] According to Haight, symbols and symbolic language are the basis of all religious experience. All language we employ to speak of the experience of the divine is symbolic. All language in the past that was employed to speak of the experience of the divine is symbolic. We cannot look at the Gospel accounts and miss the theological significance of "Twelve men," for example, as explained earlier.[14] Understanding how a theology of symbol functions in theology allows us to cultivate the capacious and just Catholic imagination that seems to be lacking in models of ecclesiology, which seem to be more invested in safeguarding masculinist power.

How does a theology of symbol function in Catholic theology? Haight works out the theology of symbol primarily in relation to Christology. Language about Jesus as the Christ is primarily symbolic. As the Christ, that is the Messiah in Hebrew, or the Anointed One in Greek, Jesus was the symbol of God for his culture and his time. Precisely as symbol, the title "Christ" takes on a vast repertoire of meanings within the burgeoning early Christian context. The title "Christ" is a cultural hybrid, resonating with important theological and religious signifiers from both the Jewish and Hellenistic cultural contexts. Thus, "Christ" as a religious symbol demands participation, in that the excess of meaning that the symbol attempts to communicate cannot be accomplished without the subjective and existential engagement and participation of the one who is attempting to grasp such meaning. The Christian symbol system took root precisely because it was created within the frames of references that had saturated meaning for its participants. Thus, the participatory nature of symbols underscores the communal nature of Catholic theology. It is only in this participatory way that the symbol Christ and the symbol Jesus become revealing of the divine, then and now. Christology in this regard needs to be able to be elastic enough so that it can draw people experientially into the range of meanings of the symbol. Jesus is a symbol because Christology creates in us a tension between the particularity of Jesus and his universal relevance:

> The tension between autonomous identity of symbol and its bearing of a meaning that transcends itself by pointing beyond itself is intrinsic to a symbol. It is therefore important to note that on an historical level Jesus' being a human being makes him universally available. Because and insofar as Jesus is a human being, he is in that degree able to be understood by all other human beings. In symbolic mediation, the universal is found in the particularity of the medium. In the case of Jesus, he was a particular person in his time, place, context and religious tradition. His individuality further distinguished him from others in his context, for example, John the Baptist. The first step in a constructive theology then, is to look not only at Jesus' humanity, but also at his distinctive individuality. Symbols release universally relevant meaning through their concreteness as individuals.[15]

Thus, symbols always point beyond themselves while utilizing the mediating potential of mundane and material objects or reality.

Precisely because symbols mediate an excess of meaning, they may not be read at face value for positivist or literal meaning, which is what leads to idolatry. Religious symbols are not magical or other than natural signs of divinity. Even as they constantly point to divine transcendence, they reveal the very human capacity to grasp the "more than" in the ordinary world. Symbols are therefore multivalent. They open up meaning and generate a plurality of meaning. A vigorous theology of symbol provides safeguards against idolatry by pointing to the excess of meaning in the theology of the incarnation. God is revealed in the mediation of relation between divine and human. As symbol of God therefore, Jesus is not merely "man for us." As *God* with us, the theology of symbol prevents reifying Jesus' masculinity or any other incidental historical attribute. Ecclesiological reflection on this view is about the symbol that "church" is meant to be—a just and holy community that embraces the human condition and human reality. Church as symbol is the enactment of the embrace of humanity by God in the incarnation. The more capacious Christology suggested by the theology of symbol permits ecclesial models that are not tied just to this or that historical incidence or attribute. Rather, in the all-embracing theology of symbol, ecclesiology takes on the potential for inclusivity and justice in the manner demanded by Jesus, the symbol of God.

It is important to understand how such a theology of symbol and Christology impact theological anthropology. For Haight, there is an intrinsic relationship between human existence and what Christians claim when they say they believe in Jesus Christ. Haight is following Karl Rahner here in asserting that there is "an internal continuity between Jesus Christ and human beings, between what happened to Jesus Christ and the destiny of all."[16] For Rahner, as for Haight, hope is the fundamental disposition of human beings arising from the realization of our continuity with Jesus Christ. Such a hope draws us into living our lives as a journey back to God. All human beings, therefore, are people of hope, people who hope for not just themselves, but have hope for the whole of created reality.

Such hope for all presents the potential to transform unjust social and political structures into structures of justice. The transformative potential of hope does not lead to a resigned and fatalistic acceptance of unjust and dominating social structures. Instead, precisely because of the continuity between human beings and Jesus Christ, we are able to found communities of love and justice in the manner of Jesus' founding of the believing community. In other words, theological anthropology, in light of a theology of symbol and Christology, is always social and relational. In such a framework, "church" means a community characterized by egalitarian relationships in which the excluded and marginalized are brought into the circle of communal care, a view underscored in feminist writing on ecclesiology.

FEMINIST PROPOSALS FOR *EKKLĒSIA*

Feminist proposals for ecclesiology have presented concrete ways in which communities of egalitarian relationships can come into view. In so doing, they draw on the strengths of the Catholic theological and intellectual tradition and the coherence of its systematic themes. The Catholic grammar of sacramentality, mediation, and communion provide the scaffolding for theological reflection in all of its forms and therefore a coherence of meaning and practice. Coherence in itself is not a value unless the system that depends on it can be shown to be sensitive and responsive to ethical demands. The work of demonstrating such coherence has fallen to feminist and liberation theologians in the face of the polemicizing dismissal by official authorities whose strategy is to point to feminism's oppositional stance as *the* problem for Catholic theology. Feminist theologians, on the other hand, see that the biggest problem for Catholic theology is its love of power, as evident in its exclusion of women, women's experience, and its narrow cultural framework. Arguing that justice become a hallmark of Catholicity, feminist theologians such as Elisabeth Schüssler Fiorenza create the opportunity for feminist theology to demonstrate the coherence of Catholic theology, precisely in its potential to redress the exclusion of women, races, cultures, and classes. She proposes the idea of *ekklēsia*, defined as "the radical equality that characterizes the already and not yet of religious community and democratic society."[17] In other words, the feminist model of *ekklēsia* challenges what she calls the "kyriarchal"[18] context in which religious and social communities operate.

One of the questions that Schüssler Fiorenza tackles head-on is why a feminist might want to remain a feminist and a Catholic in an overtly discriminatory church.[19] People often present the choice of departure as a "better" one. Feminists who are not Catholic will also assert that Roman Catholic feminists should leave the institutional church altogether. Leaving the church reinforces the idea that the most useful feminist strategy is nonengagement with the history, and the potential for redress and solutions to be found within the tradition. Consequently, Schüssler Fiorenza is convinced that feminist theology has two equally important strands that must be woven together. Catholic feminists must possess the ethical and intellectual sensitivity to point out the ways in which official ecclesiology shores up traditional anthropology and triumphant Christology, but also must have the imagination and vision to suggest alternatives to these exclusive paradigms. Thus, Schüssler Fiorenza's prophetic feminist theological anthropology grounds her proposals for a "reconstructive-reformist"[20] model of ecclesiology that is very critical of the dominant theology of "woman" operating within official Roman Catholic theology.

She argues for a theological anthropology that is inclusive for women through the "de facto clerical status of professional women ministers in the church."[21] It is important to grasp this move in Schüssler Fiorenza's methodology. Her critique of kyriocentric theological anthropology undergirding the exclusion of women from sacramental participation is based on the complex relationship between the history of women's activity in the Church and official reception of such activity by the institutional church, which continues to maintain the status quo. While the official church keeps advancing arguments against the full participation of women in the sacramental life of the Church, the official church also neatly omits the tremendous professional and spiritual leadership of women in various moments in its history.

Yet the active presence of women in many pastoral positions within the German context in 1964, in fields such as pastoral care, catechetics, and Catholic action, was predicated on the problematic ideology of the eternal feminine. Here she points out how the theology of the "eternal feminine," which replaced an earlier theological assumption of women's inferiority and sinfulness, is shored up by the dominant cultural ideology of woman's nature and biological/essential difference from man. The idea of the "eternal feminine," therefore, is the basis of gender essentialism, which is the idea that women and men have "essences" that are eternal and immutable. "Under the veil," women, in particular nun women, were permitted to contribute significantly to the life of the church precisely as *traditional* women. Moreover, their ministerial contributions were limited by the reason for their inclusion: the shortage of priests. Religious women's ministerial practice, therefore, had no impact where there were enough priests. In such a world, she argues, women are understood solely in relation to that of men and their relation to the divine embedded in kyriarchal language. The emphasis on the "eternal feminine" is most clearly seen in traditional notions of ideal womanhood, the most insidious of which is the emphasis on (heteronormative) motherhood. Women are exalted to the extent that they uphold the ultimate patriarchal value of reproducing a patriarchal society in which men's superiority is never challenged. Thus, women's capacity to be in relation is dependent on the essentialized and idealized presentation of their reproductive capacity, making their primary relational context one of sexual reproduction. The politics of such an essentialist move obscures the vested interest of official Catholic theology to maintain the status quo of women's relationality being derived solely from men.

In contrast, Schüssler Fiorenza argues that the inclusion of women on their own terms has the potential to reorient the institution towards the sacramentality, mediation, and potential for communion. Ecclesiology, which limits the role of women to traditional roles, simply reveals the extent to which institutions and, therefore, ecclesiology itself reflects kyriarchal concerns. She writes:

> How little theologians have scrutinized and corrected the traditional Catholic image of woman comes to the fore in the new edition of the *Lexicon fur Theologie und Kirche*. Here one finds the following statement under the entry "nature of woman": God has called woman to be the mother of life (Gen 3:20) and placed on her the main burden of propagation (Gen 3:16). Her essential nature therefore is motherhood. Motherhood is rooted in receptivity and productivity; it matures into joyful sacrifice and never-ending surrender. . . . The contemporary, almost Catholic image of woman is that of motherhood, of surrender, of service and of care, of the silent rather than visible contribution of woman to the creative vocation of man in the world.[22]

To the extent that Christian churches and theologies perpetuate the "feminine mystique" and perpetuate the perception of women's supposed inferiority through institutional inequalities, a feminist critical theology seeks both to critique and provide alternative visions for the restructuring of cultural images and roles of men *and* women.[23] In the constructive move following such critical work, feminists need to take care not to repeat the opposite ideological problem. Schüssler Fiorenza writes: "It is neither the patriarchal God nor matriarchal Goddess, neither the Masculine nor the Feminine, neither divine Fatherhood or complementary Motherhood [which] expresses the Divine."[24] These particular symbols are unviable since they are symbols which are created in a kyriarchal framework. All kyriarchal symbols are interrogated by a feminist theology of symbol that critiques the construction of language for the divine.

When justice becomes the mark of a feminist ecclesiology, we are able to recast the manner in which we speak of the divine and thus envision the community of worship of the divine. God-talk, that is, the way in which we speak of the divine, reveals to us how the symbolic imaginary of divine language is tainted with power. Thus, "God" is always named in the interests of the powerful.[25] In fact, all discourses of the transcendent and the Divine reveal political interest, beginning with the ubiquitous presence of masculine language to speak of divine transcendence. As is well known, feminists have consistently challenged and deconstructed the preferred language of traditional theology to speak of God in terms of human masculinity. To accuse feminists of politicizing the issue of language for the divine obscures the idea that all discourses of the divine are created and sustained by systems seeking to maintain power and status quo. In fact, the very word "God" is itself a loaded word that is gendered. Schüssler Fiorenza consequently presents the grapheme G*d as a challenge to the idea of "God" and to remind us that religious language in employing symbols points to the excess of meaning that cannot be contained in literal perceptions of language. She further points out that the naming of the divine emerges from the manner in which societies are organized: the imperial structures of Rome and medieval feudal society, for example, emphasized language of God as Father, King, and Omniscient Ruler. Or, in the time of the Reformation and the Renaissance, G*d as "authoritative unity" and "Absolute Subject" functioned to authorize the sensibility about human personality and behaviors considered to be good and desirable. God-talk, in this way, reinscribes how society in any given culture or context imagines power. Since most human societies take masculine power and privilege for granted, speech about G*d reflects such anthropological assumptions. Schüssler Fiorenza's constructive move here is to ask us to be mindful of the rhetorical effects of speech about the divine in reverse. The way in which we talk about God can affect the way in which we respond to each other in our differences, particularly the difference of gender. It is clear from her proposal that she is invested in a particular political deconstruction of language for the divine. However, in view of the feminist commitment to justice, such a deconstruction of traditional language of the divine and reconstruction in light of feminist interest challenges kyriarchy and hopes for transformation.

Emphasizing the manner in which wo/men (women and men) relate to the divine in their quest for wholeness expands the symbolic universe to include language and experience from all members of the community. The inherent idolatry of masculinist language and the positivist and essentialist positions it reinscribes are overturned here. God is not "male," and priests need not only be male. Priests necessarily need to be those who have the capacity to be in deep relationship with God for the sake of the community. A selective and literal reading of Christian history maintains the status quo, but in doing so it distorts Catholic theology and the potential of its liberating grammar. Thus, it is not constructive feminist proposals that are being selective in their theological emphases; traditional Catholic ecclesiology has always been selective and judicious in presenting one singular aspect of the tradition in place of the whole of the tradition.

When liberation and justice become the primary concerns of ecclesiology, we have ekklēsia. Ekklēsia is not the same as "church," but is an "alternative" to imperial forms of church and society (keep in mind that the original meaning of the term *ekklēsia* as a Greek political term denoted a democratic assembly or congress of full citizens[26]). Schüssler Fiorenza argues that fundamentalist literalism and academic positivism in church theology go hand in hand with the logic of domination and control—the logic of empire. In other words, if we look closely at the manner in which "church" is rhetorically deployed, we note that literalism and positivism are the marks of the imperial church. The worldview provided by such imperial logic gives rise to Christological triumphalism and the subordination of any other religious worldview. Such imperial worldviews gave rise to the history of colonization in which the institutional church played a significant part. When "church" moves to "ekklēsia," as in feminist proposals, such forms of imperial thinking are profoundly challenged, leading to "decolonized" thinking and language. The very space of church, therefore, undergoes a change from the concretely managed spectacle of soaring bricks and mortar, to a space as a political hermeneutic space.[27]

Such utopian space engenders the radical democratic imagination so vital for contemporary feminist theology. The ekklēsia of women is a "theoretical symbolic construct," which is neither about exodus (leaving as an option for feminists) nor about a comfortable home. As a symbolic construct, it has four interlocking dimensions underlying its theological framework. The first, the political dimension, understands ekklēsia an "imagined community." I would argue that ekklēsia as imagined community deepens the mark of church as "catholic." Rhetorically, the imagined community is a space that provides political, rather than a biological or cultural basis for alliance. It is, therefore, not only a virtual utopian space, but an already partially realized one of radical equality and site of feminist struggle. But this site of radical equality and struggle for women's dignity is precisely the content of the claim of universality that marks catholic.

Two, the linguistic-semantic dimension alerts us to the idea that ekklēsia is a "linguistic tool and semantic means of critical reading and political conscientization."[28] *Ekklēsia* is a term for hospitality to diversity and is not a place where social, cultural, political, or class-based sameness is presumed. Only in such a space can the "totalizing gender reading which naturalizes the sex-gender system"[29] be overturned. Here justice deepens the claim of apostolicity. The church can claim its deepest connection to its founder by being the exemplary site of just relations in the manner that Jesus already showed us. Tradition now becomes a vehicle for justice, not a vehicle for maintaining and shoring up cultural and masculinist ideals of authority and purity.

Further, ekklēsia acts positively in the symbolic sphere to actively deconstruct patriarchal, symbolic constructs without sacrificing its understanding that the sphere of positive action remains the historical and communal. In other words, the concrete practice of ekklēsia occurs in community. In this context, justice is enacted in communal relations. The mark of oneness, which is a significant value for the Catholic Church, is deepened by the call to justice to mend the age old division created by the sex/gender paradigm. Thus, oneness is less about a homogenous identity and far more about a unity based on a Catholic sacramental view of the world and the difference created and sustained by God.

Finally, ekklēsia has a global and spiritual dimension in that it imagines society as a community of support and an alliance of equals. Justice deepens the call to holiness as a community committed to avoid the sin of sexism and discrimination. This rhetorical construction of ekklēsia is methodologically undergirded by the process of "decolonization." Here, logics of empire, which are usually constituted by domination and subordination forms of thought, are disabled through radical egalitarian relationships. Ekklēsia is, therefore, a historical and theoretical alternative to empire. Such a space provides a symbolic alternative to other spaces than the biological or cultural:

> [Such a] Feminist theology does not ask for the integration of women into patriarchal ecclesial structures, nor does it advocate a separatist strategy, but it works for the transformation of Christian symbols, tradition and community as well as for the transformation of women . . . to speak of the *ekklēsia* of women, does not mean to advocate a separatist strategy or to mythologize women. It means simply to make women visible as active participants and leaders in the Church, to underline women's contributions and suffering throughout Church history and to safeguard women's autonomy and freedom from spiritual-theological patriarchal controls.[30]

In sum, this essay has presented the idea that when justice marks what is catholic in Catholic ecclesiology, sexism, literalism, fundamentalism, and triumphalism, all marks of injustice and imperial domination begin to be erased. Only with justice can we become one, holy, catholic, and apostolic church. Catholic theology, with its capacious sacramental and symbolic sensibility, is the basis for feminist ecclesiological proposals.

ECCLESIOLOGY ROUNDTABLE

Jeannine Hill Fletcher, Laura M. Taylor,
Elena Procario-Foley

What does it mean to rethink "church" from a contemporary feminist and Catholic perspective? Drawing on the experiences of women in the church and the insights of feminist theologians, the authors in this section answer this question from their own unique point of view. Since it is not the nature of feminist thought to give absolutist or definitive answers, each response provides women with one way among many to speak of themselves as rightful participants in the Body of Christ and to revision the sacramental nature of the Church accordingly.

As this volume has repeatedly demonstrated, the voices and experiences of women have been marginalized within official Church teachings and practices. Although women constitute the majority of Church membership, they have continuously been denied full participation in the Church by virtue of their sexed/gendered identities. For many women, the consistent devaluing of their gifts and resources has led to a dilemma: "Should we stay or should we go?"

Feminist ecclesiology sits at the heart of this quandary and pushes the boundaries in all directions. Over the course of the last several decades, feminist theologians have sought to formulate liberating alternatives to the patriarchal ecclesial discourses that have prevented the flourishing of women in the Church. Yet as Natalie

Watson proposes, "The question feminist ecclesiology has to answer is not whether or not women have to 'leave' or 'stay,' but how it is possible to rethink what it means to be church within a theological paradigm which aims at reconsidering the basics of Christian theology and practice in feminist terms."[31]

To this end, the feminist ecclesiologies constructed in this volume not only ask what is the church, but also *who* is the church, and what it entails to be church in and for the world. Each of these questions is rooted in the lived reality of Catholic women, such as Krista, the undergraduate student, who was fired up with love for Christ; Elvira Arellano, the grassroots mother who called Christian churches into political action for immigration reform; and the eight-year-old Susan Abraham, who wanted desperately to be a priest while watching an ordination at her parish in Mumbai. In short, these ecclesial reconsiderations take into account the ways in which the church has been both a space of oppression and a site of significant meaning for women. They honor the complex and ambiguous relationship of women with the church and, in so doing, seek to open up an area of theology and church life that has been largely dominated by elite, male clerics.

Taken as a whole, the strength of the essays can be found in the way in which the understanding of the Church is widened from an institutional structure (Groppe) to an active public engagement with the world (Carbine), to, finally, a utopian vision of justice (Abraham). As individual moments in a broader movement, they indicate women's desire to be part of a Church without being part of the oppressive structures it produces. Yet, in order to re-vision the Church as an inclusive entity, each essay necessarily grapples with the magisterium's interpretation of theological anthropology and Christology, which has contributed in part to the marginal role and status of women in the Church. Likewise, each essay reclaims the notion of sacraments for women, dislodging it from traditional patriarchal interpretations that have excluded women based on androcentric understandings of the Incarnation. In the end, each essay proposes a creative and constructive reading of ecclesiology, which is both uniquely feminist and Catholic.

Elizabeth Groppe's essay entitled "Women and the *Persona* of Christ: Ordination in the Roman Catholic Church," asks what it means to act in the image and person of Christ. Noting through the eyes of her students that there are many ways in which women can and do contribute to the traditional structures of the Church, Groppe also notes that the people in the Church who are able to make decisions about the direction and life of the Church are men. If we can recognize Christ in both male and female persons, she asks, why have women been prohibited from standing *in persona Christi* at the altar? Her essay answers this question by leading the reader through a concise overview of the theological debate on the ordination of women, which includes biblical and theological perspectives from both the Vatican and its interlocutors. Groppe concludes with her own response to this disputed question, which focuses on the priesthood as an instrumental and sacramental sign of the Wisdom of God that ultimately transcends the category of male and female by bearing public witness to the rich content of the mystery of Christ and the unending compassion of God.

Rosemary Carbine's essay, "Artisans of a New Humanity: Re-Visioning the Public Church in a Feminist Perspective," shifts the focus from the inner ecclesial praxis of the church to its public, political praxis. Like Groppe, Carbine acknowledges the ways in which women already are Church, but have not been recognized as such due to official Church teachings that claim women cannot be representatives of the church, broadly construed. By developing a theology of the public church based on a feminist reading of *Gaudium et Spes*, Carbine hopes to enable women to recover their rightful place as political actors in the church. She does so by countering the magisterium's rigid, patriarchal understandings of theological anthropology and Christology with a dynamic alternative rooted in the biblical Wisdom tradition. Such an understanding, she argues, focuses not on masculine symbols or the maternal status of women, but rather on the broader notion of the works of Christ. This interpretation, coupled with a feminist construal of *GS*, allows Carbine to cite the feminist public church as a sacramental and performative sign of divine presence in the world that propels us toward greater love and generativity. As a result, she retrieves faith-based political engagements as one way for women to usher in a new understanding of humanity for the Church.

Finally, Susan Abraham's essay, "Justice as the Mark of Catholic Feminist Ecclesiology," serves to deepen the claims of universality in Catholic theology by recognizing justice as the fifth mark of the church. She argues that feminist Catholics need to infuse the traditional marks of the Church—unity, holiness, catholicity, and apostolicity—with justice in order to rethink the problematic of gendered identities in the church. The ability to do so, she claims, stems from the Catholic potential to think symbolically and challenge literalist and positivist assertions of ecclesiology. Drawing specifically from Roger Haight's notion of symbol and Elisabeth Schüssler Fiorenza's understanding of ekklēsia, Abraham contends that church is not only about member-ship or a certain set of beliefs, but is also a way to envision the world and respond to the needs of the whole community. She concludes that a capacious Catholic imagination provides one way for feminist eccle-siological proposals to recast the manner in which we speak about the divine and envision the Body of Christ that worships the divine.

The pedagogical implications of the authors' reclamations of sacrament are vast. When we remember that habit is traditionally a synonym for virtue, we understand that the habit of taking the incar-nation seriously leads to the virtue of fierce and tenacious care for the world in which we live. In other words, when sacrament is not limited to seven ecclesially-regulated actions, our eyes are opened to wonder. The universe is grace-saturated, and creation, as Genesis 1 says, is very good. Our unity, holiness, catholicity, and apostolicity are not limited by gender and canon law, but derive from the grace mediated to us by creation itself. Creation, incarnation, and salvation are simultaneous and ongoing, not limited episodes in finite history.

As such Catholic sacramentality teaches us to be in the world as church, a community of equals devoted to the well-being and care of the other, and to be Church as a community of equals dedicated to the justice of Jesus. Feminist ecclesiology demonstrates the porous boundary between church as community in the world and Church as specific, ecclesial community, while demanding an equal commitment to structures of justice in each community. Feminist ecclesiology exposes these boundaries of being c/Church in multiple ways and challenges us to be schooled by the grace mediated through our material world in the virtues of compassionate justice.

The various renderings of "Church" in the essays demonstrate a commonplace in feminist theology. Feminists inhabit a variety of social locations and make distinct choices with respect to enacting a feminist response to contemporary Catholic Christianity. Feminist theology is, after all, articulated by different persons under unique circumstances with a variety of backgrounds, horizons, and interests in mind. While this variety is confirmed, the essays also demonstrate what may be one of the real sites of agreement among Catholic feminist theologians: the critique of unjust practices within the Church. It is difficult to call to mind ever having read or heard a contemporary Catholic feminist agree with the practice of excluding women from the priesthood. While they may or may not take up this issue as a primary concern within their writing, Catholic feminist theologians do seem to stand in agreement on the fact that excluding women from the priesthood stands contrary to the sacramental embrace of the body and the fundamental search for justice that should mark Catholic Christianity.

Simultaneously, the variety of responses within the essays demonstrates that there is no one way that the protest against this practice is enacted. From employing one's gifts for the transformation of an unjust practice, to the private resistance of nonparticipation, or the public claiming of women's work as the work of the church, and the utopian imaginings of a more perfect community, Catholic feminist theologians display a multiplicity of responses. This multiplicity is evident not only among Catholic feminists, but "within" the Catholic feminist herself. That is to say, at any given moment, the Catholic feminist of today may choose to follow any one of those paths or to engage more than one response simultaneously. This reflects both ambiguity and multiplicity at the same time: multiplicity in the varied options open for responding to glaring ecclesial exclusionary practices and ambiguity, in that many of us today are not finally settled on any one response as sufficient. The Catholic feminist may choose one day to claim the space of writing, working, and arguing for the transformation of an unjust Church, while another day (or that same day) find herself walking away from a community that excludes us, only to return to reclaim a space in a community saturated with grace. It is a vacillation born of ambiguity and hope—hope in the possibilities that justice might indeed reign among those who follow Jesus, ambiguity in that we have seen this possibility shattered as often as we have seen it realized. The shifting alliance with Catholicism as an institution and the Church as the organized form of that institution signals, at the same time, a commitment to follow the Jesus of justice and to refuse, as he would, all that dehumanizes.

This ambiguity, no doubt, connects us with our foremothers in the struggle. From Mary Daly's *Church and the Second Sex* and *Beyond God the Father*, to Elisabeth Schüssler Fiorenza's *In Memory of Her* and *Discipleship of Equals*, a similar ambiguity and tension run through the work of the pioneers of feminist ecclesiology. But by the time these classic texts were taught to the next generation, they had been rendered only mildly ambiguous—one trajectory representing a rejection of the Church and a subject-position termed "post-Christian" and another trajectory demonstrating a commitment to change in the Church, recognizably still Christian. The option laid before us as we began our work as Catholic feminist theologians was dualistic: stay or leave. "Christian" or "post-Christian" marked the paths available. And yet many of us wanted to take both paths as we felt in our hearts the radical critique of a Church that refused to change and continued to control women's bodies and reject women's gifts, while we also felt in our souls the deep nourishment that comes from struggling and gathering and celebrating together. No doubt our foremothers experienced this ambiguity as well, but their ambiguity was channeled into two distinctive paths when it was finally communicated to us. They felt the ambiguity, but it is perhaps for us today to embrace that ambiguity and to claim it as the place from which feminist ecclesiology is written. Simultaneously embracing and rejecting the Church is not schizophrenic, but a realistic response to a "Church" that is not any one thing but is multiple in its many different expressions. As "post–Vatican II" Catholics, we were born into a church already changed by the fresh air of the Second Vatican Council. In terms of ecclesiology, this means we were milk-fed on the idea that the Church is not a building, but the people; the Church is not best described as a hierarchy, but as the "People of God." This means that we *are* Church in all our ambiguity, in the grace and sinfulness that simultaneously mark us as human, and in the hope for justice that marks us as followers of Christ.

In the ambiguous space of Catholic feminist ecclesiology today, there are times when we look longingly at the past for options that are more clearly delineated. For many of us, our Catholic upbringing was in the saturated community of parish life, and we may look back at what we perceive to be simpler days when the Catholic community was at a peak. Following Catholic commentator Eugene Kennedy, sociologist James Davidson describes this era of Catholicism in America as Culture I Catholicism in which the Church was our "refuge."[32] In this space of Church, all of life was encompassed by the rites, roles, and rituals of the Catholic community. We lived in the same neighborhoods, prayed together, went to school together, and played together. This was a Church that was then made fresh by the winds of Vatican II. The clarity of faith and doctrine of Culture I Catholicism joined with Culture II Catholicism and its emphases on the baptismal dignity and responsibility of the laity, the people of God, and the need to be leaven for a suffering world. Who wouldn't want to be a part of it? The parish picnics, liturgical dance, vibrant music ministry, living stations of the cross, competitive education, and sports teams—who wouldn't want to stay and celebrate the change? It is only now that we can see the underside of this community brought to light, that while we prayed and played together, the young men and women of our generation were being preyed upon by our priests. Who would want to be a part of this Church? Who wouldn't want to leave and denounce the evil manifest in this community?

Catholic Christian feminist theologians have inherited this ambiguous Church, and we respond with ambiguity. We have great hope in the future of Jesus' justice and commit ourselves to being part of the grace-filled creation of God's kin-dom, but we stand with ambiguity with respect to a Church that may, or may not, ultimately be a part of that grace and justice. Finally, with the essays as representative, we insist that "being Church" is not (just) about "going to Church" and claim our place in Church as a site of both community and resistance. In doing so, the essays underscore together the ethical demands of being Church, for any form of writing the faith forward must be conscientiously and consistently dedicated to justice.

QUESTIONS FOR DISCUSSION AND REFLECTION

1. Summarize the theological reasons for and against the ordination of women in the Catholic Church. Why do those who support women's ordination and those who oppose it come to different conclusions? Which position do you think is more cogent theologically, and why?
2. Read one of the Gospels. Based on this reading, what do you think it means to act as an image or representative of Jesus Christ? Who, in your own experience, acts in this manner?
3. Explain in your own words the theological notion of the public church. Based on your independent research of contemporary U.S. and/or global news, give a few examples of religious

or faith-based engagement in social and political life. In your examples, analyze: (a) the issues that are addressed, and (b) the presence and roles of women.

4. How does the theological notion of the public church connect with other models or symbols of the church found in other chapters in this section, such as the church as prophetic or as the body of Christ? Identify some of the religious and political implications of such models or symbols for women's empowerment in the church and in society, as well as wider human and worldly well-being.

5. How does justice transform ecclesial and theological structures?

6. Does Catholic theology possess the resources to change imperial and dominating forms of theology?

FOR FURTHER READING

Steven M. Avella and Elizabeth McKeown, eds., *Public Voices: Catholics in the American Context* (Maryknoll, N.Y.: Orbis, 1999). A documentary history from colonial to the present-day United States that focuses on how bishops, political representatives, and everyday Catholics addressed issues such as slavery, war, social and international policy, sexuality, and so on from a religious perspective.

Eugene C. Bianchi and Rosemary Radford Ruether, eds. *A Democratic Catholic Church: The Reconstruction of Roman Catholicism* (New York: Crossroad, 1992). Rather than reflect on how Catholics engage in democratic politics, this collection of essays examines various theological perspectives from which to rethink internal church structures with regard to a more democratic and participatory form of Catholic Church polity, ministry, and so on.

Sara Butler, *The Catholic Priesthood and Women: A Guide to the Teaching of the Church* (Chicago: Hillenbrand Books, 2006). An exposition of the church's teaching on the reservation of the priesthood to men, a summary of the critiques of the church's teaching, and theological responses to these critiques in support of the church's position.

William J. Collinge, ed., *Faith in Public Life: Annual Publication of the College Theology Society* (Maryknoll, N.Y.: Orbis, 2008). Essays that retrieve the insights of Catholic mysticism, liberationist theologies, and social teaching to address such wide-ranging issues as poverty, war, immigration, religion and science, and church-state relations.

Edward P. Hahnenberg, *Ministries: A Relational Approach* (New York: Crossroad, 2003). A clear and comprehensive guide to the history and theology of ministry in the Catholic Church, with an emphasis on the trinitarian foundations of the new diversity of ministries in the post–Vatican II church.

Gary Macy, *The Hidden History of Women's Ordination: Female Clergy in the Medieval West* (New York: Oxford University Press, 2008). This historical study documents the variety of ministries to which women were ordained from the first through the twelfth centuries, after which the meaning of *ordination* changed and referred only to a sacrament that conferred a sacred power and was reserved for men.

Susan A. Ross, *Extravagant Affections: A Feminist Sacramental Theology* (New York: Continuum, 2001). A constructive feminist sacramental theology with particular attention to body, gender, symbol, ethics, and worship that highlights the complexity and ambiguity of sacramental practice and theology.

Peter Scott and William T. Cavanaugh, eds., *The Blackwell Companion to Political Theology* (Malden, Mass.: Blackwell, 2004). Explores major Christian figures, theological claims, and social movements—historical and contemporary, Catholic and Protestant—that highlight the interrelationship of Christianity and the political/public sphere.

Margaret O'Brien Steinfels, ed., *American Catholics in the Public Square*, 2 vols. (Lanham: Sheed and Ward, 2004). Examines Catholic social theology that underlies grassroots, lay, and institutional examples of the Catholic Church's sociopolitical presence and activism in the United States.

U.S. Conference of Catholic Bishops, *Forming Consciences for Faithful Citizenship: A Call to Political Responsibility from the Catholic Bishops of the United States* (Washington, D.C.: USCCB, 2007), available at http://www.faithfulcitizenship.org/church/statements. Advocates a broad social justice agenda in U.S. civic life and public policy based on the fundamental moral principles of Catholic Social Teaching, namely, the protection and promotion of human dignity and the common good.

Natalie K. Watson, *Introducing Feminist Ecclesiology* (Cleveland: Pilgrim, 2002). An overview of major topics in feminist ecclesiology, such as feminist theological reconstructions of the church's self-understanding, liturgical theology and praxis, ministry, and sacraments.

NOTES

PREFACE

[1] See Anne M. Clifford, *Introducing Feminist Theology* (Maryknoll, N.Y.: Orbis, 2001), 16–38, for a succinct, historical summary of forms of feminist thought and feminist theology.

[2] See Elizabeth A. Johnson, *She Who Is: The Mystery of God in Feminist Theological Discourse* (New York: Crossroad, 1992), 216–22, for a discussion of these feminist themes within the context of Trinitarian theology.

[3] Johnson, *She Who Is*, 216.

[4] Johnson, *She Who Is*, 29–30. See also Clifford, *Introducing Feminist Theology*, 35, for a somewhat different delineation of the methodology.

[5] Rosemary Radford Ruether, *Sexism and God-Talk: Toward a Feminist Theology* (Boston: Beacon, 1993), 18–19. Note that this is the tenth-anniversary edition.

CHAPTER 1

1. Michel de Certeau, *The Practice of Everyday Life,* trans. Steven F. Rendall (Berkeley: University of California Press, 1984), 115.

2. For a riveting analysis of how "we are all hybrids," particularly in relation to the world's religions, see Jeannine Hill Fletcher, *Monopoly on Salvation? A Feminist Approach to Religious Pluralism* (New York: Continuum, 2005), 82–101.

3. Gregor Mendel, *Experiments in Plant-Hybridisation* (1866; repr., Cambridge: Harvard University Press, 1938).

4. See Homi Bhabha, *The Location of Culture* (London: Routledge, 1994); Robert J. C. Young, *Colonial Desire: Hybridity in Theory, Culture and Race* (London: Routledge, 1995); and Samira Kawash, *Dislocating the Color Line:*

Identity, Hybridity, and Singularity in African-American Narrative (Stanford: Stanford University Press, 1997).

5. "Sen. Barack Obama Addresses Race at the Constitution Center in Philadelphia," http://www.washingtonpost.com/wp-dyn/content/article/2008/03/18/AR2008031801081.html (accessed March 21, 2008).

6. Gen. 1:27 NRSV.

7. Gen. 2:21-22 NRSV.

8. John 2:3-4 NRSV.

9. The notion of Jesus as "host" carries over into the liturgical tradition where Jesus becomes the host through ritual and memory through the sacrament of the Eucharist. Arguably, in proposing that through communion, "we recognize him in those around the table, we repent our collusion and complicity in their suffering and oppression, we ask his and their forgiveness, we share the body of the Lord, we *become* the body of the Lord," M. Shawn Copeland posits the Eucharist as an event illustrative of what I call "claiming hybridity," whereby solidarity has the potential to emerge through God's presence in the overlapping and intertwining stories with others. See M. Shawn Copeland, "Body, Race, and Being," in *Constructive Theology: A Contemporary Approach to Classical Themes*, ed. Serene Jones and Paul Lakeland (Minneapolis: Fortress Press, 2005), 115–16.

10. Luke 14:12-14 NRSV.

11. For groundbreaking and innovative feminist theological readings of table fellowship and table sharing, see Letty M. Russell, *Church in the Round: Feminist Interpretation of the Church* (Louisville: Westminster John Knox, 1993); and Elisabeth Schüssler Fiorenza, *In Memory of Her: A Feminist Theological Reconstruction of Christian Origins*, Tenth Anniversary Ed. (New York: Crossroad, 1994).

12. Jones and Lakeland, *Constructive Theology*, 168.

13. For more on the theopolitical implications of a hybridized "Jesus/Christ," see Kwok Pui-lan, *Postcolonial Imagination and Feminist Theology* (Louisville: Westminster John Knox, 2005), 171–74.

14. See Gloria Anzaldúa, *Borderlands/La Frontera: The New Mestiza* (San Francisco: Aunt Lute Books, 1987). See also, Roberto S. Goizueta, *Caminemos con Jesús: Toward a Hispanic/Latino Theology of Accompaniment* (Maryknoll, N.Y.: Orbis, 1995).

15. See Victor Anderson, *Beyond Ontological Blackness: An Essay on African American Religious and Cultural Criticism* (New York: Continuum, 1995).

16. Serene Jones, *Feminist Theory and Christian Theology: Cartographies of Grace* (Minneapolis: Fortress Press, 2000), 70.

17. For a discussion of the four avenues by which bias occurs, see *Collected Works of Bernard Lonergan*, ed. Frederick E. Crowe and Robert Doran, vol. 3, *Insight: A Study of Human Understanding* (Toronto: University of Toronto Press, 1997), 214–20.

18. For an interesting discussion of the connections between mother-hood and spiritual development, see Trudelle Thomas, "Becoming a Mother: Matrescence as Spiritual Formation," *Religious Education* 96, no 1 (2001): 88–105.

19. This romanticized notion of mother can be found in the work of Swiss theologian Hans Urs von Balthasar among others. For explicit ecclesio-logical and implicit anthropological claims related to his understanding of sexual difference and motherhood, see Hans Urs von Balthasar, "Woman's Answer," in *Theo-Drama: Theological Dramatic Theory*, vol. 3, *The Dramatis Personae: The Person in Christ*, trans. Graham Harrison (San Francisco: Ignatius Press, 1992), 283–360, and "The All-Embracing Motherhood of the Church," in *The Office of Peter and the Structure of the Church*, trans. Andrée Emery (San Francisco: Ignatius, 1986), 183–225.

20. For more on the myths around motherhood, see Susan J. Douglas and Meredith W. Michaels, *The Mommy Myth: The Idealization of Motherhood and How It Has Undermined All Women* (New York: Free, 2004), and also see Shari L. Thurer, *The Myths of Motherhood: How Culture Reinvents the Good Mother* (New York: Penguin, 1994).

21. For more on how strategic essentialism can be used in construc-tive feminist theological projects, see Jones, *Feminist Theory and Christian Theology*, 59–61.

22. Julia Kristeva, "Motherhood according to Giovanni Bellini" in *Desire in Language: A Semiotic Approach to Literature and Art*, ed. Leon S. Roudiez, trans. Thomas Gora, Alice Jardine, and Leon S. Roudiez (New York: Columbia University Press, 1980), 237.

23. Cristina Mazzoni, *Maternal Impressions: Pregnancy and Childbirth in Literature and Theory* (Ithaca, N.Y.: Cornell University Press, 2002), ix, 206.

24. Christina Baker Kline, introduction, in *Child of Mine: Writers Talk about the First Year of Motherhood*, ed. Christina Baker Kline (New York: Hyperion, 1997), 6.

25. For her groundbreaking work, see Adrienne Rich, *Of Woman Born: Motherhood as Experience and Institution* (New York: Bantam Books, 1976). See also Judith Plaskow, "Woman as Body: Motherhood and Dualism," *Anima* 8, no. 1 (1981): 56–67; Sara Ruddick, *Maternal Thinking: Toward a Politics of Peace* (Boston: Beacon Press, 1989); and Julia Kristeva, "Stabat Mater," in *Tales of Love*, trans. Leon S. Roudiez (New York: Columbia University Press, 1987), 234–63.

26. Rich, *Of Woman Born*, 3.

27. Ibid., 2.

28. Kline, introduction, 3.

CHAPTER 2

1. This is a turn on the word *latinamente*, which serves as an adjective to mean (roughly) "a Hispanic way of being." It was used by Miguel Díaz

in his book *On Being Human,* in the following context: "U.S. Hispanic theological anthropology can be defined as the effort by U.S. Hispanic theologians to elucidate the relationship between God and what is 'Hispanically' or *Latinamente* human" (Maryknoll, N.Y.: Orbis, 2001, 24). The emphasis that I have placed in the word highlights the particular nature of Latina and Latin American female humanity, which is the focus of this essay.

2. I was first made aware of the enormity of the sexual slave trade through the prophetic witness of Mu Sochua, Nobel Prize nominee, Cambodian ambassador and activist, whose work is highlighted in the documentary *The Virgin Harvest* (http://www.priorityfilms.com/harvest.html). See also Agnes M. Brazal and Andrea Lizares, eds., *Body and Sexuality: Theological-Pastoral Perspectives of Women in Asia* (Manila: Ateneo de Manila University Press, 2007). From this awakening, I was led to resources that documented the plight of Latin American girls and women being sold by their own families in similar fashion (http://www.libertadlatina.org/Index.htm).

3. The norm of heterosexism exacerbates this dynamic, as seen in the contributions of the authors of *The Sexuality of Latinas,* Norma Alarcón, Ana Castillo, and Cherríe Moraga, eds. (Berkeley: Third Woman Press, 1993), particularly, Claudia Colindres' "A Letter to My Mother" and Moraga's "The Obedient Daughter." See also Marya Muñoz Vásquez' "The Effects of Role Expectations on the Marital Status of Urban Puerto Rican Women," in *The Puerto Rican Woman: Perspectives on Culture, History and Society*, 2nd ed. (New York: Praeger, 1986).

4. http://www.unodc.org/unodc/en/hiv-aids/people-vulnerable-to-human-trafficking.html.

5. Pope John Paul II, *Man and Woman He Created Them: A Theology of the Body*, trans., intro. and index by Michael Waldstein (Boston: Pauline, 2006), 257.

6. In his introduction to the main text, Waldstein outlines Cardinal Wojtyla's convergence and divergence with the philosophy of Immanuel Kant around the themes of personalism, autonomy, and their implications toward an interpretation of sex and marriage; John Paul II affirms that we are who we were called to be from the beginning (Genesis) when we give of ourselves to others, when we "express the love by which man, through masculinity or femininity becomes a gift for another," *Man and Woman He Created Them,* 258.

7. Michelle A. Gonzalez, *Created in God's Image: An Introduction to Feminist Theological Anthropology* (Maryknoll, N.Y.: Orbis, 2007), 159.

8. David Kelsey, "Human Being," in *Christian Theology: An Introduction to Its Traditions and Tasks*, ed. Peter Hodgson and Robert H. King (Philadelphia: Fortress Press, 1985), 177.

9. Roberto Goizueta, *Caminemos con Jesús: Towards a Hispanic/Latino Theology of Accompaniment* (Maryknoll, N.Y.: Orbis, 1995).

10. Ibid., 48.

11. Ibid., 205.

12. Gonzalez, *Created in God's Image*, 69.

13. Díaz, *On Being Human*, 109.

14. By this term "double cross," I suggest that the double scourge of HIV/AIDS and human trafficking, *as well as* the distortions of religion and culture, have created an unbearable burden which Latin American women and Latinas have been forced to bear.

15. This is called *simpatía*, in which the importance of nonconfrontational relationships is emphasized. See Peragallo et al., "Latinas' Perspectives on HIV/AIDS: Cultural Issues to Consider in Prevention," in *Hispanic Health Care Internationa* 1 (2002): 11–22; and Miguel de la Torre, *Beyond Machismo, The Annual of the Society of Christian Ethics* 19 (1999): 213–33.

16. Ivone Gebara, *Out of the Depths: Women's Experience of Evil and Salvation* (Minneapolis: Augsburg Fortress Press, 2002), 88.

17. Paragraphs 599–623 outline the theological foundations of Roman Catholic Church teaching on Christ's redemptive death in God's plan for salvation. *Catechism of the Catholic Church* (Mahwah, N.J.: Paulist, 1994), 155–61.

18. Both Martin Luther and John Calvin offer a vision of God who, while no longer requiring wrathful retribution, needs to substitute the fall of humanity with the rising of the new Adam. Luther claims that Jesus died the death of a guilty person, a thief, according to the law of Moses: "He has and bears all the sins of men in His body—not in the sense that he committed them but in the sense that he took these sins, committed by us, upon his own body in order to make satisfaction for them with his own blood." Similarly, Calvin places humanity's reconciliation and peace with God on the mantle of Jesus' suffering and death: "Because trembling consciences find repose only in sacrifice and cleansing by which sins are expiated, we are duly directed thither; and for us the substance of life is set in the death of Christ." See Martin Luther, *The Galatian Lectures* on Galatians 2:16 and 3:13 (1535), and John Calvin, *Institutes of the Christian Religion*, 2.12–17.

19. Eleazar S. Fernandez, *Reimagining the Human: Theological Anthropology in Response to Systemic Evil* (St. Louis: Chalice, 2004), 13.

20. Ibid., 187.

21. John Paul II, "The Song of Songs," in *Theology of the Body*, 548–92.

22. Fernandez's third chapter, "A Theological Reading of the Interlocking Forms of Oppression," underscores the ways in which systemic sin, which he equates with evil, "demands not only individual confession and conversion but also the transformation of our collective ways of being, acting

and thinking. . . . What must happen is social conversion or social transformation," *Reimagining the Human*, 69.

23. Gonzalez, *Created in God's Image*, 160. In addition, the work of Ada María Isasi-Díaz, particularly in *Mujerista Theology: A Theology for the 21st Century* (New York: Orbis, 1996, 129), emphasizes that *"familia/comunidad* for Latinos/as does not subsume the person but rather emphasizes that the person is constituted by this entity . . . the individual person and the community have a dialogical relationship through which the person reflects the *familia/comunidad."*

24. Christopher J. Morse, "Salvation," in *Not Every Spirit: A Dogmatics of Christian Disbelief* (Valley Forge, Penn.: Trinity, 1994), 231–39.

25. "To theologically speak of grace . . . means that we speak (and can only speak) about the human experience of grace,"Orlando O. Espín, "An Exploration into the Theology of Grace and Sin," in *From the Heart of Our People: Latino/a Explorations in Catholic Systematic Theology*, ed. Orlando O. Espín and Miguel H. Díaz (Maryknoll, N.Y.: Orbis, 1999), 123–24.

26. John Paul II, 75:3, in *Theology of the Body*, 421.

27. Donald DeMarco, "The Virgin Mary and the Culture of Life," in *The Virgin Mary and Theology of the Body* (Stockbridge, Mass.: Marian Press, 2005), 74–75. DeMarco draws from the writings of St. Edith Stein to emphasize his point that the fallen and perverted feminine nature, as marked by Eve, can be restored to purity and health only through surrender to God, marked by the Virgin Mother. "Paradoxically, it is through this surrender that a woman achieves her fulfillment both as a woman and as a human being."

28. Ivone Gebara, *Out of the Depths: Women's Experience of Evil and Salvation*, trans. Ann Patrick Ware (Minneapolis: Fortress Press, 2002).

29. Ibid., 106.

30. Ibid., 107.

31. According to the Centers for Disease Control, African American women have the highest rate of HIV/AIDS infection in the United States, with a diagnosis rate of 50 percent of all cases in 2005. This is both frightening and appalling, reflecting the reality of present-day slavery, not simply as a legacy of the past. Also, African and Asian women are trafficked across borders within their respective continents as much as Latin American women are in the Western Hemisphere. See also M. Herrera, "Who do you say Jesus is? Christological reflections from a Hispanic woman's perspective," in *Reconstructing the Christ Symbol* (Mahwah, N.J.: Paulist, 1993), for a Latina reconstruction of Christology grounded in the contemporary context of Latinas in the United States.

32. Delores S. Williams's seminal work on black women's surrogacy experience (on which her full-length book *Sisters in the Wilderness* [Maryknoll, N.Y.: Orbis, 1993] is based) is reprinted in *Cross Examinations:*

Readings on the Meaning of the Cross Today, ed. Marit Trelstad (Minneapolis: Augsburg Fortress, 2006), as well as JoAnne Marie Terrell's work on sacrifice, treated more fully in her text *Power in the Blood? The Cross in the African American Experience* (Maryknoll, N.Y.: Orbis, 1998).

33. Williams, *Sisters in the Wilderness*, 166–67.

34. Terrell, *Cross Examinations*, 48–49.

35. Marcella Althaus-Reid, *From Feminist Theology to Indecent Theology: Readings on Poverty, Sexual Identity and God* (London: SCM Press, 2004), 39.

36. Ibid., 31–32.

CHAPTER 3

1. This title is borrowed from Diana L. Hayes's book, *Hagar's Daughters: Womanist Ways of Being in the World* (Mahwah, N.J.: Paulist, 1995).

2. Emilie M. Townes, *Womanist Ethics and the Cultural Production of Evil* (New York: Palgrave Macmillan, 2006), 29–55.

3. Some African American women self-identify as womanists because they resonate with its ethos, which is characterized by an affirmation and celebration of black women,women of color, and their communities.

4. I use the descriptors black and African American interchangeably in this essay.

5. Cyprian Davis, *The History of Black Catholics in the United States* (New York: Crossroads, 1990).

6. Patricia Hill Collins, *Black Feminist Thought: Knowledge, Consciousness, and the Politics of Empowerment* (New York: Routledge, 1999), 69ff.

7. Jacques Steinberg, "All Forgiven: WIMUS-AM Is on a Roll," *New York Times*, February 3, 2009, http://www.nytimes.com/2008/02/03/weekinreview/03steinberg.html?pagewanted=print (accessed on February 3, 2009).

8. M. Shawn Copeland, "Womanist Theology," in *New Catholic Encyclopedia* (2003), 14:822.

9. Cyprian Davis and Jamie Phelps, eds., "Stamped with the Image of God": African Americans as God's Image in Black (Maryknoll, N.Y.: Orbis Books, 2003).

10. Alice Walker, *In Search of Our Mothers' Gardens: Womanist Prose* (New York: Harcourt Brace Jovanovich, 1983), xi.

11. Ibid., xi.

12. Ibid., xii.

13. Katie G. Cannon, Allison P. Gise Johnson, and Angela D. Sims, "Living It Out: Womanist Works in Word," *Journal of Feminist Studies in Religion* 21, no. 2 (2005): 137.

14. Cannon, Johnson, and Sims, "Living It Out," 137.

15. Stephen J. Duffy, *The Graced Horizon: Nature and Grace in Modern Catholic Thought* (Collegeville, Minn.: Liturgical, 1992), 13.

16. Ibid., 13.

17. Roger Haight, "Sin and Grace," in *Systematic Theology: Roman Catholic Perspectives*, vol. 2, ed. Francis Schüssler Fiorenza and John P. Galvin (Minneapolis: Fortress Press, 1991), 109.

18. Ibid., 110.

19. Mercy Amba Oduyoye, "The African Experience of God through the Eyes of an Akan Woman," *Cross Currents* 47, no. 4 (1997–1998): 494.

20. Ibid., 494.

21. Zora Neale Hurston, *Their Eyes Were Watching God* (New York: HarperCollins, 2000), 17.

22. Valerie Boyd, *Wrapped in Rainbows: The Life of Zora Neale Hurston* (New York: Simon & Schuster, 2003), 263.

23. Edward Schillebeeckx, *Christ: The Experience of Jesus as Lord* (New York: Crossroad, 1980), 737.

24. Ibid., 738.

25. Ibid.

26. Ibid., 739.

27. Ibid., 740.

28. See Paula J. Gidding's *A Sword among Lions: Ida B. Wells and the Campaign against Lynching* (New York: HarperCollins, 2008) and M. Shawn Copland, *The Subversive Power of Love: The Vision of Henriette Delille* (New York: Paulist, 2009).

29. Schillebeeckx, *Christ*, 740.

30. Ibid.

31. Ibid.

32. Copeland, "The New Anthropological Subject at the Heart of the Mystical Body of Christ," *Proceedings of the Fifty-Third Annual Convention of the Catholic Theological Society of America* (1998): 53:27.

33. Ibid., 37.

34. Gustavo Esteva and Madhu Suri Prakash, *Grassroots Post-Modernism: Remaking the Soil of Cultures* (New York: Zed, 1998), 16–17.

35. Renita Weems, *Just a Sister Away: Understanding the Timeless Connection of Women Today and Women in the Bible* (New York: Grand Central Publishing, 2005).

36. This is borrowed from Delores S. Williams's seminal book *Sisters in the Wilderness: The Challenge of Womanist God-Talk* (Maryknoll, N.Y.: Orbis, 1993).

37. Patricia Hill Collins, *Black Sexual Politics: African Americans, Gender, and the New Racism* (New York: Routledge, 2005), 283.

38. From the Center for Minority Health, Department of Health and Human Services, http://www.omhrc.gov/templates/content.aspx?lvl=3&lvlID=537&ID=6456 (accessed on February 7, 2009).

39. From the Centers for Disease and Control Prevention, Department of Health and Human Services, http://www.cdc.gov/hiv/topics/women/resources/factsheets/women.htm (accessed on February 7, 2009).

40. Borrowed from Cyprian Davis and Jamie T. Phelps, *Stamped with the Image of God: African Americans as God's Image in Black* (Maryknoll, N.Y.: Orbis, 2004).

41. See St. Irenaeus *Adversus haereses* IV.20.7.

CHAPTER 4

1. Kwok Pui-lan, "Engendering Christ: Who Do You Say That I Am?" in *Postcolonial Imagination and Feminist Theology* (Louisville: Westminster John Knox, 2005), 171.

2. This is Roland Robertson's term. See his "Church-State Relations and the World System," in *Church-State Relations: Tensions and Transitions*, ed. Thomas Robbins and Roland Robertson (New Brunswick, N.J.: Transaction, 1987), 39–52.

3. Elisabeth Schüssler Fiorenza, *The Book of Revelation: Justice and Judgment*, 2nd ed. (Minneapolis: Fortress Press, 1998), 4.

4. Tina Beattie, *God's Mother, Eve's Advocate: A Marian Narrative of Women's Salvation* (New York: Continuum, 2002), 39.

5. Nancy Julia Chodorow, "Gender, Relation, and Difference in Psychoanalytic Perspective," in *Feminist Social Thought*, ed. Diana Tietjens Meyers (New York and London: Routledge, 1997), 11. Reprinted from *Socialist Review* 9, no. 46 (1979): 51–69.

6. Judith Butler, revisiting Sigmund Freud's theory of separation and mourning in *Gender Trouble: Feminism and the Subversion of Identity*, 2nd ed. (New York: Routledge, 1990), 78.

7. Recent writings on the role of Mary in Christian theology have tended to see her importance as "mother of God" substantively in the form of her accepting impregnation, providing the site for gestation, and birthing a savior into the world. See, for example, *Mary, Mother of God*, ed. Carl E. Braaten and Robert W. Jenson (Grand Rapids: Eerdmans, 2004). Feminist reclaimings of an alternative portrait include the historical-critical work of Elizabeth Johnson, *Truly Our Sister* (New York: Continuum, 2006) and earlier in the work of Rosemary Radford Ruether, *Sexism and God-Talk* (Boston: Beacon, 1983).

8. Judith Butler, "Beside Oneself: On the Limits of Sexual Autonomy," in *Undoing Gender* (New York: Routledge, 2004), 18.

9. Catherine Keller, "Seeking and Sucking: On Relation and Essence in Feminist Theology," in *Horizons in Feminist Theology: Identity, Tradition and Norms*, ed. Rebecca S. Chopp and Sheila Greeve Davaney (Minneapolis: Fortress Press, 1997), 58.

10. Morwenna Griffiths, *Feminisms and the Self: The Web of Identity* (New York: Routledge, 1995), 92.

11. Linell Elizabeth Cady, "Identity, Feminist Theory and Theology," in *Horizons in Feminist Theology,* ed. Chopp and Davaney, 24.

12. Elisabeth Schüssler Fiorenza, *In Memory of Her: A Feminist Theological Reconstruction of Christian Origins* (New York: Crossroad, 1992) 135.

13. Clement of Alexandria, *The Instructor,* 1.6. on Paul's 1 Corinthians 3:2, in *AnteNicene Fathers: Translations of the Writings of the Fathers Down to AD 325,* vol. 2, ed. Alexander Roberts and James Donaldson (Grand Rapids: Eerdmans, 1951), 218.

14. Caroline Walker Bynum, *Jesus as Mother: Studies in the Spirituality of the High Middle Ages* (Berkeley: University of California Press, 1982), 114.

15. Ibid., 117, quoting Bernard of Clairvaux, Letter 322, PL 182: col. 527.

16. Ibid., 123, quoting Aelred *De institutione,* chap. 26, *Opera omnia* 1:658; trans. M. P. Mcpherson, in *The Works of Aelred of Rievaulx* 1: *Treatises and Pastoral Prayer* (Spencer, Mass.: Cistercian Fathers, 1971), 73.

17. Margaret R. Miles, *A Complex Delight: The Secularization of the Breast 1350–1750* (Berkeley: University of California Press, 2008), 33–53.

18. According to Gail Paterson Corrington, the earliest Christian use of the image of lactating mother echoes pre-Christian religious traditions in the figure of Isis lactans. Corrington's argument is that the image itself becomes dissociated from real women's experiences as it gets transferred to a God-imaged male. See Gail Paterson Corrington, "The Milk of Salvation: Redemption by the Mother in Late Antiquity and Early Christianity," *Harvard Theological Review* 82, no. 4 (Oct. 1989): 393–420.

19. I am especially aware of the diversity of reasons why women do and do not breast-feed—ranging from cultural practices to economic need *not* to breast-feed—and women for whom breast-feeding is a source of death for the child, for example, in the lives of women with AIDS. My aim is not to identify breast-feeding as the desired practice, but rather, recognizing that it is a practice for some women, to draw from this experience theological insights.

20. Valerie Saiving Goldstein, "The Human Condition: A Feminine View," *Journal of Religion* 40, no. 2 (April 1960): 100–112.

21. Butler, *Undoing Gender,* 24.

22. This quote is from *The Philosophical Challenge of Religious Diversity,* ed. Philip L. Quinn and Kevin Meeker (New York: Oxford University Press, 2000), 2. It represents how interreligious dialogue is often conceived as a conflictual comparison, rather than the source of theological insight and cooperative solidarities.

23. This comes from Aelred of Rievaulx (d. 1167), quoted in Bynum, 124.

24. Homi Bhabha, keynote address of Conference on *Sex and Religion in Migration,* Yale University, September 15, 2005.

25. Lina Gupta, "Affirmation of Self: A Hindu Woman's Journey," in *Women's Voices in World Religions*, ed. Hille Haker et. al. (London: SCM, 2006), 90.

26. See, for example, Elizabeth Cady Stanton, *Eighty Years and More: Reminiscences 1815–1897* (Boston: Northeastern University Press, 1993).

27. Delores S. Williams, "Black Women's Surrogacy Experience and the Christian Notion of Redemption," in *After Patriarchy: Feminist Transformations of the World's Religions*, ed. Paula M. Cooey, William R. Eakin, and Jay B. McDaniel (Maryknoll, N.Y.: Orbis, 1991), 1–14.

28. Leila Ahmed, *A Border Passage: From Cairo to America—A Woman's Journey* (New York: Penguin, 2000).

29. Radha Kumar, *The History of Doing: An Illustrated Account of Movements for Women's Rights and Feminism in India 1800–1990* (London: Verso, 1993).

30. It is important to note that these constructions of "mother" may or may not have been created by those who inhabit them, and may or may not be willingly inhabited. Whether or not a particular construction of mother is liberating and life-giving requires closer analysis of the context and the lives impacted by a particular way of framing motherhood.

CHAPTER 5

1. For an early use of this phrase, see Leonard Swidler, "Jesus Was a Feminist," *Catholic World* (Jan. 1971): 177–83.

2. See Rosemary Radford Ruether, *Faith and Fratricide: The Theological Roots of Anti-Semitism* (New York: Seabury, 1974), for an early study by a Catholic feminist theologian of the development of anti-Jewish theology and its effects on Christology.

3. See Mary Christine Athans, "Anti-Semitism? or Anti-Judaism?" in *Introduction to Jewish-Christian Relations*, ed. Michael Shermis and Arthur E. Zannoni (New York: Paulist Press, 1991), 118–44 for an introduction to the terms, the relationship between the terms, and the relationship of both terms to the *Shoah*.

4. Jules Isaac, *The Teaching of Contempt: Christian Roots of Anti-Semitism*, trans. Helen Weaver (New York: Holt, Rinehart, and Winston, 1964).

5. See, for example, Heinz Schreckenberg, *The Jews in Christian Art: An Ilustrated History* (New York: Continuum, 1996).

6. See *Guidelines on Implementing the Conciliar Document Nostra Aetate, 1974, Guidelines on Preaching and Catechesis in the Roman Catholic Church, 1985,* and *We Remember: A Reflection on the Shoah, 1998.* These documents are issued by the Vatican's Commission on Religious Relations with the Jews and are available at http://www.vatican.va/roman_curia/pontifical_councils/chrstuni/sub-index/index_relations-jews.htm.

7. Judith Plaskow, "Christian Feminism and Anti-Judaism," *Cross Currents* (Fall 1978): 306–9 (308).

8. Mary Boys, "Patriarchal Judaism, Liberating Jesus: A Feminist Misrepresentation," *Union Seminary Quarterly Review* 56:3–4 (2002): 50.

9. Rosemary Radford Ruether, "Motherearth and the Megamachine: A Theology of Liberation in a Feminine, Somatic and Ecological Perspective," in *Womanspirit Rising: A Feminist Reader in Religion,* ed. Carol P. Christ and Judith Plaskow (San Francisco: Harper and Row, 1979), 43–52.

10. Ruether, "Motherearth and the Megamachine, see esp. 47–48.

11. Susannah Heschel, "Feminism and Jewish-Christian Dialogue," in *Introducing Jewish-Christian Relations,* ed. Michael Shermis and Arthur E. Zannoni (Mahwah, N.J.: Paulist, 1991), 233.

12. Amy-Jill Levine, "Lilies of the Field and Wandering Jews: Biblical Scholarship, Women's Roles, and Social Location," in *Transformative Encounters: Jesus and Women Re-Viewed,* ed. Ingrid R. Kitzberger (Leiden: Brill, 2000), 329–52. "Second Temple Judaism, Jesus, and Women: Yeast of Eden," *Biblical Interpretation* 2, no. 1 (1994): 8–33.

13. See Paula Fredriksen, *Jesus of Nazareth King of the Jews: A Jewish Life and the Emergence of Christianity* (New York: Alfred A. Knopf, 1999), 197–207, for an accessible account of the significance of purity legislation in the late Second Temple period; see also 104–10 and passim.

14. Levine, "Lilies of the Field," 335–37.

15. Levine directs the reader to Joanna Dewey, "The Gospel of Mark," in *Searching the Scriptures: A Feminist Commentary, Vol. II,* ed. Elisabeth Schüssler Fiorenza (New York: Crossroad, 1994), 481.

16. Levine, "Yeast of Eden," 11.

17. Dewey, "The Gospel of Mark," 481.

18. Turid Karlsen Seim, "The Gospel of Luke," in *Searching the Scripture,* ed. Schüssler Fiorenza, 739.

19. See note 13; Fredriksen guides my thinking in this section, but others such as Levine and Boys also argue for understanding Jesus as a Jew in his time.

20. Fredricksen, *Jesus of Nazareth,* 203.

21. Heschel, "Feminism and Jewish-Christian Relations," 241.

22. Levine, "Lilies of the Field," 332.

23. See note 14 and Judith Plaskow, "Blaming Jews for Inventing Patriarchy," *Lilith* 7 (1980): 11–12, 14–17.

24. Ibid., 12.

25. Ibid., 12.

26. See, for example, Amy-Jill Levine, "Women Like This," in *New Perspectives on Jewish Women in the Greco-Roman World* (Atlanta: Scholars, 1991); and Ross Shepard Kraemer, *Her Share of the Blessings: Women's Religions among Pagans, Jews, and Christians in the Greco-Roman World* (New York: Oxford University Press, 1992).

27. For a classic, systematic treatment of the dynamics of Jewish feminism, see Judith Plaskow, *Standing Again at Sinai: Judaism from a Feminist Perspective* (New York: Harper Collins, 1990), esp. chap. 2 "Torah: Reshaping Jewish Memory."

28. See 1 Peter 3:15.

CHAPTER 6

1. Here, it is important to acknowledge that oppression of women is not symmetrical. As feminist thinkers have illustrated, a woman's identity is simultaneously constructed by the multiple categories of race, class, sexuality, age, nationality, physical ability, and so on. Because women are not a homogenous group, feminists are called to recognize the particular mixture of identities, as well as the multilayered and disproportional experiences of oppression that it entails. For further reading on "intersectionality," see Kimberlé Crenshaw, "Mapping the Margins: Intersectionality, Identity Politics, and Violence against Women of Color," in *Identities: Race, Class, Gender and Nationality,* ed. Linda Martín Alcoff and Eduardo Mendieta (Malden, Mass.: Blackwell, 2003), 175–200.

2. Elizabeth Johnson, "The Maleness of Christ," in *The Power of Naming: A Concilium Reader in Feminist Liberation Theology,* ed. Elisabeth Schüssler Fiorenza (Maryknoll, N.Y.: Concilium, 1996), 307.

3. Sandra M. Schneiders, *Women and the Word: The Gender of God in the New Testament and the Spirituality of Women* (New York: Paulist Press, 1986), 50.

4. Rosemary Radford Ruether, *Sexism and God-Talk: Toward a Feminist Theology* (Boston: Beacon, 1983), 117.

5. Sacred Congregation for the Doctrine of Faith, "Declaration on the Question of the Admission of Women to the Ministerial Priesthood," written and published at the behest of Pope Paul VI, October 15, 1976; available at http://www.newadvent.org/library/docs_df76ii.htm.

6. Ibid.

7. Ibid.

8. Ruether, *Sexism and God-Talk,* 116–38.

9. Gregory of Nazianzus, *Letter to Cleodonius.*

10. Lisa Isherwood, *Introducing Feminist Christologies* (Cleveland: Pilgrim, 2002), 28.

11. Daphne Hampson, *Theology and Feminism* (Cambridge, Mass.: Blackwell, 1990), 50–81.

12. See Mary Daly, *Beyond God the Father: Toward a Philosophy of Women's Liberation* (1973; repr., Boston: Beacon, 1985) and Naomi Goldenberg, *The Changing of the Gods: Feminism and the End of Traditional Religions* (Boston: Beacon, 1979).

13. For an overview of these Christologies, see Isherwood, *Introducing Feminist Christologies*.

14. Pope John Paul II, "On the Dignity and Vocation of Women: *Mulieris Dignitatem*," August 15, 1988; available at http://www.vatican.va/holy_father/john_paul_ii/apost_letters/documents/hf_jp-ii_apl_15081988_mulieris-dignitatem_en.html.

15. Karen Trimble Alliaume, "Disturbingly Catholic: Thinking the Inordinate Body," in *Bodily Citations: Religion and Judith Butler*, ed. Ellen T. Armour and Susan M. St. Ville (New York: Columbia University Press, 2006), 97–102.

16. Ibid., 100.

17. Ibid., 100–102.

18. Ibid., 97.

19. See Judith Butler, *Gender Trouble: Feminism and the Subversion of Identity* (New York: Routledge, 1990).

20. Ibid., 137–40.

21. In her work, *Undoing Gender*, Butler recalls attending a drag show and realizing that "some of these so-called men could do femininity much better than [she] ever could, ever wanted to, ever would." See Judith Butler, *Undoing Gender* (New York: Routledge, 2004), 213.

22. Ibid., 105–6.

23. Ibid., 104–6.

24. Ibid., 102.

25. Ibid., 102.

26. Ibid., 100–102. Alliaume's essay offers two performative readings of feminist Christologies: the Roman Catholic woman priest movement, which "illicitly" ordained several women to the priesthood, and Eleanor McLaughlin's essay "Feminist Christologies: Re-dressing the Tradition," which likens Jesus to a transvestite. For Alliaume, these Christological citations "recontextualize" the body of Christ by inciting the simultaneous recognition of two supposedly incompatible things, specifically womanhood and priesthood. See 108, 109–16.

27. Butler, *Undoing Gender*, 109.

28. Ibid., 102.

29. Karen Trimble Alliaume, "The Risks of Repeating Ourselves: Reading Feminist/Womanist Figures of Jesus," *Cross Currents* 48, no. 2 (Summer 1998): 198–217.

30. Alliaume, "Disturbingly Catholic," 98.

31. Elizabeth Conde-Frazier, "Latina Women and Immigration," *Journal of Latin American Theology* 3, no. 2 (2008): 54–75.

32. Ibid.," 58.

33. What follows is my summary of the story as told by Conde-Frazier. in Ibid., 67–74.

34. Lisa Isherwood, "The Embodiment of Feminist Liberation Theology: The Spiralling of Incarnation," *Feminist Theology* 12, no. 2 (2004): 145.

35. Michael J. Himes, *The Mystery of Faith: An Introduction to Catholicism* (Cincinnati: St. Anthony Messenger, 2003), 19–28.

36. Rosemary Radford Ruether, "Christology and Patriarchy," in *Thinking of Christ: Proclamation, Explanation, Meaning*, ed. Tatha Wiley (New York: Continuum, 2003).

CHAPTER 7

1. Pontifical Biblical Commission, "Can Women Be Priests?" *Origins* 6 (July 1, 1976): 92–96.

2. See Gary Macy, *The Hidden History of Women's Ordination: Female Clergy in the Medieval West* (New York: Oxford University Press, 2008); Phyllis Zagano, *Holy Saturday: An Argument for the Restoration of the Female Diaconate in the Catholic Church* (New York: Crossroad, 2000).

3. Cited in Zagano, *Holy Saturday*, 95.

4. Gary Macy, "The Ordination of Women in the Early Middle Ages," *Theological Studies* 61 (September 2000): 490–93.

5. Miriam Therese Winter, *Out of the Depths: The Story of Ludmila Javorova, Ordained Roman Catholic Priest* (New York: Crossroad, 2001), 177, 227.

6. *Lumen gentium*, ¶10, pars. 39–42.

7. Ibid., ¶29; Zagano, *Holy Saturday*.

8. For references, see the notes in Leonard Swidler's "Introduction" to *Women Priests: A Catholic Commentary on the Vatican Declaration*, ed. Leonard Swidler and Arlene Swidler (New York: Paulist, 1977), 3–18. One of the first studies was Haye van der Meer's 1962 dissertation directed by Karl Rahner and published in English as *Women Priests in the Catholic Church? A Theological-Historical Investigation* (Philadelphia: Temple University Press, 1973).

9. Canon Law Society of America, "Women in Canon Law," *Origins* 5 (November 1975): 260–64.

10. See http://www.nd.edu/~icl/nd_study.shtml.

11. For a study of twenty Catholic parishes administered by women, see Ruth Wallace, *They Call Her Pastor: A New Role for Catholic Women* (Albany, N.Y.: SUNY Press, 1992).

12. Congregation for the Doctrine of the Faith, *Inter Insigniores* or the "Declaration on the Admission of Women to the Ministerial Priesthood," *Origins* 6 (1977): 517–24.

13. Albert Descamps, "Significance for Us Today of Christ's Attitude and of the Practice of the Apostles," in *From "Inter Insigniores" to "Ordinatio Sacerdotalis": Documents and Commentaries*, Congregation for the Doctrine of the Faith (Washington, D.C.: United States Catholic Conference, 1996), 92–93.

14. Elisabeth Schüssler Fiorenza, "The Apostleship of Women in Early Christianity," in *Women Priests*, 135–40; idem, "The Twelve," in *Women Priests*, 114–22.

15. John H. Wright, S.J., "Patristic Testimony on Women's Ordination in *Inter Insigniores*," *Theological Studies* 58 (1997): 526.

16. Dennis Michael Ferrara, "The Ordination of Women: Tradition and Meaning," *Theological Studies* 55 (1994): 706–19.

17. Hans Urs von Balthasar, "The Uninterrupted Tradition of the Church," in *From "Inter Insigniores" to "Ordinatio Sacerdotalis*," 99–106.

18. Carroll Stuhlmueller, "Bridegroom: A Biblical Symbol of Union, Not Separation," in *Women Priests, A Catholic Commentary on the Vatican Declaration*, ed. Swidler and Swidler, 283.

19. Thomas Aquinas, *Summa Theologiae*, ST Suppl. Q. 39, a 2 ad 4; Ferrara, "Ordination of Women: Tradition and Meaning," *Theological Studies* 55 (1994): 716–17.

20. Sara Butler, "Quaestio Disputata: 'In Persona Christi': A Response to Dennis M. Ferrara," *Theological Studies* 56 (1995): 80.

21. Sandra M. Schneiders, *Women and the Word* (Mahwah, N.J.: Paulist, 1986), 54. See also David N. Power, "Representing Christ in Community and Sacrament," in *Being a Priest Today*, ed. Donald J. Goergen (Collegeville: Minn.: Liturgical, 1992), 116.

22. Sara Butler, *The Catholic Priesthood and Women: A Guide to the Teaching of the Church* (Chicago: Hillenbrand Books, 1997), 102.

23. According to the University of Chicago's 1998 General Social Survey, 65 percent of Catholics in the United States favored the ordination of women. This was also the position of 18 percent of Catholics in the Philippines, 29 percent of Catholics in Poland, 58 percent of Catholics in Italy, 67 percent of Catholics in Ireland, and 71 percent of Spanish and German Catholics.

24. Pope John Paul II, "*Ordinatio Sacerdotalis*: Apostolic Letter on Ordination and Women," *Origins* 24 (1994): 49, 51–52.

25. Congregation for the Doctrine of the Faith, "Response to a 'Dubium' on Ordaining Women to the Ministerial Priesthood," *Origins* 25 (1995): 401, 403–5.

26. Ladislas Orsy, "The Congregation's 'Response: Its Authority and Meaning," *America* 173, no. 19 (December 9, 1995): 4–5; CTSA Board, "Study, Prayer Urged Regarding Women's Ordination 'Responsum,'" *Origins* 27 (1997): 75–79. See also Francis A. Sullivan, "Guideposts from Catholic Tradition," *America* 173, no. 19 (Dec. 9, 1995): 5–6.

27. The creed of Chalcedon, which became a classic formulation of Christology, reads: "One and the same Christ, Son, Lord, Only begotten, made known in two natures [which exist] without confusion, without change, without division, without separation; the difference of the natures having been in no wise taken away by reason of the union, but rather the

properties of each being preserved, and [both] concurring into one Person (*prosopon*) and one *hypostasis*—not parted or divided into two persons (*prosopa*), but one and the same Son and Only-begotten, the divine Word (*Logos*), the Lord Jesus Christ." English translation from the Greek taken from Robert Sellers, *The Council of Chalcedon: A Historical and Doctrinal Survey* (London: SPCK, 1953), 211.

28. Aquinas, *Summa Theologiae*, IIIae, Q. 2, Q. 16, and Q. 17. For commentary, see Eleonore Stump, "Aquinas' Metaphysics of the Incarnation," in *The Incarnation*, ed. Stephen T. Davis, Daniel Kendall, S.J., and Gerald O'Collins, S.J. (New York: Oxford, 2002), 197–218; Joseph Wawrykow, "Hypostatic Union," in *The Theology of Thomas Aquinas*, ed. Rik van Nieuwenhove and Joseph Wawrykow (South Bend, Ind.: University of Notre Dame, 2005), 222–51. That the Word of God is properly identified as conceived wisdom or begotten wisdom (as distinct from the wisdom that is of the essence of God) is Aquinas's position in the *Summa Contra Gentiles* IV, chap. 12. For commentary, see Gilles Emery, *The Trinitarian Theology of Saint Thomas Aquinas* (New York: Oxford University Press, 2007), 192–95.

29. Elizabeth A. Johnson, *She Who Is: The Mystery of God in Feminist Theological Discourse* (New York: Crossroad, 1992), 150.

30. On God as neither male nor female—and yet the origin of the perfections of both male and female persons—see Elizabeth A. Johnson, "The Incomprehensibility of God and the Image of God Male and Female," *Theological Studies* 45 (1984): 460.

CHAPTER 8

1. This chapter draws on my scholarly papers delivered for "Vatican II, 40 Years Later: Legacy, Leadership and Unfinished Agenda," held at Saint Mary's College in 2005, and for the Theological Anthropology session at the Catholic Theological Society of America in 2005 and 2008. I am grateful to my colleagues at those conferences and in this anthology for their constructive comments.

2. In keeping with historian Martin E. Marty, who coined this phrase and its associated field, the "public church" in this essay refers to Christian churches, organizations, and groups that are concerned with U.S. public life, whereas "Catholic Church" or "Church" denotes the political concerns and contributions of U.S. Catholic churches, organizations, and groups. Marty, *The Public Church: Mainline, Evangelical, Catholic* (New York: Crossroad, 1981).

3. "Pastoral Constitution on the Church in the Modern World: *Gaudium et Spes*," in *Vatican Council II: The Basic Sixteen Documents*, ed. Austin Flannery, rev. trans. (Northport, N.Y.: Costello, 1996).

4. J. Bryan Hehir identifies these paragraphs as hermeneutical keys to interpret Vatican II's perspective on the church's social role; J. Bryan Hehir,

S.J., "The Social Role of the Church: Leo XIII, Vatican II, and John Paul II," in *Catholic Social Thought and the New World Order*, ed. Oliver F. Williams, and John W. Houck (South Bend, Ind.: Univ. of Notre Dame Press, 1993), 29–50, at 36–38.

5. See Mary E. Hines, "Ecclesiology for a Public Church," *CTSA Proceedings of the Fifty-fifth Annual Convention* 55 (2000): 23–46.

6. W. Clark Gilpin, *A Preface to Theology* (Chicago: University of Chicago Press, 1996), 167–68.

7. For such clericalist histories of American Catholic public/political participation since 1900, see Mark A. Noll and Luke E. Harlow, eds., *Religion and American Politics: From the Colonial Period to the Present*, 2nd ed. (New York: Oxford University Press, 2007), chaps. 11 and 15.

8. Yvonne Abraham and Brian R. Ballou, "350 Are Held in Immigration Raid," *Boston Globe*, March 7, 2007, available at http://www.boston.com/news/local/articles/2007/03/07/350_are_held_in_immigration_raid/; and Louis Sahagun, "L.A. Church in Forefront of Sanctuary Movement," *Los Angeles Times*, March 23, 2007, B1.

9. For profiles of other undocumented mothers and children in sanctuary, see Sasha Abramsky, "Gimme Shelter," *The Nation* 286, no. 7 (February 25, 2008): 24–25.

10. Maria Cristina Garcia, " 'Dangerous Times Call for Risky Responses': Latino Immigration and Sanctuary, 1981–2001," in *Latino Religions and Civic Activism in the United States*, ed. Gaston Espinosa, Virgilio Elizondo, and Jesse Miranda (New York: Oxford University Press, 2005), 159–73.

11. Rev. Alexia Salvatierra, "Sacred Refuge," *Sojourners* 36, no. 9 (September–October 2007): 12–20.

12. James Barron, "Churches to Offer Sanctuary," *New York Times*, May 9, 2007, B1 and Saul Gonzalez, "Immigrant Sanctuary Movement," *Religion and Ethics Newsweekly*, June 15, 2007, available at http://www.pbs.org/wnet/religionandethics/week1042/feature.html.

13. Karl Rahner, "The Theology of Symbol," in *Theological Investigations*, vol. 4, trans. Kevin Smyth (London: Darton, Longman, and Todd, 1974), and Bernard Cooke, and Gary Macy, *Christian Symbol and Ritual: An Introduction* (New York: Oxford University Press, 2005).

14. Elizabeth A. Johnson, *Quest for the Living God: Mapping Frontiers in the Theology of God* (New York: Continuum, 2007).

15. Pope John Paul II, "Letter to Women," June 29, 1995; available at http://www.vatican.va/holy_father/john_paul_ii/letters/documents/hf_jpii_let_29061995_women_en.html.

16. "Letter to the Bishops of the Catholic Church on the Collaboration of Men and Women in the Church and in the World," May 31, 2004; available at http://www.vatican.va/roman_curia/congregations/cfaith/documents/rc_con_cfaith_doc_20040731_collaboration_en.html.

17. Tina Beattie utilizes postmodern feminist theory and theology to unpack the complex theological discourse about sex and gender differences that is embedded in the institutional Church's interpretations of such nuptial imagery. See Beattie, *New Catholic Feminism: Theology and Theory* (New York: Routledge, 2006).

18. Deborah Halter, *The Papal No: The Vatican's Refusal to Ordain Women* (New York: Crossroad, 2004). For a critical feminist response, see Anne M. Clifford, *Introducing Feminist Theology* (Maryknoll, N.Y.: Orbis, 2001), 139–48.

19. Feminist theologians counter such dominant ideologies about Mary with a more historicized portrait of Mary among prophetic witnesses around Jesus. See Elizabeth A. Johnson, *Truly Our Sister: A Theology of Mary in the Communion of Saints* (New York: Continuum, 2003).

20. Feminists and womanist theologians have long criticized anthropologies of servanthood and self-gift that are predicated on kenotic Christologies, or the divine self-emptying of Jesus in the incarnation and crucifixion celebrated in some early Christian hymns (Phil. 2:1-11). See Maryanne Stevens, ed., *Reconstructing the Christ Symbol: Essays in Feminist Christology* (New York: Paulist, 1993); and Rosemary P. Carbine, "Contextualizing the Cross for the Sake of Subjectivity," in *Cross Examinations: Readings on the Meaning of the Cross Today*, ed. Marit Trelstad (Minneapolis: Fortress Press, 2006), 91–108, esp. 98–99.

21. The council fathers failed to contest human domination of nature, but rather took it as basic to theological anthropology, based on the creation of humanity in the image and likeness of God (*GS*, pars. 9, 12, 15, 33, 34, 57).

22. See the recent documentary by Dorothy Fadiman, *Stealing America: Vote by Vote* (Menlo Park, Calif.: Concentric Media, 2008).

23. See Michael Stogre, "Commentary on the Pastoral Constitution on the Church in the Modern World," in *The Church Renewed: The Documents of Vatican II Reconsidered*, ed. George P. Schner (Lanham, Md.: University Press of America, 1986): 19–36, esp. 25–27; Walter Kasper, "The Theological Anthropology of *Gaudium et Spes*," *Communio* 23 (1996): 129–40, at 129; William C. McDonough, "The Church in the Modern World: Rereading *Gaudium et Spes* After Thirty Years," in *Vatican II: The Continuing Agenda*, ed. Anthony J. Cernera (Fairfield, Conn.: Sacred Heart University Press, 1997), 113–33, esp. 122, 125–26; and, John J. Markey, *Creating Communion: The Theology of the Constitutions of the Church* (Hyde Park, N.Y.: New City, 2003), 84–99.

24. Some theologians argue that *GS* does not adequately link anthropology and Christology, thereby creating a central tension; Kasper, "The Theological Anthropology of *Gaudium et Spes*," *Communio* 23 (1996): 135–38, 140; and David L. Schindler, "Christology and the *Imago Dei*: Interpreting *Gaudium et Spes*," *Communio* 23 (1996): 156–84, esp. 157–63. This essay

shows that such tension can give rise to fruitful theological reflection, in this case, feminist theological reflection on the church's political praxis.

25. David Hollenbach, S.J., "Commentary on *Gaudium et Spes*, Pastoral Constitution on the Church in the Modern World," in *Modern Catholic Social Teaching: Commentaries and Interpretations*, ed. Kenneth R. Himes, O.F.M. (Washington, D.C.: Georgetown University Press, 2005), 266–91, at 271.

26. Christine Firer Hinze, "Straining toward Solidarity in a Suffering World: *Gaudium et Spes* after Forty Years," in *Vatican II: Forty Years Later*, ed. William Madges (Maryknoll, N.Y.: Orbis, 2006), 165–95, esp. 170–75.

27. As Peter Phan states, "Eschatology is anthropology conjugated in the future tense on the basis of Christology." Phan, "Contemporary Context and Issues in Eschatology," *Theological Studies* 55, no. 3 (1994): 507–36, at 516.

28. Elizabeth A. Johnson, "The Maleness of Christ," in *The Power of Naming: A Concilium Reader in Feminist Liberation Theology*, ed. Elisabeth Schüssler Fiorenza (Maryknoll, N.Y.: Orbis, 1996), 307–15, esp. 307–8; idem, *She Who Is: Mystery of God in Feminist Theological Discourse* (New York: Crossroad, 1992), 151–53.

29. On the limitations of *GS* from a feminist theoethical perspective, see Anne E. Patrick, "Toward Renewing the 'Life and Culture of Fallen Man': *Gaudium et Spes* as Catalyst for Catholic Feminist Theology," in *Feminist Ethics and the Catholic Moral Tradition*, ed. Charles E. Curran, Margaret A. Farley, and Richard A. McCormick, S.J. (New York: Paulist, 1996), 483–510. Recent commentaries on *GS* pay little attention to feminist movements that preceded and followed Vatican II, such as David Hollenbach, S.J., "Commentary on *Gaudium et Spes*, Pastoral Constitution on the Church in the Modern World," in *Modern Catholic Social Teaching: Commentaries and Interpretations*, ed. Kenneth R. Himes, O.F.M. (Washington, D.C.: Georgetown University Press, 2005), 267–69.

30. Mary Catherine Hilkert, "Imago Dei: Does the Symbol Have a Future?" *The Santa Clara Lectures* 8, no. 3 (April 2002).

31. Kasper, "Theological Anthropology of *Gaudium et Spes*," *Communio* 23 (1996): 137.

32. The previous paragraph summarizes the insights of Elizabeth Johnson, *She Who Is: The Mystery of God in Feminist Theological Discourse* (New York: Crossroad, 1992) 86–100, and idem, "Redeeming the Name of Christ: Christology," in *Freeing Theology: The Essentials of Theology in Feminist Perspective*, ed. Catherine Mowry LaCugna (New York: HarperCollins, 1993), 115–37, esp. 120–27.

33. Johnson, "The Maleness of Christ," 313; idem, "Redeeming the Name of Christ," 129.

34. Hilkert, "Imago Dei," 15, 18.

35. Susan A. Ross, *Extravagant Affections: A Feminist Sacramental Theology* (New York: Continuum, 1998), 33–34, 36–38, 138–42.

36. Anne E. Carr and Mary Stewart Van Leeuwen, eds., *Religion, Feminism, and the Family* (Louisville: Westminster John Knox, 1996) and Elisabeth Schüssler Fiorenza, *Discipleship of Equals: A Critical Feminist Ekklesialogy of Liberation* (New York: Crossroad, 1993).

37. Feminist theologians and ethicists have employed the notion of generativity to reinterpret sacramental practices in light of women's experiences of giving and sustaining life. See Ross, *Extravagant Affections*, chap. 5, and Christine E. Gudorf, "The Power to Create: Sacraments and Men's Need to Birth," *Horizons* 14, no. 2 (1987): 296–309.

CHAPTER 9

1. Catholicity as a mark of the church emphasizes its universality, inclusiveness, and openness to truth. Oneness, or unity, is a mark of the church that speaks to the unifying presence of the Holy Spirit in the church. Holiness is a mark of the church that emphasizes that it is a community on its way to being transformed by the indwelling of the Holy Spirit. Apostolicity, as a mark of the church, identifies its faith and practice with those of the apostles. See Richard McBrien: *Catholicism* (New York: HarperSanFrancisco, 1994), glossary of key terms.

2. May 30, 2008: http://www.cwnews.com/news/viewstory.cfm?recnum =58760.

3. Literalism is a modern reading strategy, arising in the context of religious fundamentalism, which seeks to persuade Christians that the Bible is the direct, inerrant Word of God, which must be accepted without question. Actually, official Catholic theology does not assume that the Bible is the direct word of God. I argue that the reliance on literalism is marshaled only in relation to the question of women's ordination.

4. Postivism is another modern reading strategy arising in the context of the scientific method and religious fundamentalism and seeks to persuade Christians that scripture and doctrines possess the assurance of absolute certitude. Positivists are to be found on both the right and left sides of the spectrum when they argue that we can derive positive knowledge of Jesus from the Gospel narratives. Positivists ignore the idea that the Gospel narratives are full-fledged theologies, making specific arguments in relation to their contexts.

5. See Richard McBrien: "Did Jesus intend to *found* a Church? The answer is 'no' if by found we mean some direct, explicit, deliberate act by which Jesus established a new religious organization. The answer is 'yes' if by *found* we mean 'lay the foundations for the Church in various indirect ways. . . . The call of *the Twelve* has to be seen in this light. The Twelve were to represent Jesus' call to all of the twelve tribes of Israel . . . as a whole." *Catholicism* (New York: HarperSanFrancisco, 1994), 578, emphases in the original.

6. Ibid., 10.

7. Ibid., 12, emphasis added.

8. Dean Hoge and Jacqueline Wenger: *Evolving Visions of the Priesthood: Changes from Vatican II to the Turn of the New Century* (Collegeville, Minn.: Liturgical, 2003).

9. Ibid., 8.

10. Ibid., 10.

11. Ibid., 11.

12. Susan K. Wood: "The Search for Identity" in Dean Hoge and Jacqueline Wenger: *Evolving Visions of the Priesthood: Changes from Vatican II to the Turn of the New Century* (Collegeville, Minn.: Liturgical Press, 2003), 167–73.

13. Roger Haight: *Jesus Symbol of God* (Maryknoll, N.Y.: Orbis, 1999).

14. See n. 5.

15. Haight, *Jesus Symbol of God*, 202.

16. Ibid., 140.

17. Elisabeth Schüssler Fiorenza, *Rhetoric and Ethic: The Politics of Biblical Studies* (Minneapolis: Fortress Press, 1999), preface. In relation to the issues raised in this essay, the complementarity model is framed by kyriarchal interests. Thus, women's "complementary" work to men always leaves women in subordinate positions, which are socially and culturally constructed.

18. Schüssler Fiorenza, *Rhetoric and Ethic*, "Kyriarchal/kyriocentric: derived from the Greek term for lord, this coinage underscores that domination is not simply a matter of patriarchal, gender based dualism but of a more comprehensive, interlocking, hierarchically ordered structures of domination, evident in a variety of oppressions such as racism, poverty, heterosexism and colonialism."

19. Elisabeth Schüssler Fiorenza: *Discipleship of Equals: A Critical Feminist Ekkelesia-logy of Liberation* (New York: Crossroad, 1993), 2.

20. Ibid., 10.

21. Ibid., 10.

22. Ibid., 22.

23. Ibid., 56–58, emphasis in the original.

24. Elisabeth Schüssler Fiorenza: "The Rhetoric of Empire and G*d-Talk," in *The Power of the Word: Scripture and the Rhetoric of the Empire*, (Minneapolis: Fortress Press, 2007), 206.

25. Elisabeth Schüssler Fiorenza: "G*d—The Many Named," in *Transcendence and Beyond: A Postmodern Inquiry*, ed. John Caputo and Michael Scanlon (Bloomington, Ind.: Indiana University Press, 2007), 110.

26. Schüssler Fiorenza: *Rhetoric and Ethic*, preface.

27. Elisabeth Schüssler Fiorenza: *The Power of the Word: Scripture and the Rhetoric of Empire* (Minneapolis: Fortress Press, 2007), 70.

28. Ibid., 75.

29. Ibid., 76.

30. Elisabeth Schüssler Fiorenza, "For Women in Men's World: A Critical Feminist Theology of Liberation," in *The Power of Naming: A Concilium Reader in Feminist Liberation Theology* (Maryknoll, N.Y.: Orbis, 1996), 9–10.

31. Natalie K. Watson, *Introducing Feminist Ecclesiology* (Cleveland: Pilgrim Press, 2002), 4.

32. James D. Davidson, "Generations of American Catholics," *The Catholic Theological Society of American Proceedings of the Sixty-third Annual Convention* 63 (2008): 1–17.

GLOSSARY

Anti-Judaism: an attitude that rejects the religion and theology of Judaism. Some scholars argue that it should not be distinguished from antisemitism, while others maintain that the theological focus of the term requires two separate words.

Antisemitism: made popular in the late nineteenth century by German journalist Wilhelm Marr, this word was used to provide a more "scientific" term to replace the German *Judenhass* (Jew hatred). It refers to a rejection or hatred of the Jewish people based on pseudoscientific theories of biology and race.

Apostolic succession: the handing on of apostolic teaching and authority from the apostles to their successors.

Body of Christ: a theological term with multiple meanings, ascribed most often to the historical human body of Jesus; the presence of Jesus Christ in the Eucharist; or the risen body of Jesus Christ, transfigured by the Holy Spirit and united in a universal way to all human life as well as cosmic reality. In ecclesiology, or theological reflection on the mission and features of the church, the model of the church as the Body of Christ refers to the people of God who are interdependently interconnected through baptism and the Holy Spirit (see Rom. 12:4-5; 1 Cor. 12:12-27; Eph. 1:22-23). Feminist and womanist theologians critically reinterpret the model of the church as the body of Christ through early Christian baptismal formulas (for example, Gal. 3:26-28) to advocate unity, equality, and mutuality in contrast to hierarchical, patriarchal understandings of the church in which Christ, the male head of the Church, saves, rules, and in other ways instructs the feminized body of the Church.

Canon Law: the norms ("canons") or laws that govern the social order of the Church. The most recent Code of Canon Law for the Latin Church was promulgated in 1983.

Catechumenate: a program of formation of persons preparing for reception of initiation into the Catholic Church that nurtures their conversion and helps bring faith to maturity.

Charism: a grace of the Holy Spirit given for the service of the common good.

Christology: theological reflection on the person of Jesus Christ.

Communion: God's way to us and our way to God is through the created community. While we may experience God in our individual selves, Catholic theology insists that such experience cannot simply be "private."

Congregation for the Doctrine of the Faith (CDF): the department of the Roman Curia responsible for safeguarding church teaching on matters of faith and morals.

Curia: A network of discasteries (departments) that assist the pope in governing the universal church. The Curia was first formally organized in 1588 by Pope Sixtus V. The most recent reorganization was undertaken in 1988 by Pope John Paul II.

Deacon/ess: in the Greek New Testament, a servant, minister, or helper (*diakonos*). In the first centuries of the Church, both the male and female deaconate flourished as an office that involved charitable, liturgical, and evangelical responsibilities. After the fifth century, the role of deacons diminished in the West. The deaconate eventually became a temporary ministry required of those preparing for priesthood. The Second Vatican Council restored the permanent, lifetime deaconate. The office is now open to both celibate and married men.

Deposit of faith: Christ's revelation handed down to the apostles and transmitted in Scripture and tradition.

Docetism: a heresy that denies the full humanity of Jesus.

Essentialism: the process by which someone is reduced to her or his biological characteristics or role in life. Essentialism is often contrasted in feminist literature to social constructionism, leading to what many have characterized as the nature/nurture debate.

Feminism, Waves of (U.S.): in the United States, the history of feminist political movements encompasses three waves. The first wave, associated with abolitionist and suffragist movements of the mid to late nineteenth and early twentieth centuries, largely focused on gaining women equal political participation via the right to vote. The second wave in the 1960s and 1970s, coincided with the African American Civil Rights Movement and focused on civil rights for women, especially via economic and racial equality. The third wave of feminism, ongoing since the late 1970s and 1980s, emphasizes differences among global women's experiences of oppression, as well as transnational solidarity among global women's struggles for justice. In U.S. Christian theology, the third wave's emphasis on difference gave rise to African American womanist (see entry below) and U.S. Latina/mujerista theologies, as well as to Asian American, ecological, postcolonial, and many other feminist theologies. See also "Types of Feminism in the United States," in the inset box on page 86.

Feminist: a designation for anyone who is committed to the flourishing of of all human and more than human life.

Fundamentalism: modern fundamentalist movements are religiously and ethnically diverse. In the context of change, however, they promise religious security, certainty of faith, and clear-cut identity. They maintain a literalist understanding of sacred scriptures and language and argue that tradition is the "will of God" and that the subordination of women is natural and ordained by God. Nevertheless, they employ the gamut of modern conveniences, including electronic media, in order to communicate their message of ethnic, religious, and gender superiority.

Hagar: the story of Hagar appears in chapters 16 and 21 of the book of Genesis. Hagar is the maidservant of Sarah, the wife of the patriarch Abraham. When Sarah is unable to have a child with her husband, Hagar is forced to bear a child in Sarah's name. This culturally acceptable practice resulted in Hagar bearing a son named Ishmael. Though never given the benefits of Abraham's firstborn, Ishmael and his mother, Hagar, have a place in salvation history.

Hybridity: see boxed inset at page 11.

Hypostatic union: the union of the divine and human natures in the one divine person (Greek: *hypostasis*) of the incarnate Word of God, Jesus Christ.

Idolatry: the worship of idols. The term applies to any tendency to equate something finite with the infinite (God).

Imago Dei: points to the theological doctrine of creation in which human beings are created to reflect God's image or essence, and hence have a special calling to live in right relationship with God and others.

Immanence: referring to the indwelling of God in creation. That is, God relates to the world by being near or close to God's creation.

Incarnation: the church teachings related to the notion that God became human.

Infallibility: the inability to err, attributable in a strict sense only to God. The term is also used in the Catholic Church in reference to a gift of the Holy Spirit that enables the church to believe and teach without error those truths necessary for salvation. This does not mean that the church can never make mistakes. Infallibility can be invoked only in certain, very restricted conditions. According to the Second Vatican Council, infallibility is promised to the church and is present when the body of bishops is in agreement that a particular teaching concerning faith and morals is to be held definitively (*Lumen gentium*, par. 25). The pope can also exercise infallibility when he speaks *ex cathedra*, in his office as pastor and teacher of all Christians, to define a doctrine concerning faith or morals.

Interreligious dialogue: the practice of communicating with people of other faiths, whether formally, as with religious leaders coming together for discussion, or informally through an ongoing relationship with persons who are affiliated with a religious tradition other than one's own.

Lactating/lactation: the process by which milk is created in a woman's breast as food for her newborn baby or young child.

Magisterium: the teaching office of the church, charged with giving an authentic interpretation of Scripture and tradition to ensure fidelity to the teaching of the apostles in matters of faith and morals.

Marcionism: a heresy that rejects the Old Testament and denies that the God of the Jews is the same God in the New Testament.

Mediation: God is available to us and acts through persons, places, events, and things. God as God is not limited to certain times, places, or events, even though these times, places, and events may serve to focus our attention on God in specific ways.

Metaphor: a literary comparison between two entities in which the second entity can shed light on the first or reveal deeper meanings of it. With respect to theology, it is indirect or analogical language for the divine that relies on known human and earthly experience, terms, and/or images to characterize, but never totally capture, the ultimately unknown and transcendent mystery of God. Metaphors: (1) preserve both the similarity and the difference between human/earthly realities and the reality of God (for example, God both is and is not like a father, a burning bush, a rock, a mother hen, to name a few prominent scriptural images); (2) defend multiple images and inclusive ways of referring to God, using more than dominant masculine language for God; (3) avoid anthropocentrism, or using only human experience to characterize God; and, finally, (4) protect religious God-language from idolatry.

Ordination: from the first century through the twelfth, the term "ordination" (*ordinare, ordinari, ordinatio*) in the Latin Church signified the designation or consecration of someone to take up a specific place or function (*ordo*) in the service of the community. From the thirteenth century through today, the term has been used more restrictively. It now refers to Holy Orders, understood as a sacrament that marks the ordained with a spiritual character and bestows a sacred power (*sacra potestas*).

Other: anyone or anything who is different. We are all others to someone.

Patriarchy: an analytical concept in feminist critical theory that problematizes sociocultural and political constructions of privilege and power. Rather than a sex/gender system of universal male dominance, patriarchy refers to multiple interconnections among gender, race, class, culture, sexuality, geopolitical identity, religion, and so on, that justify hierarchical power relations, as well as ultimately idealizing an elite, white, male, Western, Christian, heterosexual paradigm of personhood. Contrary to its literal translation as "the rule of the father," patriarchy connotes a multilayered complex system of dominance, which some feminist theologians have renamed "kyriarchy" (the rule of the lord or master) and some womanist theologians have called "demonarchy" (the rule of dehumanizing powers).

Positivism: an outcome of the "scientific" method, it avows objectivity, disinterestedness, and value neutrality in order to control and legitimize the "true" meaning of texts. Consequently, positivism goes hand in hand with literalism, which assumes that textual meaning is static, positively established, and proven. Positivism and literalism are marks of fundamentalist thought and abjure the idea that all knowledge is constructed and sustained in a system of power relations.

Praxis: the interrelation of action and theory at the heart of Marxist theory and liberationist theologies that challenges a one-way linear relation from theory to action. As elaborated by Latin American and Euro-American liberation theologians, praxis emphasizes a mutual, dialectical relationship between action and theory, which, when applied to theology, refers to the ways in which everyday lived religious practices, especially, but not only for social justice, shape and are reshaped by theological claims.

Religious pluralism: the reality that there are many different religious traditions in the world that shape different understandings, beliefs, and identities.

Sacrament/al: the ritualized or, as is more generally understood, presence of God's offer of grace to humanity in everyday life.

Sacramentality: all reality is potentially and in fact the bearer of God's presence. This is so because we understand reality to be created by God.

Scotoma: refers to a visual impairment, which Bernard Lonergan uses to interpret individual and group sin.

Second Vatican Council (Vatican II): called by Pope John XXIII, and lasting from 1962 until 1965, this council or gathering of bishops, lay theologians, and observers was oriented to rethinking Catholic theology and practice in the light of the modern world. The Council produced sixteen major documents and initiated reforms in terms of liturgical theology and practice, the self-understanding of the church as the people of God, church-world relations, and ecumenical, as well as interreligious, dialogue, to name some of the salient issues.

Sin: the brokenness that occurs among individuals and groups as a result of any number of social and psychological factors.

Solidarity: sharing a concern for those who are suffering, whether one is experiencing the suffering or not. Acting in collaboration with others with a deep feeling of commitment to the other's well-being.

Theological anthropology: this branch of theology engages the question, "What does it mean to be human in a world imbued with God?"

Transcendence: refers to the idea that God is self-sufficient and apart from the world. That is, God relates to creation by approaching creation from beyond.

Womanist theology: this liberation theology makes the varied experiences of African American women the center of the theological project. The word *womanist* was coined by Pulitzer prize—winning author Alice Walker in her book *In Search of Our Mothers' Gardens: Womanist Prose*. Womanism celebrates black women's gifts of curiosity, self-care, and critical consciousness, and their ability to "make a way out of no way."

INDEX